D1563835

In Memory of Self and Comrades

In Memory of
Self and Comrades

Thomas Wallace Colley's
Recollections of Civil War Service
in the 1st Virginia Cavalry

EDITED BY MICHAEL K. SHAFFER

Voices of the Civil War
Michael P. Gray, Series Editor

The University of Tennessee Press
Knoxville

The Voices of the Civil War series makes available a variety of primary
source materials that illuminate issues on the battlefield, the home front,
and the western front, as well as other aspects of this historic era.
The series contextualizes the personal accounts within the framework
of the latest scholarship and expands established knowledge by
offering new perspectives, new materials, and new voices.

LIBRARY OF CONGRESS CATALOGING-IN-PUBLICATION DATA
Names: Shaffer, Michael, 1961- editor.
Title: In memory of self and comrades : Thomas Wallace Colley's recollections
of Civil War service in the 1st Virginia Cavalry / edited by Michael K. Shaffer.
Description: First edition. | Knoxville : The University of Tennessee Press, [2018]
| Series: Voices of the Civil War | Includes bibliographical references and index.
| Identifiers: LCCN 2018027834 (print) | LCCN 2018028742 (ebook) |
ISBN 9781621904311 (pdf) | ISBN 9781621904304 (hardcover)
Subjects: LCSH: Colley, Thomas Wallace, 1837- | Confederate States of
America. Army. Virginia Cavalry Regiment, 1st. |
United States—History—Civil War, 1861–1865—
Personal narratives, Confederate. Classification: LCC E605 (ebook) |
LCC E605 .I5 2018 (print) | DDC 973.7/82092 [B] —dc23
LC record available at https://lccn.loc.gov/2018027834

To Charlene Roche and Bob Colley,

descendants of Thomas Wallace Colley;

thank you for sharing your family history,

providing images of Thomas,

and offering unending support.

CONTENTS

ILLUSTRATIONS

Maps

INTRODUCTION

As the clouds of war dotted the landscape of the United States in early 1861, many young men, North and South, rushed to volunteer. Whether they eventually donned the blue or the gray, thousands never returned home, having given the full sacrifice on some distant battlefield. Others did return, often carrying horrid memories of their wartime experience. Those fortunate to escape serious wounds or amputation still struggled with mental stress from the horrific sights and sounds they experienced during the Civil War. Many veterans carried guilt over their return, while comrades had fallen, a factor further complicating their readjustment to civilian life.

Thomas Wallace Colley, born November 30, 1837, outside Abingdon, Virginia, grew up around the hard work of farm life. As a youth, he hardened his stamina and developed a solid work ethic, which would hold him in good stead later in life. In May 1861, along with the other members of the Washington Mounted Rifles, he left his home in Washington County, Virginia, and reported to camp in Richmond. During the war, Colley received wounds on three different occasions: first at Waterloo Bridge in 1862, again at Kelly's Ford in 1863, and finally, at Haw's Shop in 1864. The engagement at Haw's Shop resulted in the amputation of his left foot, thereby ending his wartime service.

Surgeons on both sides performed thousands of amputations during the war, and the limbs most frequently severed were fingers, hands, and feet.[1] Many other soldiers, North and South, could have returned home after receiving similar wounds, and many did, yet Colley struggled to recover and report to his regiment. Finally, absent a limb, he joined with thousands of other soldiers who had feared "they would be blown apart or would return home with wounds and scars . . . [and] that such injuries would reduce them to the status of slaves, without individuality or humanity."[2]

While the term Post Traumatic Stress Disorder (PTSD) did not enter the popular lexicon until 1970—as doctors began diagnosing returning

Vietnam veterans—recent scholarship has indicated soldiers from earlier conflicts suffered likewise. Several Civil War veterans displayed PTSD-like symptoms, diagnosed at the time as "nostalgia" or "irritable heart." Historian Eric T. Dean, in his landmark work *Shook Over Hell: Post-Traumatic Stress, Vietnam, and the Civil War*, described the signs, which included "rage, guilt, flashbacks, nightmares, [and] depression," often leading to "psychiatric problems," thus creating difficulties in gaining employment.[3]

Perhaps Colley too struggled, in varying degrees and at different times during his life, from PTSD. The loss of a child or other family member weighed heavily upon former soldiers. For one already struggling to resume some degree of normalcy in their life, losing a loved one, especially a child, "seemed to produce the most potent mental shock."[4] Colley lost four of his children, each at a very young age: son James, shortly after his birth in 1873; two daughters—Sally, age 2, and Ella, age 4—in 1886; and son Charles, who died in 1898 at age 3. Many veterans, including Colley, tried to lead somewhat normal lives despite the physical and mental trauma from the war. As Dean suggests in his narrative, "one could be diagnosed as having PTSD and still be entirely functional—married, with children, owning a home, pursuing a successful career."[5]

Many struggled. The inability to cope with postwar stress intensified for those who had received serious wounds and amputations (Colley endured both); they often "sought relief in alcohol, patent medicines, and suicide. . . ."[6] Expectations, especially in the South, for men to serve as the provider for the family, despite physical disabilities or mental issues, presented challenges. Many veterans, unable to overcome these various stress factors, eventually ended up in an insane asylum after family members gave up on their efforts to provide in-home care.

Participating in religious activity helped many veterans begin to cope with everyday life. Churches of various denominations took on added importance, as they raised money to help needy veteran families and provided a welcoming environment for all in the communities they served. However, the assistance "came at the price of conformity to the churches' behavioral standards."[7] Colley makes several references to God throughout his journals. He also writes of the church, and his faith. Recalling a revival in 1872, he stated: "I was soundly 'converted' and cleansed from all my past sins and was made to feel and know that 'God' for Christs sake has power to cleanse a sinners heart and that he can feel and know it for himself." From his promise at Kelly's Ford to repent if God spared his life; to his donating land and building materials and giving money for the construction of Washington Chapel Church in 1866, one can glean a Christian attitude in Colley before 1872. However, he still had demons to defeat.

An estimated 20,000 Confederate soldiers underwent amputation during the war.[8] Like many amputees—as Brian Craig Miller notes in his *Empty Sleeves: Amputation in the Civil War South*—Colley relied on the "local charities and benevolent organizations to survive."[9] His church membership aided him in overcoming a dependency on alcohol (another PTSD symptom, and one he openly discusses in his journals) and afforded him the faith needed to provide shelter and a livelihood for his family. Writing to a relative of his foot injury, Colley declared, "I thought I would have it amputated before I would risk suffering what I am." Having some say in the surgeon's request to amputate his foot, afforded him the opportunity to "take back some of the control that many men perceived as lost in the context of warfare, when they were ordered to march, work, kill, and die."[10]

On several occasions after the war, Colley displayed a short-temper, quick to retaliate against those harboring thoughts that differed from his own. Anger is commonly associated with PTSD, and this could help explain Colley's disposition. However, he might have had a short-fuse all his life, as evidenced by descriptions from former comrades in the 1st Virginia Cavalry. Referring to Colley as "the Big Indian," the men portrayed him as "brave as the bravest but somewhat reckless, would rush into danger when circumstances did not warrant him in so doing."[11]

Differing from many amputees—"only a small minority took up authoring as a hobby or profession in the postwar years,"—Colley sought to enhance his education.[12] In 1870, He attended Bryant and Stratton College in Baltimore, where he took courses in penmanship. The lessons learned spawned a lifetime love of writing. During the war, he kept a small diary for a brief period in 1862. The original diary, housed in Richmond's Museum of the Confederacy, offers only basic information, as Colley primarily noted the daily weather conditions. Beginning in 1903, he started work on a multi-volume narrative of his life. Writing from memory many years after the war, he often consulted former members of his regiment, especially Mike Ireson, to fill in details he could not recollect.

In researching the events Colley recounted, this writer found the majority of the information fairly accurate. Colley's constant work in drafting articles and other correspondence possibly helped keep his memory sharp, even in his later years. He attempted to recount not only his service during the war, but also the struggles common for many veterans, especially those missing a limb. His writings often mirrored the Lost Cause mentality of the period, which Jubal Early and other Virginians had helped establish when they took over leadership of the Southern Historical Society and began formulating—immediately after the death of Robert E. Lee—a strategy for creating their own recollections of the war.

Colley continued to write, keeping yearly diaries until his death on September 24, 1919. Many of the daily entries simply noted the weather conditions; occasionally, especially if someone came to visit, he would elaborate on their discussions. However, each year, on March 17, he would take special notice of the day he almost lost his life at Kelly's Ford. Colley not only wrote, but others wrote to him. Several pieces of correspondence from Fitz Lee numbered among his most treasured documents. He thought highly of Lee, naming one of his sons Fitzhugh Lee Colley (1876–1904).[13] Colley included two of Lee's letters in an article he wrote for *Confederate Veteran* in 1899. The first, dated January 26, 1895, read: "Your kind letter received. I am glad that you are well, and that you take the proper view of life, with its burdens. We are all apt to have business misfortunes and domestic losses and troubles, but with brave hearts and clear consciences we can surmount them. Remember me to any of old Company D you may meet. Alas! We are all growing old now, and our ranks are being thinned rapidly, all of which should make us—the old soldiers of the State—cling closer and stand together in all things. I shall always be glad to hear from you."

The second letter, dated October 22, 1866, stated: "I am always pleased to hear from and of any of my old soldiers, particularly from those I am able to recall as having proved themselves good ones, and in that class I shall always place you."[14] The Thomas W. Colley Collection at Virginia Tech contains yet another letter from Lee, this one a testament to Colley's service, and perhaps documentation for a pension application:

Habana, Cuba
March 29, 1898

I certify that Thos. W. Colley was a soldier under my command, that he performed his duties well during the war of 1861 to 1865. That he was wounded in 1862, and again in 1863, March 17th at the cavalry battle of Kelly's Ford, being shot through the body and left on the field for dead. He was again wounded on May 28th, 1864, losing his left foot at the ankle joint. It will be readily seen that his soldier's record is excellent.

Fitzhugh Lee[15]

Working to establish two United Confederate veterans camps, one in Enoree, South Carolina, and a second in Abingdon, Virginia, Colley served in leadership positions with both camps. He deviated from the norm in this role, as many amputees "did not share a desire to join a group that would force them to relive the memories of a war that had produced so much personal suffering." Also, those missing a limb typically "participated only marginally in events that smacked of the Lost Cause."[16] Colley assumed the responsibility to serve as the official scribe, especially for the Abingdon camp. He wrote obituaries for passing members and submitted them to various publications, including the *Southern Historical Society Papers, Confederate Veteran,* and local newspapers.

Several historians believe the Lost Cause efforts helped Confederate veterans acclimate to society and escape the effects of PTSD. Others maintain these arguments are speculative and unproven. PTSD sufferers tended to "forget all the killing and to remember only the camaraderie."[17] Colley demonstrates this trait in his recollections, describing, often in vibrant detail, life in camp and the strong bond formed between messmates. He also compiled several biographical sketches of his former comrades. Seemingly, they occupied a strong position in his memory.

Struggling to find stable employment after the war, Colley held several different jobs. Elected sheriff of Washington County in 1871, he joined the ranks of several amputees, as people in the South sent "limbless men to all levels of the political process."[18] During his career in law enforcement, Colley dealt with a circumstance one historian described as "a carnival of crime." A state of lawlessness existed in many sections of the country, and with violence on the rise, civilians blamed "lax law enforcement."[19] Amid these conditions, Colley tried to maintain order but continued to struggle with an artificial limb and alcohol. Finally, thanks to the influence of the Temperance movement, he put down the bottle, joined the church, and began to turn his life around.

Getting his affairs in order allowed him to marry, as did many former soldiers, especially those missing limbs. Amputees harbored concerns about their ability to "court women and have children."[20] The Colleys—Thomas and Ann Eliza—eventually had 12 children. In 1897, to find stable employment and maintain his identity as a provider for his household, Colley moved his family to Enoree, South Carolina. Once settled in the Palmetto State, he recalled, "The children all went to work in a few days after we got there and soon learned up in the various floor or departments to which they were all assigned by the superintendent of the mills." Colley accepted "the public work of wives and other family members as a necessary part of their survival."[21] Despite the displacement from his native land and his wife's sincere desire to return—Colley remarked that "she would give a thousand dollars if she was back at home"—Colley understood the combined income of a couple greatly assisted in eking out a living.[22] He demonstrated time and again his resilience in providing for his family. Many veterans did likewise, as "anxieties about their manliness and the assumption that they could no longer perform manual labor" emboldened especially amputees, who "had both an emotional and an economic stake in appearing publicly whole."[23]

L. Thompson Cosby penned Colley's obituary for the *Confederate Veteran*. Cosby noted, "He was one of the most daring Confederate soldiers in the cavalry service. He was a man of powerful physique and was conspicuous in any crowd, clad, as he always was, in a suit of gray. He took great interest in looking after the welfare of all his comrades and of every man who was a true Confederate."[24] In the end, after struggling to overcome lingering physical and mental residue of war, Colley developed a degree of steadfast determination to make the best of his situation in life. When compiling his biographical sketches, he simply stated of himself, "Let someone else speak for him." Hopefully, within these pages, his words will "speak," allowing readers to connect with a soldier and his memory of a war that altered, shaped, and forever changed his life.

Editorial Notes

This writer owes a debt of gratitude to Charlene Roche, a direct descendent of Colley. She made possible the opportunity to transcribe, edit, and annotate this soldier's words. One volume of his journals remains lost to history—the portion covering December 1862 to early 1863—perhaps destroyed during a fire many years ago. In the opening paragraphs, Colley referred to himself in the third person, but quickly shifted to the first-person style. He also had the very unusual practice of capitalizing most words beginning with the letter "L," and frequently misspelled "cavalry" as "calvary," a rather common occurrence from the period. As is typical in many Civil War soldier letters, he used punctuation very sparingly. To enhance readability, this editor corrected (except in Colley's wartime letters) the shift from first to third person, changed misspellings, added punctuation, and inserted paragraph breaks, all while refraining from altering Colley's original meaning. For the sake of eliminating clutter, these editorial corrections do not have brackets.

My sincere appreciation goes to Bob Colley, another direct descendant, who graciously shared his ancestor's writings and photographs. Thanks to John Coski with the Museum of the Confederacy in Richmond. John provided a copy of Colley's wartime diary and informed this writer of the existence of a second Colley photograph in the museum's collection; both images appear within these pages. Marc Brodsky and the staff in the Special Collections Department at Virginia Tech pulled Colley's letters and other documents, allowing this researcher to spend productive time in Blacksburg. Kudos to Jonah Inestroza and the team at Appalachian State University's Special Collections group for providing documents in their library. Much appreciation goes to the reviewers of this manuscript. Their collective efforts have helped clarify certain points, shed light on various topics, and resulted in a more engaging narrative. Michael Gray, Scot Danforth, Jon Boggs, Tom Post, Linsey Perry, and the whole team team at the University of Tennessee Press have provided tremendous support along the way! Without their input, this project would have never happened. Any mistakes in relating Colley's story remain this writer's responsibility.

Thomas W. Colley

1

A Signal without a Word of Command

THE SUBJECT OF THIS SKETCH, Thomas W. Colley was born in Washington County, Virginia, Nov. 30th, 1837 of poor but respectable "parentage." I was sent to the old field schools [on the job training] until 14 years of age, when I was apprenticed to the "Blacksmith trade" at which I served for some two years and then by concent of my father decided to quit that trade and learn the Brick Masons trade which I continued to work at until April 1861. I learned to make & burn brick and to lay them up, and also learned the "Plasters business," and became quite an expert in the Plasters part of his trade. The war between the States coming on in 1860 & 61 I volunteered on the 7th of April 1861 in a cavalry company then being organized at Abingdon, Va., the county seat of my county, by Captain Wm. E. Jones [William Edmondson Jones], [who had served] previously as a Lieut. in the Mounted Rifles U.S.A. In honor of his old command, Jones named this co. the Washington Mounted Rifles.[1]

We were known as such until we merged into the 1st Regiment of Virginia Volunteer Cavalry first as Co. G and afterwards as Co. D. This regiment was composed of companies from the upper and lower Valley of Virginia with one Co. from Amelia County and one from Maryland. At first the "Maryland Co" & the Washington Mounted Rifles formed the 1st squadron in the regiment and were armed with carbines and were used as sharpshooters.[2] Afterwards all the companies were armed with rifles & the whole regiment were sharpshooters and continued in that line of service until the closing scenes around appomatox C.H. April 9th 1865.

I was constantly with my command from the day I left home for Richmond until I was finally disabled and wholy unfit for any kind of duty. I was in the Valley of Virginia with my regiment in front of Gen. Joseph E. Johnston whose forces in June 1861 and up till July 21st were at Winchester. My command was on picket duty in the medical front [the position Colley references as "medical front" is unclear] and scouting in the country watching the movements of Gen. Patterson [Major General Robert Patterson, Pennsylvania Militia]. Was on camp guard the morning Gen. Patterson advanced towards Winchester in his "first" movement to hold Johnston there, while he went to the aid of Gen. Banks [Major General Nathaniel Banks] at Manassas and in this advance,[3] where I heard the first shell "fired" from an enemy gun; the thing most dreaded by raw recruits "the peculiar whizzing sound of those missiles of death" as they pass through the air caused the hair to rise on one's head and a creepy horrible sensation run over his flesh and a great desire to be back at home with Ma. And at this particular time and place this horrible feeling seized almost the entire regiment and they started down the Pike, one co. actually going into Winchester 12 miles from the point they started from.

At the time the shell passed over us Co. D was drawn in marching order by 2, with horses heads turned toward Winchester. Captain Jones was on the front with the advance picket watching the enemys movements. Some of the boys were dismounted searching among a lot of blankets & other camp equipment that had been thrown away by a stampeded wagon driver. We had been hurried out of camp and left our baggage to the care of the wagoners. I was among the dismounted ones and would have sworn the shell that passed over the mounted mens heads some 50 or so feet in the air did not miss me 2 inches. This was a signal with out a word of command.

The whole mounted positions hit out down the pike. Captain Jones seeing or hearing the movements dashed up cursing the cowardly wretches for running away. Came in time to save me from running with the rest. Captain sent Lieut. Blackford [William Willis Blackford] after the boys, and he over hauled them and brought them back.[4]

The captain gave us a lecture on the harmlessness of these terrible missiles, especially if they were as high in the air as that one was; in 12 months from that time the sound of artillery and the whizzing of shells would only lull a soldier to sleep. He ordered me to dismount and open a place in the fence so our company could be drawn up in line to oppose any forward

Brigadier General
William E. "Grumble" Jones.
Courtesy Historical Society of
Washington County, Virginia.

General Joseph E. Johnston.
Library of Congress.

Major General Robert Patterson.
Library of Congress.

Lieutenant William Willis Blackford.
Courtesy of Mounted Clippings
Collection, Special Collections,
University Libraries, Virginia
Polytechnic Institute and
State University.

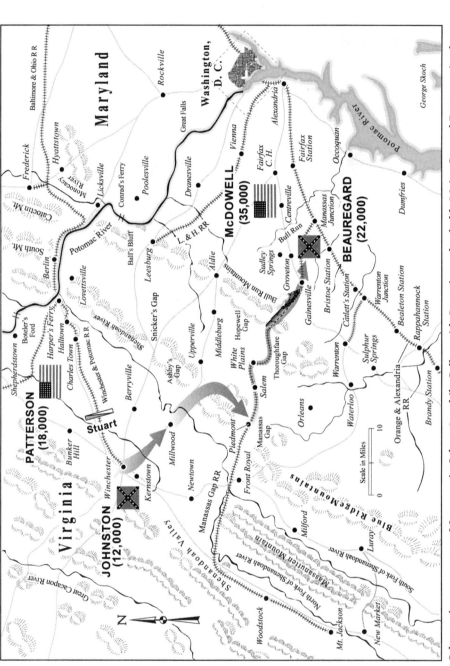

Johnston's movement to Manassas in July 1861, while Colley, with Stuart's cavalry, holds Major General Patterson in place.

movement of the enemy. General Johnston succeeded in deceiving Gen. Patterson after all his shrewd maneuvers and left him in the lower valley.[5]

Whilst Johnston was rushing the whole force to Manassas to join Gen. Beauragard [Pierre Gustave Toutant Beauregard] Gen. Stuart [at the time, Colonel James Ewell Brown Stuart] took all the companies of the regt. and pressed on with Johnston except our co. under Captain Wm. E. Jones. We were left to hover around the front of Pattersons army and keep up a bold front until the line was joined at Manassas. We left for Manassas and arrived there Saturday, and were there, ready for the memorable 21st Sunday morning, a day never to be forgotten by any who participated in its terrible coverage. I shall never forget I know, until my eyes close in death. I was out on one of the advanced picket posts near Jermanna [Jermantown] Ford on Bull Run. Just as the sun was brightening the tops of the trees "the signal gun was fired." A tremendous gun. I thought I never heard such a report and the whizzing and whining of that awful shell, "I thought it would never stop."

It went far out across the Manassas Plains into the skirting forrest. I thought if we had to charge and capture such tremendous guns, there would be none of us left to tell the tale. But I was not permitted to summarize or reflect long on these terrible unforseen results. The picket firing commenced all along the line and the cavalry were all drawn together and were moved here and there all day through clouds of road dust so thick we could not see the horse in front of us. We were finally ordered at about 2 pm to support Gen. Bartows [Colonel Francis Stebbins Bartow] & Be Brigades [Brigadier General Barnard Elliott Bee, Jr.] near Stone Bridge, and arrived there at the time they were both killed.[6] My stirrup leathers broke and I had to fall out of ranks and repair them. As I came over a hill I could see the enemys batterys and masses of infantry to my left. Farther up on the hill I saw two or three officers and I rode up to them and asked where my regiment was, and Col. Thomas G. Preston pointed out to me the direction they went, and I was satisfied it was a soldier's duty to be with his command.[7]

When the fight was on, and about that time of day it was on in all its fury and fearfulness, the face of the hill in my front was literally rent and torn with shells and shot. How I was ever to pass through that spot I could not tell, but my duty led in that direction and I must go. So I put spurs to my horse and ran the gauntlet safely and soon found my command drawn up in line in a small ravine. I had hardly goten over my run before the Hampass Legion [Brigadier General Wade Hampton's Legion] of S.C., whose officers had been killed and who were badly cut up and stampeded, came running down through a clump of pines and our company commenced cursing and abusing them for running. I asked who they were & they said South Carolinians. Damn you. You were the first to secede, now you are the first to run. It was always shocking to me to see a soldier run and especially at that time, our first fight. They said we are whiped and ruined, our cause is gone. We told them they were liars, we were not whiped there.[8]

About this time Col. Stuart took 3 companies of our regt. and charged the 14th Brooklin Zouaves, "Red Briches" fellows.[9]

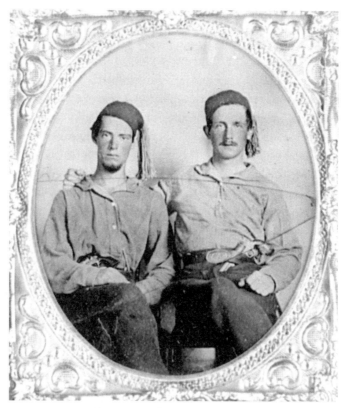

New York Zouave Soldiers. Library of Congress.

He broke their lines, and fresh forces were coming on through the night. They soon gone away, and the greatest stampeed and run for dear life that was ever imangerated since history commenced recording the events of the various ages. We were soon in the chase. The first fellow I saw on crossing Bull Run Bridge was an ambulance driver; his horses had ran away with him and stradled a tree, broke the breast yoke and smashed the front end of the vehicle up against the tree and smashed the drivers face up and tumbled him out insensible. He was just coming to when we run up on him and we wanted to know what he was doing over here invading our country. Some of the boys wanted to kill him and others thought best not to hurt the poor fellow. We had not learned then that wagoners and ambulance drivers were not at all dangerous. As beligerants we soon left him and went on after the fleeing blue coats [underlined in original].

We followed them to Cub Run and there the bridge crossing that stream was blockaded with wagons and other vehicles disabled by our artillery.[10] If we had known as much that night as we did 2 or 3 years later, not many of the boys would have ever reached Washington D.C. That night it was getting quite dark and we were brought back over the battlefield. The excitement of the dog "gone" and now it was our time to see and hear the shreaks and groans of the wounded and dying of both armys. I thought "oh horrors of horrors" is this war? It was a terrible scene. We could hear the awful groans and sighs and the calls for water and the torches going in every direction searching for friends. We were hurried on towards the junction where we started from.[11]

In the morning we had no rations, our baggage wagons had been left far in the rear. We were taken out in an old field, we soon fell asleep and had it not been for a pretty hard rain in the night I would never awakened until sunrise, but the rain struck me fair in the face and awoke me. I drew my blankets up over my head and was soon in dream land again. When we were aroused, the sun was up and shining brightly everywhere. Capt. Jones came around with a few cracker crumbs in a sack and said a friend had given them to him and he was personally carrying them around and giving each man a small handful, saying at the same time "boys this is all I can do for you this morning."

We were marched out in the evening and encamped in a grove of small scruby timber near the Manassas Plains. In the evening at about

4 p.m., a wagon brought us some corn for our horses & 2 sacks of meal; no cooking vessels nothing but meal & water. A cousin of mine W. W. Morrel [William W. Morell], a man who was always ready for anything and everything in camp or on the battlefield, suggested that we make up some fires and burn embers and ashes. The whole company was soon in the most active preparation for cooking. My mess procured some large leaves that grew on some of the trees there and wrapped up our corn dough in them. We used the mouth of the sack for a bread pan; soon all were satisfied. Some got rocks and some shaved out sticks and rolled their dough on them & held them in the fire until burnt or cooked so they could eat it. Our small mode was the best. Ours was rolled up in those large leaves and placed on the hot ground where a large pile of brush had been recently burned, and then covered with hot embers and ashes and nicely roasted. It was the sweetest bread I think I ever tasted.

Tuesday morning we started out on the trail of Uncle Abrams [President Abraham Lincoln] "bad" boys [quotations in original]. We did not come up on any live ones but plenty of dead ones and some who had been knocked down or shook out of ambulances and wagons. They were litterly ground up or mashed to pieces by their wagons and artilery wheels. We soon found plenty to eat, good coffee and crackers and canned goods of all kinds. At Munsons Hill we found a fine table spread loaded with everything good. It was prepared for Mr. Lincoln and some of his cabinet and those high in authority.[12] The boys were rather afraid to attack it for some time, for fear it was poisoned. But they soon learned there was no poison there, that it was abandoned through fright as the tide turned the wrong way, and they had no use for their hand cuffs they had brought out for Jeff Davis [President Jefferson Davis] and our officers.

We could have went to Washington City and got Uncle Abe at that time if we had "wanted him" [quotations in original] but despite all our forbearance and pleadings to be let alone to govern our own affairs, another stupendous effort was made, urged on by spite and malice and a cry for the preservation of the Union.[13]

2

I Suppose the Yankees Are Human and Will Not Murder Me

UNCLE ABE was soon able to muster another large army to invade our homes. Some wonder why southern soldiers suffered so much so many deprivations, half starved and scantly clad and ill equipped and always on the march. The answer is plain, they were fighting for everything that is dear to a patriots heart "Home," Personal and Constitutional Liberty, and I am glad that we fought until we were whittled down to a sharp point. That when they got what little earthly possesions we had left it was not enough to do them any good and still the indamitable and unconquerable spirit still lived in every true Southern "Soul," and is there today, and will go on with them into the presence of their God and live throughout all eternity.

We were engaged picketing and scouting from July until December from Leesburg on the Potomac to the mouth of the Pohick Creek near "Mount Vernon." We had numerous skirmishes. I and two of my comrades captured a sergeant, & two privates one day at a farm house where they had walked out to get a square meal. One had a pecular gun, the only one of the kind I ever saw, the cylinder—a 6 chambered concern—worked paralel with the barrel. The tubes were in the center near the screw on which the cylinder revolved. Dr. Will Dunn appropriated it. The sergeant had a fine opera glass; he was very much concerned about loosing it. It belonged to his captain he said. The other had a six shooter, Whitneys patent. I got it, first pistol I ever captured and I prized it highly.[1] Dr. Baker [Dr. John A. P. Baker] got the glass near Annandale in Fairfax County.

The yanks fixed a trap for us. They stretched telegraph wires across the road one night and placed some men in ambush and sent out a small party

Alfred Waud sketch of the 1st Virginia Cavalry. Library of Congress.

to draw us in to it. Captain Jones with 2 companies charged into it in the dark. We were all piled up in a mass. Captain Jones's mare was shot and fell on his leg and pinned him to the ground. He called out lustly for shot guns to advance on the right and left. The enemy fled in terror. They fired a volley into the mass of horses and men piled up in the road. Captain Jones's mare was the only thing hit. The enemy had no cavalry force of any consequence, and they never came out. All their work was done with infantry. They would come out at night and creep up on our pickets and some times capture or kill them.

About this time I had a sad experience. I came near killing one of my comrades. He and two others had got frightened and ran off their post one night, and I was teasing him about it. At the time, we were carrying brush to make booths to sleep under. I had an armful of brush, and he had told me if I continued to tease him he would kill me or run his saber through me. Of course, I paid no heed to that. At this moment, he had

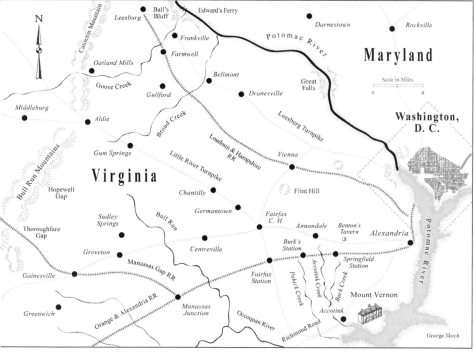

Leesburg to Mt. Vernon, Virginia. This is the area where Colley
spent the winter of 1861–62 picketing.

thrown down his brush and drew his saber. I had no arms but my carbine,
which was swinging around my shoulders. I dropped my load of brush
and grabbed the carbine, cocked it and told him to stop or I would shoot
a hole through him. At this moment W. W. Morrell [William W. Morell]
stepped between us and said "don't do that," and I said "let him put up
his saber," which he did. He had a spite at me after that. When we were
in camp at one time and had furnaces in our tents. He hit me in the head
and started to run back in his tent, but as he stooped to enter, I seized him
in the coat collar and I shoved him forward in the furnace. His head and
face in a bed of hot embers, it burnt him considerably. A mess mate of his
grabed us and pulled us out of the fire. We made friends then in this same
camp.

Early in November 1861, one of my mess mates—and an old schoolmate
—was shot by the accidental discharge of a double-barreled shot gun in
the hands of a comrade in another company, located just above our line.

We were going to roll call and inspection of arms in the evening just about sun down. Each company were required to go up to their captains' tents or quarters, which was in a line at the head of each company. Wm. F. P. Clark [William Franklin Page Clark], my comrade who was shot, was moving up the line. Dr. Gilbert C. Greenway was on the opposite side of him walking with his hand on comrade Clark's shoulder at the fatal moment, when the comrade came out of his tent with his gun muzzle in front of the flap of the tent. He caught the hammer of his gun and raised it enough to explode the cap and discharge the piece, which was loaded with some 16 or 18 buck shot; some 8 or 9 of them struck comrade Clark. It entered his Testament which he usually carried in his side pocket; it was at that time immediately over his heart and saved him from instant death. Two shots went in his left arm and three in his hip, and the one that passed through his stomach, which caused his death about four o'clock next morning. One shot passed through Dr. Greenway's pants behind and cut the skin. Two more went through Captain Gaither's [George Riggs Gaither, Jr.] tent at the top. This accident brought a deep gloom over the whole regiment and especially over his underrated company. He was a brave noble hearted young man, a man of great promise as a soldier and beloved by all, as especially his two most intimate companions, W. W. Morrell and myself. We were the only two who stood by him that long gloomy night.[2]

He suffered terribly at times, vomiting up the blood that accumulated in his stomach; it made him deathly sick. We had provided him as good a bed as our united blankets and company would afford. It was an awful night, one of those dismal dark rainy nights. It looked at times as if the tent would be actually flooded with water. We had to go out as many as three times in the night with our sabres and cut ditches around the tent. We were wet to the hide and weary with watching for the last flicker of life to go out of the mortal body of a dearly beloved companion. It is hard to die at home surrounded by mothers, fathers brothers and sisters, with all the comforts home can afford. This was the first death in camp. It made an awful impression on me and I resolved to be a better man, but also for humane resolutions. It was soon shaken off and amid the stiring scenes of camp life; all good resolves were soon forgotten, but still they would not stay down. They would come back in the lonely night watches out in some old Piney field, or at some lonely crossroads, many times expecting the enemy to creep up and shoot or stab me to death in the dark.

We procured a coffin and had the lifeless body of our comrade encased and sent home to his grief-stricken parents; a sad task to us and doubly so to those at home. Who had only a few short months ago parted with him in the bloom of his young manhood, filled with all the bright prospects of the future. But there is a bright light in every cloud, only our dull eyes cannot discern it, blinded as they are by the veil of mortality.

A great many of our comrades took the bilious[3] and Typhoid fever. I took yellow jaundice shortly after this occurence and moped around. All I wanted to eat was "Brown Sugar" [quotations in original]. I used every strategy to get a supply and generally succeeded. I was on guard at the commisary department one night. They had just opened a barrel of the best New Orleans brown & ropey; I filled my haversack. All good soldiers were careful of their haversacks as they were with their arms and ammunition. An empty haversack was only carried by a lazy do less soldier. When it could be possibly avoided, even if one was on the watch and move all the time day & night if need be, he always found rations enough to keep him alive.

A good cavalry soldier had a double duty to perform in his line. He had his horse to provide for in addition to himself, but it very often happened that while he was looking for one he found both [food for man and horse]. About this time, we were moved back behind the infantry camps and built winter quarters. Each mess built huts according to their inteligence in such matters and the willingness to work. My mess—ten of us—we had two masons and one carpenter. We built a double pine log cabin with chimney in center with two fireplaces. We had quite comfortable quarters and good spring mattresses composed of pine poles covered with straw or sagegrass, and a blanket or gum cloth spread over that for a sheet, and our coats for pillows.

A few days before Christmas my company was returning from picket duty. We passed General J. E. B. Stuart's headquarters, as the boys and especially my mess were looking out for fun and something to eat. Comrade Thos. W. Bailey [Thomas White Bailey] and W. W. Morrell spied a fine turkey gobbler the General had up in a coop, fattening him for his Christmas dinner. The boys said they were going to have him that night. I tried to disuade them, told them we had plenty. Will Morrell had just received a large box from home, with ham cakes and two large dressed turkeys in it, and we had combined and bought three more from our sutler. At this stage of the war we had plenty of all kinds of rations. We threw away a large quantity of good meat at this time that we would have been glad to have picked up out of the mud in two or three years. The boys went out that night and got the Generals gobbler. We had a colored cook hired at that time and were having a good time generally. We had our cook to clean & prepare the large fat gobbler that night.

Next day, General Stuart's colored cook was around through the camp hunting for his turkey. Our old cook and him had a long talk about the stolen turkey. At the same time, Uncle "Brady" [likely the cook Colley and his messmates had hired] had him in the camp kettle. He told Stuart's cook "the young men had plenty of turkeys and would not of course thought of such a thing as stealing 'Massa' Stuart's turkey." Of course, Uncle Brady had distroyed all signs of the butchery: the entrals and all the feathers were carefully burned up. The General's "rage" was terrible. If he could have discovered the guilty culprits, no doubt he would have reaked vengance on them in the shape of confinement in the guard house and double duty and other vile things, that kind officers inflicted on all who did not come up to the strict rules of the military "Discipline;" such as standing on a flour barrel head and being tied up by the thumbs to a pole, or carrying a large fence rail for 12 or 15 or 24 hours on a stretch. But our regiment was never subjected to such treatment, and especially our company.

I do not remember of ever seeing more than three or four of my company punished in any way. The boys were sometimes lodged in the guard house for a short time. We ate the turkey all the same and had many a hearty laugh over the General's discomfort over his loss. One of our mess Robb J. Sanders [Robert J. Sanders] had a severe sick spell in our winter quarters; he was discharged and sent home. Afterwards, I missed him all the time. He was a good soldier, but one of those high tempered, pecular kind of beings. Nothing ever pleased him. It took patience and courage to wait on him. None of the boys would have anything to do with him. W. P. Clark, Will Morrell, and he and I were having a little social game of cards in the tent one day. Sanders and Will Morrell fell out over the game and passed the D-Lie [perhaps Colley references a dead-line, as found in most Civil War prisons]. Will drew his knife and would have stabed him, had not Will Clark and I interfered. I caught Sanders and threw him out through the back of the tent. Will Clark pushed Will Morrell out at the front. We had hard work to keep them apart but finally succeeded, and then I told them no more cards for me, "if the war lasted a thousand years and I lived that long." I would never engage in another game and I kept my vow so far as camp games were concerned. Sometimes I would play a game with ladies at home, but seldom I allowed myself to do that even.

I took down in February 1862 with Malaria Fever. I went about until I fainted and fell off my horse one day. I had goten up and stepped out side the door of our quarters, had made some two or three steps when everything turned green and down I went in the mud about half leg deep. It was quite cold and but few of the boys were stiring. A cousin of mine, David H. Morrell, happened to be at the door of his hut and saw me fall and ran to my assistance, and called for help. They carried me in and placed me on my bunk, where the doctor told me to stay; I was there for some 3 weeks.

At this time General J. E. Johnston had determined to evacuate Manassas and move his men to Yorktown to meet General McClellan's [Major General George Brinton McClellan] second on to Richmond movement, as that seamed to them the most direct route.[4] Orders were given to send all the sick to hospitals in the rear. One morning—I see by date of furlough in my possession: February 27th 1862—news came to me through my mess mates that I would have to go to a hospital. I had visited some of our boys that were sick and in a Confederate Hospital. All the bedding I saw was a blanket spread on the floor and I was determined, in my own mind, I would never enter one as long as I had power to resist. I told my companions altho I was yet too weak to sit up but for a short time, I was not going and requested them to load and cap my pistol and give it to me, which my cousin Will Morrell did. They all went out and left me alone, none of them wishing to get into trouble for breach of military discipline.

I knew all the ambulance drivers did not have much ambition for a sudden and tragic death, and I would not have much trouble in ridding myself of them pretty soon. One drove up to the door of our shack and opened it and walked in and said "good morning." I said "howdy, what do you want here?" He said, "I came to take you to the hospital." I said, "the hell you did." I had my pistol concealed under the blanket, cocked and ready for use. I drew it out and leveled it at his body and said, "I am not going alive and you get out of here as soon as you can or I will fix you for a

Major General George B. McClellan.
Library of Congress.

Hospital or a hole in the ground." One look was enough for him. I expect I was a pretty frightful looking object any way, beard and hair both long and tangled and I all emaciated, bony and haggard. He left in a rush, did not take time to shut the door.

Some of the boys came in, they did not know what the result would be. Our old Captain, Wm. E. Jones, a rigid discipline man, was Colonel of the 1st then. We did not have long to wait. As soon as the driver reported to headquarters, the Colonel came tearing in and the first thing I knew he was in the middle of the room. He said in his short quick way, "Colley they say you won't go to the hospital." I said, "no sir I will not." He said "what the hell will you do then?" I said "I do not know sir. That is one thing I am not going to do while I am alive." He went on to state to me "General Johnstons" orders,[5] and stated the army would fall back in a few days and

I would be left to the mercy of the Yankees. I said "very good I have a good comfortable bed here and I suppose the Yankees are human and will not murder me and it is almost certain death to go to a hospital under present arrangements." He said, "well I dont know what to do with you." I said, "Colonel I can tell you what to do, send me home to my mother, where I can get good nursing and kind treatment and I will be well and back to my post of duty in a few weeks." He said, "I will do it if the Doctor says you can stand the trip." As soon as he went back to his quarters, he sent the doctor and he concluded I could go.

We had another sick man in our company, Rufus Williams [Rufus Chapman Williams]. He had been down with fever; by my stubborn insubordination we both got furloughs home. It was not two hours from that time until we had our papers signed up and were in the ambulance on our way to Haymarket, the nearest railroad station to our camp. We were both quite weak but busied up with the hope of getting home where we could [eat] food prepared by our mothers' loving hands. We had to stay over until next morning awaiting the train. We did very well until bedtime, when our landlord told us we would have to go upstairs to sleep. Neither of us could have stepped up a flight of steps to have saved our lives. We both tried it by the help of the hand rail but failed. Where there is a will there is always a way. I said "if I can not walk up I can crawl up," so down on my knees I went, and Rufus followed suit. We were soon landed in a good comfortable bed and off in the Land of Dreams. We both awoke much refreshed by our good nights sleep. We arose and dressed and went down to the office, or sitting room rather, and soon had breakfast announced. Of course, neither of us had any appetite much for anything; we both ate some.

We were more interested about the train arriving than anything else. It was due at 9: am. and came in on time. We were soon out. We had steps to climb to get to the platform at the depot. We got up them the way we got up the stairway. Persons standing around, seeing our weak conditions and feeble also, assisted us on the train. We found a friend from our county, Colonel Buck Edmondson. He had two sons in our company, and he had his daughter with him. She had been to Winchester to see her husband who was encamped there; he belonged to Stonewall Jackson's Division. We came on all right until we arrived at Lynchburg Va. It was hard to get hotel acommodations as there was so many sick on their way to and from home. We stopped at the Orange House [a boarding house] and Colonel Edmondson prevailed on the landlord to let us sleep in the parlor. They brought in mattresses and placed them on the floor for Colonel Edmondson and his daughter to sleep on. There was two large sofas; Rufus and I occupied them. We all rested comfortably and was up and ready for the long ride of 284 miles to our home in the brave south-west.

We came on to Christiansburg and found the recent heavy rains had washed a trestle away, and the train that left Lynchburg the day before was there. My father was on it; he had been to Richmond, Virginia with horses and mules for the Government.[6] He was purchasing agent "at that time." Rufus and I were all right when we got with him. We were on the train all night and up till next day about 11: pm. We came to Marion. A mile above the town we came to another wash out. The bridges were all gone for some 10 miles at this point. We walked out about a mile on the McAdam [macadamized] road.[7] It was tuff on us but we took our time. We came to the house of an old friend of my fathers, Mark Harper by name. His good wife fixed up a nice dinner for us. After dinner, Mr. Harper hitched up his wagon and hauled us to the residence of Captain Jacob Merchants.[8] The train on that side of the break being gone, we had to content ourselves until next day. Mrs. Merchant was a kind motherly old lady, she got up something for Rufus and I to eat, and we slept and was refreshed. We gained strength rapidly. We stayed with these good kind people until noon next day. Father and I got off the train near our home, through the kindness of the conductor, and Rufus went on to Abingdon. We had a short mile to walk to get home. I was glad, mother and sisters were glad too.

My long trip, and eating everything I could get, brought on a relapse of fever and our old family physician had to be called in. He had me about straight again in a few weeks and then I had a good time with the girls. Two, I remember, came near coming to blows about which should have me. At this time I was very bashful in the presence of ladies. I was invited to a quilting where there was a number of young ladies. The lady of the house requested me to sit at the foot of the table, her husband being absent that day. She had two nice fat hens roasted with dressing, and she politely requested me to carve them. That was one thing I had never attempted to do in a scientiffic "manner," and being considerably embarassed any way made the task that much harder. I tugged and sawed away trying to get a wing off and the girls set into giggling and laughing and poking fun at me. Finally, the hostess came to my releif. It came very near spoiling all my fun that day, but we must all live and learn.

My old commandeo R R Cassel [Rufus R. Cassell] was at home at the same time on furlough. He was very much struck on a couple of young ladies, one of which he afterwards made his wife. One was from an adjoining county, the other was teaching school near our homes. He laid around the school house a great deal. I wrote him a note [Colley pretending to be the teacher] and requested him to come oftener, that she could not live with out his presence. He tore off in a high state of bliss and showed her the note. She disclaimed all knowledge of it, and the hunt commenced for the author. At last they saddled it on me. I generally wrote his letters for him to his other girls. I wrote one for him one day, and in a day or two I wrote an answer; by the aid of the Postmaster I got it in the mail. It was a scorcher. It upbraded him for his unfaithfulness to her, about his courtship with the other lady, and declaring she wanted nothing more to do with him. Of course I had to read it to him and console him the best I could. He was in a terrible state for a few days. He at length concluded to go and see her and try to bring about a reconciliation, and that forced me to tell him I had played a trick on him. He and I stayed at home until the last of April 1862, when we left for our command which was at that time on the peninsula near Williamsburg, Va.[9]

3

The Wonderful Feat Accomplished
by a Few Cavalrymen

WE WENT TO RICHMOND and put up at the Columbian Hotel.[1] He nor I either had ever been in a big city Hotel, we were as green as green could be. One of our company, W. D. Barber,[2] was in the city. He had been a page in Congress in his boy hood and was up to city life. When he found us, he had us moved to his room and some spirits ordered by the underground route as "martial" law was enforced and nothing stronger than water or wheat, or rye coffee could be found above ground. But Billy knew the ropes.[3] We furnished the money and he procured the spirits. He took us to the Theater and let us see Wonders performed there.

Next morning at breakfast, the bill of fare was handed each of us. Cassell said to the waiter who presented it, "I dont want to read I want to eat." We teased him about that till the end of the war. I knew as little about a bill of fare as he did. I had read or heard of such tings but had never saw one before. A soldier did not want to be fooled with, they were used to seeing things on the table. When they were called to a meal at home, and in camp when a meal was ready, all we had to do was to come to the camp kettle or frying pan if we had such. We ate with a wooden spoon out of the camp kettle, or if we had gravy or soup "we soped our bread in the frying pan" and laughed and jested. We grumble and growl now about clean cooking; if we could see a meal prepared by a dirty, lousy soldier, it would almost turn the stomach of a botlentot or a Digger Indian.[4]

Wheat dough mixed up on a dirty gum or oil cloth that he had slept on or under, and rode on per chance, or used as a saddle cloth for months. Meat, if he had any cooked, just as it came from the butcher's hand, or bacon or pork as it came from the crate or barrel. Hands washed by one comrade pouring water from the mouth of a canteen, or one and sometimes two or three at a time when water was scarce; there was but little used for washing hands or face. When we had time, and came to a river or large water course we would take a general wash, strip off our shirts and wade out in the water and give them [shirts] a cold bath and spread them out on the ground or hang them on a bush to dry. If they got too thick with vermin on them, or eggs, we would build up a fire and boil them in a camp kettle. Such was camp life "in the Confederacy."

We suffered all these hardships and endured them all and thousands more for "Constitutional Liberty," and still there is men and women in these United States that would have us teach our children we were Rebels and were all wrong and that we were sorry and all those kind of things. Our northern brethern can not understand how we are truly loyal to the U.S. Government and were not wrong in waging war against the invasion of the sacred soil of their several states, their homes, and firesides.

Comrade Cassell and myself left the city for Williamsburg next morning and arrived the night after the Battle of that place.[5] We were in time for the retreat up the Peninsula covering "the rear of General Joe Johnston's Army, picketing and scouting first on the James River and then on the York River. We got hold of some oysters in the shell. We had a nice time roasting them in the shell using a little salt and pepper; those who were fortunate enough to have any on hands. We had a good time eating oysters and fish. Rations were quite plentiful at this time in April 1862.

I was on picket on a high point on James River where I had spent the night, and the noise of the frogs "I thought I never heard such a den in all my life, little squeaky frogs and then some on a higher key," and then the Great Wide Mouthed Bull frog with his hoarse and enormous "Voice calling out Jug-o-Rum Jug-o-Rum," and then the millions of mosquitos that swarmed around my head and covered my face and hands. It was enough to cause a Roman Sentry to desert his post. You can imagine how I longed for day light to come, and how I welcomed it, when I could see the first bright streak of light in the far distant east. With my eyes fixed in that line, down the waters of the majestic James, a sight greeted my vision that made me shutter. It was an eminence color of black smoke shot up into the sky, and presently the awful sound of a terrific explosion, and

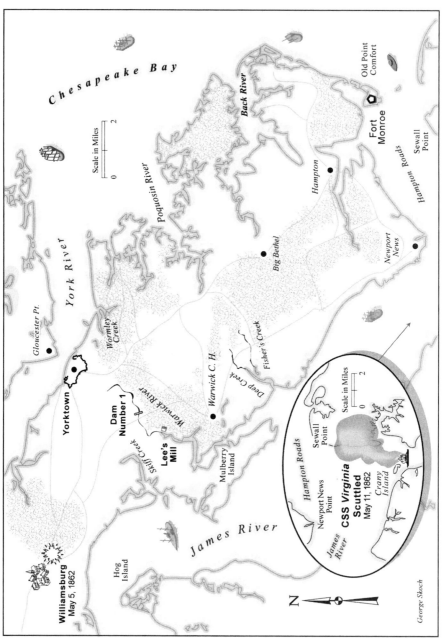

The Peninsula Campaign, showing the scuttling of C.S.S. *Virginia*. Colley witnessed this event.

George Skoch

then the awful 'far and shaking of old mother earth.' It was the death of the *Merrimac*, the Ironclad monster which had so recently cursed [and] shook havoc and consternation to "Uncle Abe" and his people.[6] I could not imagine what had taken place. I thought probably the "yanks" had invented some great 'Machine that was to blow us all up and send us on our way Heavenward or Hellward, where they wished we were a many a time,' and where we would have 'consigned' them if we had had the power to direct their shipments, and especially just after such a night's 'experience' as I had just endured. After a good meal and a comfortable nap, and the companionship of comrades, all this passed off and all were jovial, and full of mirth and fun.

After several days of marches in mud and rain, we fell back behind the treacherous swamps of the Chickahominy, where many brave and noble souls went out of their tenements of clay to 'meet their God,' Who gave them unseen by mortal eyes. Whose bones are today buried in the black murkey mud and leaves that fill this dismal place. Nothing cheerful but the tall majestic Camphor trees that raise up out of the black waters. A host will come up at the 'Great Day,' both of Blue and Gray out of the murkey depths of this stream.

When we came back to Richmond our camp was 'established' on Brook Avenue, some 4 miles out of the city limits. That threw us on the extreme left of General Johnston's position. We could do but little out side of picket duty, and that on the beaten highways. We were here some month or six weeks until General J. E. B. Stuart conceived the driving idea of making his celebrated 'raid' around McClellans 'vast' army. One morning, the bugle sounded boots and saddles; we had already drawn 3 days rations and we knew something was on the move. The head of our colum was turned towards Ashland, and our conjectures were, we are on our way to the Valley to join Jackson. But it is well that the great mass of the army do not know where they are going until they get there. We have one instance of how a considerable army was reduced by the proclamation that who-so-ever is fearful and afraid let him return and depart early from Mt. 'Gilead,' and there returned 20 and 2000.[7]

We marched all day northward, and marched some hours after dark, and camped in a thick pine forest. We were hurried out by dawn and in the evening; began to come in contact with enemys cavalry out posts, which

Burial of Latané. Library of Congress.

we soon demolished or captured near 'Old Church' [where] the Brave Captain Latané was killed and left.[8]

He was buried by the Brave Virginia Women of that 'vicinity.' Our 1st regiment took the front and charged an out post at the top of a high old road hill. There was a tremendous mud hole, and the 1st set of fours in the column all went down. I had a fresh and high-spirited horse. He cleared the mass of horses and men at one tremendous bound, it was at least 20 feet, and some of the yanks sat on their horses and watched us. We were on them in an instant We asked them "why they did not make their escape?" and they said "they wanted to see us fall in the mud." They remarked "that if that had been them, they would have all tumbled in the mud in a pile."

Just beyond this, to the right of the road, was their camp and tents. We were soon in among the camp. I found a fine little silver watch in one tent, it was in the vest pocket of an officer, who in his haste, had left it hanging in his tent. I sent it home to a cousin of mine to keep for me. At the time of the Stoneman Bridge raid through south west Virginia, she and her sister put all their valuables in a trunk and hid them out in the woods, where a tree had blown up and covered it with leaves. The yanks soon saw the fresh signs and uncovered and rifled it of its contents, 'my watch' going up with the other things.[9] As I left this camp and was attempting to regain the highway, my horse came near being swamped in the treacherous quick sand; as luck would have it, only his hind feet. We caught, and he made three desperate 'lunges' before he could extricate himself; came near unhorsing me.

We moved on with our prisoners some 2 miles from this point. About twenty-five cavalry men came up to the rear guard, and surrounded, they thought they were entirely cut off from their army. They frightened one of my company who was at a private house 'pirating,' as we called it, hunting for grub. The house was some distance from the road. When he saw the yanks pass, he thought they were pursuing our colum, and he was cut off so he had no other alternative, only to swim the Pamunkey River and make his way back to Richmond. He came in some three days after our return to camp.

We came to Turnstall's Station about dark and tried to intercept a train on the York River Railroad. The engineer seeing or hearing something of what was up put on steam and rushed over our obstructions, which had been hastily thrown on the track. A few shots were fired at him as he passed. It was reported that the engineer and all plunged into the York River [false report] at the "White House," as it was only a short distance from where we fired into it.[10] A detachment of our men was sent there and destroyed several transports and a lot of army stores and brought in several prisoners. I was helping to guard prisoners that night. A Lieutenant Cummings [Lieutenant John S. Cummings] of our regiment attempted to pass us as we were halted in the road. In doing so his horse slipped and fell on his leg, pinning him to the ground, or mud rather. He ripped out a terrible oath, ordering some one to get down and move his horse off his leg. Some started to obey. I told them to get back. I would see him in 'Hell' before I would turn a hand to help him, until he addressed me in more gentlemanly terms. He soon said, "please men, some of you get down and remove my horse." I said, "that sounds right, get down and help him."

We had come in contact with sutlers' wagons and the Federal Hospitals in the rear of the army. The boys had gotten a lot of whiskey and some were getting lively. We had to leave one of our company 'a German who had come to our company as a substitute' for a man who wished to get out to marry a wealthy woman, she furnishing the money to pay for the substitute. He was as gallant a cavalryman as ever strode a horse. He served to the end and came home with his comrades and made his home in our midst. He married a good, industrious, poor girl and made a good living. He professed 'Christ' and lived a Christian life for several years before his death. All honor to such disinterested 'Patriots' as Jacob Savarty.[11] Peace to his ashes. His only fault was he loved the ardent spirits too well, and would get full if there was enough to fill him. I passed him that night, he was down by a 'keg' of some 20 gallons on the truck. Some fellow had turned it on end and knocked the head out, so all who passed could help themselves either by cup or canteen. It was well coated with horse hairs and dust. When I passed it, I had a couple of nice quart bottles of Rye I had gotten from a sutler's wagon. I did not need any of that, it caused poor Jacob a few months recreation at Fort Delaware.[12]

All night long we were swinging around General McClellan's rear and towards the James. As day light began to dawn, we realized where we were. A little squad of cavalry with 2 pieces of 'Pelham's Battery' in the rear of that vast army, with water, swamps, and mud, in our front. The wide, and the turbid James on our left, with its waters covered with gunboats and transports.[13] On our right, the York; in our rear, the little narrow strip of land on which we could possibly retreat to the Chesapeake Bay. Our leader had no thought of being trapped as long as he and his men could wade or swim or fight their way out.

About midday we came to a fence in the 'Chickahominy' where had been an old road in time; it had not been used for 20 years, so the citizens said. We had to bridge a narrow channel to get our artillery across on an island, and then we could make the balance of the route seven miles through this 'bog,' which sometimes hardly covered our horses hoofs, and sometimes ran over their backs. What made us 'cringe' most was those sharp cone shaped Cypress. They were as sharp as a bayonet, and long enough to run through a horse and man both. I thought it certain death if my horse should fall on one of those things or stumble and throw me on one of them. I would have prefered charging a brigade of 'Infantry' and running the risk of escaping unhurt, as I stated.

We had a bridge to build, the piers or uprights were already standing. All we had to do was to put on sills and lay a floor. This was soon

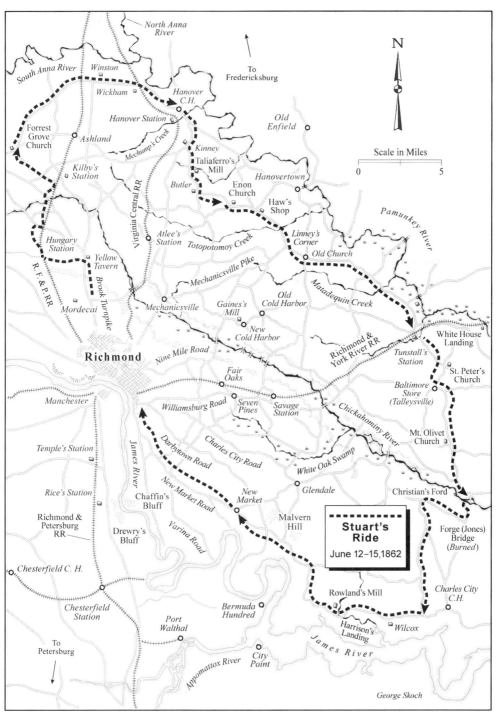

Stuart's first ride around McClellan, June 12–15, 1862.

accomplished by tearing down a large barn near by and carrying the timbers and planks. It was awful hot weather. Our noble commander J. E. B. Stuart and all the officers, or the principal part of them, were all working like beavers. General Stuart was in an old flatboat helping to get the sills across. While we were doing this, the best swimmers were swimming our horses across this channel. By the time the bridge was done, all the horses were over on the island. We rolled the artillery over by hand and carried our saddles and blankets over on the bridge. When all were saddled up we crossed the island and plunged into the swamp. We had to swim some distance on the start. I remember a laughable incident. Among the prisoners was an Irish man. He caught James W. Byar's [James M. Byars] horse by the tail, and by that means swam over. When he landed he said "be Jesus, your horse's tail saved me life."

We had to leave one of our caisson here after it got hung on a Cypress tree and could not be gotten loose in the deep water and mud. The bridge was set on fire as soon as we crossed it and the enemy ran some pieces of artillery out on the high ground in our rear and gave us a few parting shells as our rear guard was going into the swamp. It was late in the evening when we emerged from the dismal and gloomy swamp and came out near one of those old Reliable Old Virginia Residences that are situated in the high grounds 'along the banks of the James River.' This was a delightful place, with a large grove of ancient oaks and the ground covered with luscious grass. We were commanded to be very quiet. We got corn for our horses, and as the road we had to travel on was for some distance in sight of the James River, we had to lay here until dark came or so we could, under cover of its cable lines, make our way safe back to our friends at Richmond.

When night came we moved out silently, and during the night frequent halts were made and "P Coats" sent out to see if the way was clear, and the caution repeated not to make any noise. [14] No clanking of sabres or jingling of spurs was heard that long night. We rode like a long line of phantom horsemen.The colum moved on. At day light, we came to 'Charles City Courthouse,' and the word went around "You are safe back in your own lines, rest." We did rest, all that day and that night.[15]

The next morning, we marched through the city and out to our camp. We were cheered on every street. The news having preceeded us of the wonderful feat accomplished by a few cavalrymen. This was the first time 'Heros Von Borcke' the noble Prushan was with us.[16] He split a Yankee's head open with one stroke of his 'broad sword' on this raid. He just halved his head, with one half falling on each shoulder. I was a large stout man but I could not hold his sword straight out at arms length. He was a man of tremendous muscular power and an expert swordsman. He was on General Stuart's staff until the Generals death. The General was very much attached to him, and when he was wounded in 1863 at or near Aldie in a cavalry fight, he placed himself between Stuart and the Yankee sharpshooters and received a sever wound. The ball entered his lungs from which he never entirely recovered.[17]

Not long after he came to our command I was on duty as sentinal at General Stuart's headquarters, which were at that time in Hanover Courthouse. I was leaning against one of the columns, sabre in hand about half asleep, when 'Von Borcke' came rushing in with his 'Dutch Gleeb.' If he gave me the pass word, I did not know any thing more about it than I would if a 'Gander' had addressed me in 'Goose Language.' I let him pass in, and stood for some time expecting to be reported for being asleep on duty. I well knew that was the worst place in the Confederacy for a soldier to be caught at; anything that was not in strict accord with military discipline. I did not nod any more that time, until I was relieved and sent to my quarters. 'I was certainly more frightened for the time than I ever was in a battle.'

4

The Air Was Literly Poluted
with the Stink of the Dead

AFTER A FEW DAYS REST we were on the move again. The '7 Pines battle' [Seven Pines/Fair Oaks] was passed.[1] We were on our extreme left, on a high point in a clump of pines. We could do nothing but listen to the deadly strife going on. The 'bog and swamps' were too much for 'horsemen,' and of course we were not engaged in the battle. We were kept out on the high ground in daylight and sent down in the swamps at night to guard the fords and bridges. Here we had to contend with those ever lasting blood suckers, the 'mosquito.' If the tortures of Hell are any worse than 'Body Lice' under the clothing, and mosquitos on the face and hands, than one in a position where he is compeled to keep quiet as a faithful sentinel on out post liable at any moment to be shot or stabed to death by the enemy scouts. The horrors of a night on an out post in the Chickahominy Swamp can never be erased from the mind of one who has experienced it. The everlasting pain caused by the croaking of millions of frogs and the chorusing of the myriads of mosquitos around his head. This was intolerable where one needed all the powers of eyes and ears to catch the faintest sound of an approaching enemy.

After sometime spent in this pleasant task, it was a great releif to receive orders to prepare 3 days rations and we were on the move again towards 'Ashland.' Just at the dawning of day we arrived at that place. To our great surprise and joy we ran right into 'Stonewall Jackson's' foot 'cavalry.'[2] We were soon exchanging greetings with some of our accquaintances of the 37th and 48th Virginia boys[.][3] Our horses' heads were soon turned down towards the enemys left flank, and all day long we moved on toward Old Church and 'Cold Arbour' [Harbor]. We were on Jackson's

Colonel Samuel Vance Fulkerson.
Courtesy of Fulkerson.org.

right to cover his movements from the enemy, and come in contact with
their out posts.

We could hear the booming of cannons at 'Mechanicsville.'[4] About 4
o'clock in the evening we came in contact with infantry and were changed
over to the left of our forces, while Jackson pressed forward on their right
wing and drove them from their works. Here the brave and noble hearted
Colonel Samuel Fulkerson lost his life while galantly leading his regiment
in one of the desperate charges on the enemys 'breastworks.'[5] We spent
the night here on the battle field in the midst of the dead and wounded,
administering to their wants as best we could by giving them water and
placing them in easy positions.

At dawn, we were ordered to move on farther to the left and rear of
the Federal army. In a short time, we came in view of the White House
Landing which had been General McClellan's base of supplies, and the
hospitals for all his sick. The sick and wounded had all been removed and
the tents and stores nearly all burned up. There was a transport with a
heavy piece of artillery aboard, which opened up on us as soon as we came
in sight. There was all so a lot of sharpshooters. Our sharpshooters were

soon dismounted and deployed in a skirmish line, and ordered to move forward across the wide bottom land. Our skirmishers here, were at that time, composed of companies D and K. As we neared the bank of the river, she [artillery on transport] gave us a few charges of grape shot along with rifle balls and shells but that did not check us at all.

There was one fellow I had a particular spite at. He was perched up in the rigging on a sixth platform around the main mast. He put balls pretty close to me and comrade John Hockett; we were on our extreme right and fartherest down the river. We were the first to reach the river bank and had a fair shot at him. As the transport passed on her way down the river, I think we got him, as there was no more shots from that quarters.[6]

As soon as the field was clean, we all came up to the landing and commenced loading up with rations and trinkets. I got a new haversack and filled it full of combs, pocket knives, blacking [boot blacking] and brushes. I had enough to start a store in 'Dixie.' I had my own haversack filled with spiced pig's feet, soda crackers, a bottle or two of wine and other good things. Some of our cavalry command got hold of something that made them quite sick, and two of the number died. The report abounded that the yanks had 'poisoned' the wells. Another report was that they had thrown their medicine into the wells to prevent them falling into our hands. The later story might have been the true one.

We were now on the extreme right and rear of the Federal army on the peninsula below the 'Chickahominy river,' and were constantly coming in contact with 'stragglers' that had been cut off from their command and were trying to make their way down to Yorktown. Sometimes, we would encounter a whole regiment. Our regiment captured a 'Major,' along with the greater part of the 2nd Virginia Federal.[7] They were the only prisoners I ever knew our boys to curse and abuse in any way. I did not, for one, engage in this because I did not think it right to disarm a man and then curse him. The ole Major was a foreigner of some nationality. He became very much enraged, and properly he said, "it was quite 'ungentlemanly' to disarm a man and then curse him." In this charge, my new haversack strap broke and it fell to the ground with all my stores. I tried to recover it, but alas, a thousand horses' hoofs had struck it and it was literally ground into dust with all its contents, and with it my fond hopes of 'Present to Loved Ones at home,' and of a speculative nature. Alas for poor weak human nature, one moment we see vast possessions and happiness, and in another moment we with all earthly possessions are hurled to the earth or ground to dust by the hoofs of time, and we with them soon pass away. And if our hopes are not stayed on 'Him' who said to Pilate "My Kingdom is not of this world," we have alas lived in vain.

My loss was soon forgotten in the excitement of the chase, as I had broken ranks to get my treasures. I thought I would have a little frolick all to myself, and left the main road and went down in the bottom land to a large fine house, where I ran two or three yanks. I told them they were in a hole surrounded on all sides. I turned them over to a squad of our men who came up at that time. Got something to eat and went on down to 'Mr. Tuckers,' who had a large farm in the Chickahominy swamps. He was glad to see a Rebel Soldier. I told him we were all around him. He said there was plenty of yanks down in his bottom fields, and they had a picket. He wanted me to go down and see them, and of course I was not allowed to do so. For fear the old gentleman would think I was a coward, I started down the main road towards the swamp. It did not take me long to find out there was yanks there and plenty of them. They made the balls whiz around my head, as they were concealed in the bushes. I could not see any of them and I came back about as fast as I went. I told the old gentleman I would go on and get reinforcements and come back and rake them in.

As the colum was moving on towards the James River, it was sometime before I caught up with my company. The night before the Battle of Malvern Hill we crossed the 'Chickahominy' to the west side, and was on our extreme left where we stayed some three days after the 7 days fight was ended.[8] One night we were moved out on the line of the battlefield. The air was literly poluted with the stink of the dead horses and men, for I ought to know. At dawn in the morning, we came to our other works of fortifications around the city and up to our old camp on Brook Avenue [in Richmond], where for the first time in fifteen days, we had a chance to change our clothing and get rid of some of our boarders, who had a long uninterrupted spell to increase their various families. To say they had not improved their opportunity would be putting it in a mild form. They were numerous and of all sizes and ages, from the 'eggs or nits' to the old gray backed Great-Great-Great Grandfather and Grandmother. Some as large, as large wheat grains, and some so small that they could hardly be

Brigadier General
Williams Wickham.
Courtesy of Ancestry.com.

seen with the naked eye. They all came in for a share of 'Rebel blood,' it mattered not about their age.[9]

I remember a sad experience I had the first night we were ordered to unsaddle our horses and take a good rest. I had a fine new gun cloth I had captured and I divested myself of my garments, and like our great ancestor 'Adam' in his primitive innocence, free from vermin, thought I would take one good night's rest as the weather was quite warm. I spread myself out on the gum cloth. I had hardly become quiet until a more deadly enemy made an assault on my nude person from head to foot—'the executive mosquito.' I cussed and stomped and swore but it all did no good. I had to crawl back into my discarded garments and let the hungry horde go to work. They were preferable to their 'brothers the mosquito.' You who know nothing about soldiers' life can form but a poor conception of the ever-lasting torture of a soldiers' life. But with all this we were cheerful and always ready for a fight or a frolick.

Our cavalry force went out to General Wickham's [at the time Colonel Williams Carter Wickham] farm near Hanover Court House and recruited up our horses.

We were here some two or three weeks. We then moved up to 'Fredericksburg' and on up towards 'Waterloo Bridge.' We were skirmishing and picketing along the 'Rappahannock River' while Pope [Major General John Pope] and McClellan were concentrating their forces and preparing for the second Great Battle at Manasses."[10] About the 23rd [22] of August 1862, I received my first wound. All the sharpshooters of our brigade were concentrated at Waterloo Bridge on the Warrenton turnpike.[11] We were on the west bank of the river and the yanks on the east bank. They were protected by a lot of tennant houses and a skirt of timber, while we were comparatively unprotected, only by a house and a temporary breast works made of a few rails taken from a fence near by.

On our right was some few large oaks. Some sharpshooters of the Blue had gotten up into the upper stories of the houses and were putting in their work with a vim. I saw a place where I could get a fair view of them and put in some good shots. I went to 'Colonel Tom Rosser' who was in command, and asked permission to crawl down a gulley to the bank of the river and get in rear of them.[12] He granted the permission and I came back along our line to try and get some of our boys to go with me. They all declined. He's a mean boy "William Meade" [William Henry Mead], who was as brave a lad as ever sighted a carbine or wielded a saber. He and I threw ourselves flat on our hands and knees and crawled along for some two or three hundred yards until we came to the trees and bushes skirting the margin of the river.

Owing to a peculiar bend in the river at this point, in the shape of a horse shoe, we worked our way up in this bend until we were completely in the rear of the houses and could see the boys in Blue busy loading and shooting obligingly along our lines. There was some 20 or 30 behind one house in there, loading and shooting alternately. As we fired, we went down to the end of the line and came up again, in turn we got a good position straight in line, and I told Billy to take the second one in line and I would take the first one. At the report of our guns the whole line went down to the earth. We knew we had no time to fool away there, as the houses and woods were alive with 'Blue Coats.' So, we moved cautiously away to look for another good place to put in a shot. We moved down some 50 yards. Billy was laying behind a large sycamore tree; there were two of them [Federal soldiers] not more than three feet apart.

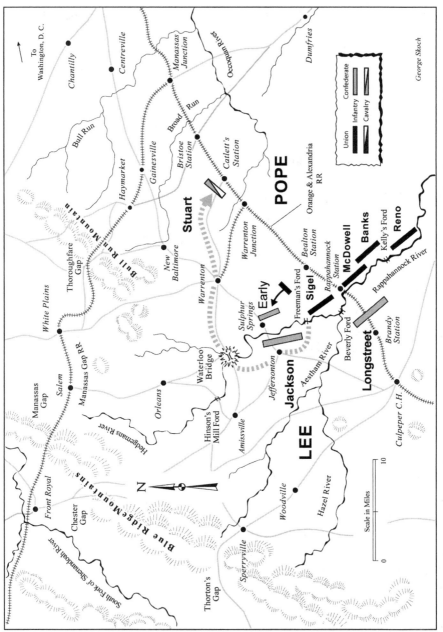

Stuart's August 1862 action around Waterloo Bridge, where Colley received his first wound of the war.

We had been here some ten minutes. I was anxious to discover if the fellow that I knew was up at a window or a tree some where on that side of the river. So, I rose up in an erect position and was looking through the bushes and vines for the smoke of his gun. He discovered me first and fired at me. The ball came close to my head and cut a piece out of my hat brim. I did not move. I was still looking for his place of concealment when another ball came spurting through the leaves and struck me on the instep of my right foot and made a slight but painful wound. It glanced off and cut off a small bush behind my heel and fell in the water back of our position. I crouched down and grunted awhile and examined my foot and saw it was not serious; by this time I had discovered his hiding place. He was up the gable of a house at a small window at the side of a brick chimney. We crawled down until we come directly opposite the window and waited for him to poke his gun out to shoot. When we both fired at the spot, we then put in a few shots through the thin weather boarding and the boys poured out in droves and made for the timber.

We moved down opposite another house and saw a yank with his elbows resting in the window sill; we put a 'quietus' on him. We were at this point in fair view of the road leading on to the bridge. At this moment, a squad of artilerists rolled a brass howitzer by hand so they could sweep our frail breast works at the opposite end of the bridge. We turned our attention to them and what was [there] ran off and left their gun. We had by this time exhausted our ammunition and made our way back to our lines. I reported to Colonel Rosser, [and] by this time my foot was so swollen I had to cut my shoe off with my knife. While I was down on the river bank, Lieutenant G. W. Litchfield [2nd Lieutenant George Victor Litchfield Jr.] was severly wounded in the hand. Colonel Rosser sent me back to the rear.

I went by our battery on the hill behind our position and told them to shell the houses on the opposite side of the river, and they soon routed the boys out of their hiding places. I went back some 3/4th of a mile to a private house and the Good Old Lady made and poulticed, and bound up my foot; it was quite painful for some 3 days. The 4th day, Charles Morrell, my cousin, came by there to see me and told me about the Great Victory our army had won on the plains of Mannasses, and I could not content myself any longer with my kind friends whose names have entirely slipped my memory. I thanked them for their kindness to me and Charles, and I set out for the front. I soon found that I could not let my foot hang down in the stirrup, so I fixed a cushion out of my blankets in front and carried my foot upon the horse withers, and on we went toward the Battle Grounds.

The next day we came to Aldie where Jacksons hospital was established. We found several of the 37th and 48th Virginia, who had been wounded at Manassas. Here we learned that our army was on their way to 'Maryland.' We struck out for Leesburg where we came up with our command and next day we crossed the Potomac at Poolesville, Maryland. We struck Maryland soil that the pedigree would rise en mas and flock to our standard, but alas we were doomed to dissappointment. Some were 'neutral,' some were Rebels, the most of them were already in the Confederate service. We had strict orders not to take anything from the 'citizens' without paying them for it.[13] We did not find much trouble in procuring anything we wanted.

We were not troubled with the boys in 'Blue' for some two weeks, but at length they began to take on a defensive attitude and made things lively for us. The first skirmish I was in was at Sugarloaf Mountain [Maryland]. We sharpshooters were dismounted. I was with our sharpshooters until we had to fall back, and then I mounted my horse and was in the skirmish line. Colonel W. M. Hopkins had command of our sharpshooters on this occasion.[14] We had a skirmishing everyday back towards South Mountain and on to Boonesborough, where my horse was wounded and I had to take him back across the Potomac at Shepherdstown.[15]

My foot had gotten about well by this time, and still having a desire for a fight, I left my horse and crossed back over to Sharpsburg on foot. I had intended to go to the 37th Virginia but could not find them. I had a great desire to show them that a cavalryman could fight. I did not get there the 1st day, but was with the 2nd South Carolina regt. in skirmish line.[16] All the next day there was skirmishing and occasional artillery firing all day. I was surprised at dark, when orders came to fall back. I had thought all day that tomorrow would bring about a great fight and I would have an opportunity of being in an Infantry engagement, but alas I was doomed to disappointment and moved on sadly towards the Potomac.[17]

I had a new pair of nice canvas shoes and did not want to get them wet, so, I sat down on a rock at the bank of the river to pull them off. The vast colums of infantry were marching straight on into the water as though there was no river there. I had a little tilt with an infantry officer. He came up with sword in hand and said, "What the hell you doing here?" I said, "I am pulling off my shoes." He said, "damn you get up and move on." I said, "I will as soon as I get ready." "What command do you belong to?" he said. I said, "Co. D first Va. Cavalry." He said "I havent got anything to do with you." I said, "I thought not," and he passed on and I slid into the Grand Old Potomac. The water was up to my knees most of the way and in some places waist deep. The periwinkle shells cut my feet so bad, sometimes I would flinch and squat. I wanted to get out of there awful bad but there was no help for it. I had to press on as best I could. When I arrived on the west bank and sat down to put on socks and shoes, my feet were cut and bleeding, but felt good when I had gotten them again encased in shoes.

I moved up on the high cliff and got out to one side and concluded I would take a nap. I did not know anything until the sun was peeping up over the Eastern Hills. At that moment, all the vast level plain below Shepherdstown was covered with wagons and artillery.[18] About that time, I was thinking about starting out to some wagon to hunt something to eat.The yanks ran some artillery on the opposite hills and commenced hurling shells into the confused mass of wagons. About this time one of the 4th Va. Infantry came up to where I was and we saw a chance to have some fun and put in a few good shots. We were up on a high cliff and had a fair view of the long gradual slope of hills on the Maryland side. The Yankee cavalry were busy running our boys who had been left on that side by being asleep. There was some quite amusing races when ever the yanks came down close, [with] the canal on their side.

They came in range of our guns and we lifted a few of them. Several of our men made their escape under our fire. We were soon compeled to move as they brought forward artillery and a line of sharpshooters. That made the place too hot for us so we moved down towards the ford and concealed ourselves. All put in a shot when ever some of the 'Blue Boys' exposed themselves. We moved again and went up behind the high cliff and banks on our side until we got up to Shepherdstown. We hunted up something to eat and then went down to the river bank to watch for some runaway yank to show his head. We were so intent at our work that we did not take any heed of time. The first thing we knew dark was coming, and the Yankee cavalry had crossed down at the ford and were moving up into Shepherdstown.

As they were moving up Main Street, we made our way up through an alley and through yards and gardens until we got clear of the town, then we pulled out on the road toward Martinsburg, some three miles out. We came on four of Jackson's men. We told them there was nothing between them and the yanks and we all pulled out for camp. I reported to the first officer I could find how matters stood and pulled out to hunt my command. History records the surprise of the yanks next morning, how old Jack hurled the advanced division of McClellan's army into the Potomac—killed and captured and drowned the whole division. How I regreted that I did not know what was going to take place; it would have been my delight to see them jumping from the high cliffs into the river below. The boys told me the river was full of them and perfectly red with their blood. They were busy preparing their breakfast when the veterans of old Jack opened on them from every side. It was as sudden and quick as a streak of lightening. This taught General McClellan that Lee was not as badly panick stricken as he imagined; things quited down, as I had no horse to ride.

I was with Co 2 [perhaps Colley meant the 2nd Virginia, as he goes on to discuss that unit]. We were at Bunker Hill and near Jackson's Division. We visited the 37th and 48th boys and had a jolly time. Quite an amusing thing took place while we were here, Tom Smith, 'Stegens' as we called him, was over at the 48th Regiment one night taking a little sociable game with the boys. He could crow like a 'Shanghi Rooster;' some time in the wee small hours of the night, the boys got him to crowing. He was not far from Colonel Williams's [Titus V. Williams] tent, the Colonel of the 37th. He woke the Colonel up and he inquired who that was and Tom gave him some imprudent answer and [the colonel] called for the officer of the guard and Tom started on a run for his quarters. In the dark, he stumbled over a wagoner who was lying on a bunch of hay near his wagon. Tom made no halt but kept straight on, on hands and knees. The guard ran up on the wagoner, arrested him, and carried him off to the guard house with all his protests of innocence; and they did not know till next morning their mistake. Stegens told us how he escaped and we all laughed heartly. After things quited down, he gave a few more loud crows to let the Colonel know he was still on the wing and out of his jurisdiction. The Colonel enjoyed the joke as well as the rest of us, when he found out how it was. The poor wagoner was the only one that could not see the fun.

Some of the boys that were with the 2nd found out there was a still house some 3 or 4 miles from camp. General Jackson had a guard over it but cavalry men did not care for guards. One night some five or six of the Buttermilk Rangers, as the Infantry dubbed us, made a raid on the Jackson foot cavalry and captured a 20 gallon keg.[19] They got it up in front of one of the men and got away before the sentinel could arouse his comrades. They fired a voley after the fleeing horsemen. It only precipitated their flight. I had a good time while this lasted. When we got scarce of rations, some one or two would go out and hunt up a vicious hog or sheep or steer that showed fright and compelled us to kill them in self defence. Ben Crawford [Benjamin C. Crawford] and I went out some two miles one evening and found a vicious yearling in a thicket and had to shoot it down. We skinned out the hind quarters and brought them in after dark. Of course, it would not do for a private soldier to be caught in day light with that much meat on hands, so if a citizen came around looking for missing stock, we would tell him Jackson's men killed it, and they would say the cavalry killed it. They soon found out it would not pay to trace up anything of that kind.

I had sent my horse back up the Valley near Harrisonburg to recuperate and get well of his wounds. I began to tire of this inactive life and wanted to go at the front. I tried the Infantry 'Gen' to get a pass to go after my horse, but they said they had nothing to do with us and I could not get to our officers, so I had no other alternative but make a pass. So, I got up a impass and started on an old broken-down wagon horse and made my way without any trouble to Mr. Cyrus Rhodes, some 4 miles from Harrisonburg.[20] The old gentleman, his wife and fine daughters, composed the family. He had two sons in the Confederate army. He had a fine farm, a large brick residence and plenty of everything around there. General Hunter [Major General David Hunter] and Phil Sheridan had not visited this part of the Valley yet.[21]

They were good old Dutch Dunkards.[22] They spun and wove and made all their own clothing. They had a bake oven and baked bread and pies twice a week. It was in the height of fruit and grape gathering time, and of course I went to work like a brother and helped the girls get wood and gather fruit and grapes. They, and I, were sure a couple more weeks rest would vastly improve my horse, and so I spent a couple of weeks quite pleasantly with these good people and they still occupy a warm spot in my affections. The time set soon rolled around, and I had set the day to depart.

After supper that night, the old folks went up stairs to their room and left us in the dining room, the girls cleaning up the table. After they got through with their work, they all said they must have a lock of my hair before I left. I had beautiful long black hair at that time, and to have a little fun with the girls I resisted. They, with shears in hand, caught me and we had a lively scuffle; but finally, the fine Large Plump Dutch Girls could easily over power one poor lame Rebel Boy. So, they clipped off what they desired and released me. They were not only stout but robust in health and strength but very courageous. They told me about five Yankee soldiers coming there to search their house for fire arms and they determined to bluff them, so the fine girls armed with carving and butcher knives, met them at the stile and told them the first one that set foot on that platform, they would carve him to pieces. After some parlaying with the girls, and seeing their determination to defend their home, they rode off and left them. While they had searched all the houses in that neighborhood, theirs [the home of the girls] was not molested at that time.

The next morning, I saddled up and started back to join my command. While I was up there having a good time, Stuart made his raid into Pennsylvania to Chambersburg.[23] The boys were full of the fun they had had with the old Dutch farmers on their trip. It was a sad regret to me that I had not known this was to come off. Nothing would have given me more unbound pleasure than this visit to Yankeetown. It would have done me good at that time to see them twist and squirm, when their property was being confiscated and turned to service in the Rebel army. I was not kept idle long.

After my return, General McClellan commenced moving his forces across the river with the intentions of getting between General Lee's army and Richmond. The cavalry was ordered to cross the Blue Ridge at 'Snickers Gap,' and retard his movements. So, we were in one continual skirmish almost day and night for some 20 days, from the Potomac to the Rapidan. I had some awful close shaves being dismounted and in skirmish lines pited against the best infantry sharpshooters in the Federal army. We generally held our own until they come with over whelming force. We were ably assisted and helped in our efforts by 'Pelham's Battery' of horse artillery.[24]

Major John Pelham.
Library of Congress.

He never missed an opportunity of giving them shot and shell at Union.[25] We had a severe scrap one morning. Our Battery was stationed on a hill just east of the village. There was a heavy body of timber some 400 yards in front. We were dismounted and ordered to move forward on this wood land. There was a high rail fence just at the edge of the woods. As our line neared and approached the fence, a whole line of Infantry pounded a volley into us. David Ryburn [David Beattie Ryburn] was mortally wounded and died.[26] RR Cassell [Rufus R. Cassell] of Company D was severely wounded in the arms. As my foot had swollen up again, I was down there on horseback. I dismounted at the fence and exchanged 7 shots with a big burley yank behind a tree, some 30 yards from the fence. When I looked around our line was broken and in full retreat up the hill towards our battery.

I did not take time to mount my horse or bid my Yankee friend good bye or to excuse me for leaving him so abruptly. I went at a brisk trot with my horse close behind me. How he and I both escaped a bullet I cannot see. Only in the way I had escaped 'thousands' before and since that time.

By the powers of the unseen Hand that has covered my unworthy 'head' from my infancy to this time. Just as I was coming up near our battery, Pelham commenced pouring the Grape and Canister into their ranks, and that put a check to their hilarity and advance. At this instance, one of our caissons was blown up, [and] killed some 3 or 4 horses and men. 'The shock was awful,' me and my horse were both thrown off our feet but were up again in an instant. In the few moments of comparative silence after the explosion I mounted and passed. [The next volume of Colley's journal is missing.][27]

5

I Am Always in the Ring

BLOODY MY SABER, our infantry comrades were always "guying me about never seeing a bloody saber or a dead cavalry man." I was so intent on pleasing my men that I never looked to the right, left or rear to see whether I had any of my comrades coming my way, that I did not find out I was alone until I ran into a squadron of Yankee cavalry drawn up behind a garden fence in the rear of a large farm house. They opened fire on me with carbines and pistols. The bullets plowed the snow up around me. I was making for a log corn crib, and a little negro boy passed me on the way to the house. He said to me "run Mister run they will kill you." I got behind the crib, stuck my old saber in the scabord, pulled up my carbine and opened up in the center of the squadron. They were in a panicky condition. The officer in command was riding up and down his line trying to get the men to stand, but they broke from the left when he rode to the right. I kept putting the hot shot into them. Just at this stage the 4th Regiment came down the road with 'a yell.' They ran them into the Infanty camps. David A. Fields came up to me just at this time and told me our regiment was on the other road, and he and I turned off across the field as there were no fences in that region at that time. We had not gone over fifty or sixty yards when we came to the brow of the hill we were on, and some 80 yards from us in a hollow there was some 20 Yankee cavalry; [with] me trying to cross a wide ditch.[1]

David Fields had let his carbine fall in the mud and was afraid to shoot it until he could get a ramrod or stick to push the mud out of its muzzle. So, I was alone. I pulled down in the center of the squad. When they spread out, one tumbled to the ground. I fired two more shots into them as they cleared the ditch and passed into the woodland beyond. As we road] down by the [fallen] man, one of our surgeons had come up to him and was examing his wound. Of course, I did not wish to see him. David and I passed by and crossed the ditch and on up the slope and to the road. We did not know where our company was so we turned to the left, which brought us back towards where we had started and it was well for us we did. We had not proceded far until we came on a squad of yanks with 3 of our company under guard. We run up to them with our revolvers and soon brought them to terms, released our comrades, took in the yanks and marched them back with us.

While we were here we could hear the 'Long Roll' beating for miles, arousing the whole of General Hooker's [Major General Joe Hooker] army and calling them to arms. We had accomplished about all we had come for and commenced moving back. Of course, when the cavalry pressed on us we turned around on them. Our regiment was in the rear and [companies] D and K, being sharpshooters, had to hold them in check. On one of these occasions David Fields and myself had captured two Yankee sharpshooters that had goten to far in front of their line. We had just brought them up to Lieutenant Rees B. Edmondson and turned them over when I spied a fine-looking man on a large Bay horse about one hundred yards from where we stood. I said to the Lieutenant "let me go and take that fellow in," He said "that is one of our officers." I said "thats a Yankee officer," and put my horse on a dead run for him.

He did not appear to notice me until I was within 20 steps of him. When he turned his horse, and started in the direction of their skirmish line, I cried, "Halt! Halt!" and brought my carbine to bear on him. He saw I had him and drew his ivory handled pistols from the holsters in his saddle and threw them down in the mud and snow and came up to me, and I troted him up to Lieutenant Edmondson. He [captive] was a Colonel and pay master of the 16th Virginia Cavalry.[2] He said he was well fixed, [he had] a fine gold watch and chain, a diamond ring and studs, and a fine grip strapped over his shoulders. It was said he had $75,000 in that grip. I did not take anything from him, a thing I never did to a prisoner during the whole of my connection with the army. I asked him for his canteen. He said he could not give me that but would give me something that was in it. We had this conversation as we were riding along back to our lines. After

I had finished cursing him for throwing his pistols in the mud, he and I took a drink as we rode back to our lines. The yanks never fired a shot at us as we came back, but as soon as we was sent to the rear they opened up on us.

Our commanders gave us all the horses we captured. That day Dave Fields and I came in with five; [I] sold my Colonel's horses to Lieutenant Edmondson with the saddle for $4.50. I kept the bridle and breast girt. I kept them until 1865. They were left by D. C. Gray together with a new McClellan saddle and a Sharps Rifle I had captured before I lost my foot at Haw's Shop in 1864.[3] Mr. Gray was bringing them home to me when the horse gave out and he had to leave him at Mr. Lanes near Appomatox Court House, where they remained until the yanks came up there on the 9th of April 1865. When, as Mr. Lane stated to me, they fell back in to the hands of the original owners.

A little incident happened to me after I had returned to camp. I loaned the Yankee Colonel's horse to one of company K to ride back to camp. I went after him next morning and the comrade refused to give him up, claiming he was a captured horse and that he had a right to keep him. Which, of course, I disputed and he ran in his tent and got his pistol and came out threatening to shoot if I did not move. Of course, being unarmed, I moved. He followed me over within a few feet of my own tent. I deliberatly walked in my tent, reached for my carbine, loaded and cocked it and drew the 'hammer' back and stepped out. He was standing with his pistol pointed at me. Just as I was bringing my carbine to my shoulder his Captain "Guss Dorsey" [Captain Gustavus Warfield Dorsey], being surprised at what was up, rushed up to his man and caught him in the collar and jerked him back and disarmed him and made him bring my horse to me and prevented a tragedy. Somebody would have certainly been hurt.

It has always been a great wonder to me that more soldiers were not killed or maimed in these little spats in camp. I never knew one settled by weapons in my regiment. They were generally settled by a fist cuff and all forgotten in a few days and like the Irishman, always ready to lend their opponent a helping hand or divide a crust of bread with him.

I was on picket post at Wheatley's Ford on the Rappahannock River below Brandy Station about the 14th or 15th of March 1863. When I returned to camp, I could scarcely sit on my horse. I was quite sick; tongue coated and severe headache and high fever. I had applied to the Doctor and he had prescribed, and on the next morning of the 17th a courier dashed into camp and reported the Yankees driving in our pickets. If the "Lieutenant" in charge of the picket post at Kelly's Ford had not made a determined stand in the rifle pits, at that point our camp would have been taken by surprise.[4] Of course all was in commotion and everything hurried to the front at this time. Fitz Lee's Brigade was very much reduced in number; so many men were on furlough for fresh horses and a great many were sick. He could only muster about 800 effective men. They were all mounted and hurried to the front in a short time.

Orders came to strike tents and move the sick and everything back to the rear of our infantry. At this news, I quickly resolved what I would do if I had to move. I staggered around and suceeded in getting my horse saddled, buckled on my arms, crawled up on his back, and started to the front. The mud was so deep and bad in the main roads that we took the Orange and Alexandria Railroad track, as it was near our camp. Just as I got to the railroad embankment and rode up, "General Fitz Lee" rode up on the opposite side and addressed me "Hello Colley, I thought you were sick." I said "I am sir but I had orders to move. As you know when there is anything to do I am always in the ring." "Yes I know that and for that reason I do not wish you to expose yourself," said Lee. He then drew his flask from his haversack and gave me a drink of very nice 'whiskey,' which revived and stimulated me. I was quite weak from not eating anything for some 3 days.

We rode on down to 'Brandy Station,' and there he sent me to carry a dispatch to C. T. Litchfield [Conley T. Litchfield], the Captain on my own company. He had charge of the sharpshooters at the front. When I rode up to him he was dismounted, standing by his horse. His first greeting was "Tom what the devil are you doing out here. You are too sick to be out of your tent." I told him I had to move and "thought there was some fun out that way." He offered me a drink and of course I could not refuse, so I took a pretty strong pull of his brandy and as 'General Lee' had ordered him, through me, to move the skirmish line forward, he and I rode on in rear of the line as it moved forwards toward 'Kellys Ford.'

As we were emerging from the woodland we were in, 'General J. E. B. Stuart' dashed up and ordered our line to be formed and to move forward. As soon as we emerged in the open fields and broad bottom land of

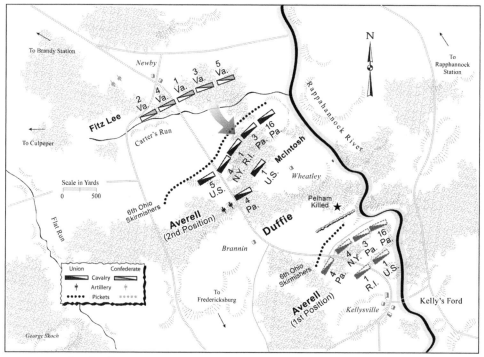

Battle of Kelly's Ford, March 17, 1863, showing Wheatly house, where Colley
convalesced after sustaining his wound during the battle.

Mr. Wheatley's farm, we were ordered to charge, [with] General Stuart
leading. As I was not in ranks, I charged with the General in front until
we came to a high stone fence at the road running from Kelly's Ford to
Wheatley's Ford. As the yanks were drawn up in solid colums on the opposite side of the fence and road, we could not get to them and were ordered
to turn the left into colums. I did not hear or notice the movement and
rode my horse up to the stone fence and commenced loading and shooting
into the dense columns of cavalry drawn up, as I stated, in an open pine
woods as far back as I could see.

Two officers opened fire on me with their pistols. I shot at them with
my carbine. Our orderly Sergeant passed down in rear of my horse and
said, "Tom what are you doing there?" I said, "I am shooting Yankees,"
and I did not move from there until I had exhausted all my ammunition. I

Sketch of the fighting at Kelly's Ford. Library of Congress.

looked around and found I was all alone. I wheeled my horse and started him across the bottom towards the pine woods that bordered them on the north. While my horse was loping along I was busy tearing the wrappers off my cartridges and placing them in their places in the top of the box. They were handy to get at, as each cartridge had a seperate hole or compartment so in dark or day light it was no trouble to load our guns.

Just as I came to the edge of the pines I came across two of my company, W. W. Morrell a cousin and mess mate of mine and a brave generous companion. With him was Joe Pendleton [Joseph H. Pendleton]; as true as steel. I rode up to them. I had on a black overcoat and they said to me, since we were in the rear of our forces, they advised me to pull off my coat. I dismounted and drew it off and buckled it on my saddle and had turned around and laid my arms up on my horse's shoulder and was looking back over the field, when all of a sudden some 15 or 20 shots came from a clump of pines at an old fence row some 80 yards away from where we stood. My comrades said, "lets get away from here" and wheeled their horses around and started. I had just dropped my right arm to my side and turned 6 or 8 inches toward my right when a bullet came under my horse's neck and struck me some 2 ½ inches on my left side, from the pit of my stomach, and passed through my body coming out some 2 inches lower down near the small of my back, slightly injuring the spinal column.

I grasped at my horse's mane but had no power to hold on. My comrades had not gotten 10 paces from me. Pendleton was nearest me and I heard him say "Tom is killed." Just as I fell to the ground, he was at my side in an instant and caught me by the shoulders, and with my determination to go away from there, he set me up on my feet but the exertion was too much. I fell back down and pulled him down with me. By that time, my cousin was there and they both laid hold of me and I said, "What are you going to do?" They said, "put you on your horse and carry you away." I said, "no I cannot ride and you will only endanger your lives, leave me and save yourselves. I am about done for anyway." So, they took my watch and arms. In lifting me to get my saber belt unfastened, it made me deathly sick. This was the last thing I remember for a long time, probably 2 hours, after biding my comrades a sad farewell.

I swooned when I came to. I heard the sound of battle and knew I was inside the Yankee lines. It was quite a cold day, snowing and freezing a little, and my first impulse was to crawl away somewhere, where the enemy could not find me. I struggled up on hands and knees and tried to move forward, but when I moved one hand from under my body to make a step I would fall over on that side. I made some 3 efforts, which caused me to swoon again and when I came to again there was a Yankee boy, about 16 years of age, standing some 3 or 4 paces from me. I said to him, "Will you please get me some water?" All the answer he gave me was "haint got no water," and then Yankee like, he started questioning me in this verse: "Where is your horse? Where is your gun? Where is your pistol? Where is your saber?" I answered him that "my friends had taken all away from me and that I had nothing to hurt him with." As my thirst was so intense, I still begged him to go and get me some water, but he declined to do so.

At this stage, a squadron of cavalry came down on the opposite side of me and the officer in command commenced cussing my young yank for being a shirker and a coward. In reply to the officer, he said "here is a wounded Rebel over here." The officer asked him if he was put there to guard me and he said he was; which I think was not true. I had not seen him before that time. The Captain rode over near me and asked me about my wound, and I told him all I knew and requested him to please get me some water. He promised me to do it. He immediately turned to his orderly and told him to detail a man with water in his canteen and send him to me. I heard a man say "Sergeant I will go," and he ordered him to go. He rode up as near to my head as he could get his horse and let his canteen down to me by the straps. I tried to grasp it but being so cold and numbed I could not hold it. The soldier kindly got down from his horse and held his canteen to my lips until I drank what I wanted. The captain told him to stay with me. He tied up his horse and sat down by me and gave me water when I called for it. I learned from him they had been repulsed by our men and were falling back. Night was coming on too.

One of the 'Generals' in command—I never learned his name—if I did it slipped my memory in that terrible crisis in my life, when for days 'my life hung in the balance,' and the weight of a hair would turn the scale for Hell or Heaven. This General questioned me as to who was in command and how many men we had. I told him all I knew. I learned afterwards that 'General Stuart' had deceived them by running the engine up and down the railroad and tooting and whistling. They thought we were bringing infantry down from Orange Court House. The General inquired about the nature of my wound and promised to send his own Surgeon to me. He was but a short distance away and came to me at once. He dismounted and examined my wound and stated to me his honest convictions, that it was impossible for me to live but a short time and desired to know if I had any words to loved ones. I told him I had none.

He had given me some good Rye whiskey, and under its stimulating influence I had began to warm up and feel better than I had during my rational moments. During that time, I had lain there for some 6 hours. My heart and soul turned towards my heavenly father until I had the assurance within me that I should not die at that time, but I did not want my Yankee friends to come to that conclusion for fear they would carry me over the river with them. I had a horror of Yankee prisons and was determined never to be a prisoner, 'if I had a inch of space to go on.' So, my good kind Doctor left me a quart bottle of whiskey and said that was all he could do for me and bade me good bye, promising to send an ambulance to take me up and asked where I wished to go. I told him he could take me to Mr. Wheatleys as I knew them. I thanked him kindly and he went his way.

The ambulance did not come promptly and my good Yankee friend who was left with me, at first to give me water, was still by my side. He proposed to ride out and see if he could find an ambulance anywhere. I thought he was gone an age. I was anxious to get in off the damp cold earth. While he was gone, a good kind Irish cavalryman rode up about four paces from me and stopped. I was wanting water and asked him if he had water in his canteen he said, "no by Jesus" I haven't got a drop of water but I have some good whiskey." I thanked him. I had plenty of that the Doctor left me. "By Jesus I'm sorry I haven't any water for you," he said. By this time, the ambulance with a herd of Barbarians [arrived] and my friend with them. He dismounted and ordered them to lift me gently and put me in the ambulance. They did not obey orders strictly, but grabed me like I was a log of wood. They hurt me and cursed me and caused me to moan with pain. My Yankee friend drew his saber and told them if they hurt me again "he would split their damn heads." They handled me like a baby after that.

I had two pocket knives in my pants pocket, and they fell out in moving me. My friend picked them up and put them back in my pocket. He ordered the driver, who was a genial whole souled Irish man, to drive out. We were at that time in a woodland, or rather in a clearing full of pine stumps. Every time the wheels struck a stone or root and jarred, the ambulance driver would stop and ask me "By Jesus does it hurt you any now?" I said "no, drive on," and I knew by the sound of our carbines that our boys were close on the retreating yanks and I did not want to be in an ambulance with a 'panic stricken driver,' so I wanted him to lose no time.

We had not proceeded far until we came by another one of my comrades who was wounded in both thighs. They put him by my side and we were soon out in the green fields, where we had made our first charge. In the morning, my friend went in to see if he could get a bed or some place to lay us on. There was no one there but two ladies, and they were frightened almost to 'death.' They were quiet poor people, and not overly stocked with household goods. The front room was entirely empty. The only thing in it being an empty flour barrel. So, my friend 'brought' me and my comrad in and placed us on the floor, 'taking his own blankets from his saddle to make me a pallet.' In moving me I swooned again and again. When consciousness returned, my Yankee friend, and some of the out lawers, were rubbing and chafing my limbs with whiskey. My feeling had begun to return and I could feel the cold.

He had the 'Hessian' out at the wood pile gathering wood to start the fire.[5] My face was fronting the door, and as one of them came in with an armful of wood, he dropped his cap and dropped it outside like a negro in slave times, and a sense of indignation raked through me at the sight of a white man dropping his hat like a negro. As near dead as I was, I had a great desire to kick him, and I thought of us having to fight such a lot of out landish degraded wretches, but being a prisoner and helpless I could do nothing or say nothing. They soon had a cheerful, blazing fire and I began to warm up and pressures of blood in the cavities around my heart and lungs became very oppressive and painful and I became restless and began to think the end was near at hand. I finally rolled over on my face, and the blood commenced gurgling out of the wound where the ball entered, like water escaping from the mouth of a jug, and I began to get easy and could do nothing but lay there and listen to my 'Life's Blood' fast trickling away.

Far from mother sisters and friends, of course my thoughts then went to him who I had been taught from my infancy was present to help in all times of need. And with all my heart, soul, mind, and strength was appealing to him who held my life and destiny in his hands. He was near me but I did not know it at that time, and not for long years afterwards. At every reoccurence of that awful day, my heart goes out in 'Gratitude' to poor sinful men like me. I lay this way for some time, and as the blood flowed out, I became perfectly easy in mind and body. By this time, the blood had saturated the heavy blanket on which I was lying and had run away into two streams toward the back of the room. There was a perfect sea of blood. It measured three inches on the wash boards in the back of the room. I had become quite weak but still knew everything that went on around me.

My Yankee friend still stuck to me like a brother. I heard the sound of our carbines drawing nearer and I did not want him to be made a prisoner,

and I began to ask him to leave me and join his own. Finally, he consented
and asked me to give him my spurs. They were fine spring steel made at
Shepherds, Virginia in 1861.[6] Of course I told him to take them as I would
in all probability never need spurs again. He unstrapped my boots and
bade me farewell. I had his card and name at the time but in the turmoil
of war times I lost it and have never been able to recall it. All I know, he
was a member of the 16th Pennsylvania Cavalry; as is shown, he proved
himself to be a friend indeed. I have tried to find him since the war but
have utterly failed up to this time. I fear he went down like thousands of
other brave generous souls on both sides before the close of the deadly
conflict then 'being waged.' My only hope now is of meeting him beyond
the confines of earth. Because one that would voluntarily come to the aid
of the enemy and administer to his needs as kind and affectionately as if
he had been a blood relation, if not a christian at that time, possessed that
goodness of heart that lead men to embrace the teachings and doctrine of
the meek and lovely Nazarene. 'Peace to him if he still lives Peace to his
ashes if dead is all I can say now.'[7]

He had not left me 15 minutes when Robert Bruce of company K, a
noble brave Maryland boy, came into my room. He was greatly surprised
to see me still alive. He stated that Will Morrell, my cousin and companion and as generous and brave a soul as ever drew a saber, had gone down
where he had left me in the morning to look for me. Bruce said he would
go and tell him where I was. It was not long until he was by my side and he
never left me until my father came 3 days later. He sent Bruce out to hunt
up one of our 'surgeons.' He came back in about one hour with Dr. Wilson
[William Randolph Wilson], the assistant surgeon of our regiment at that
time. He was a general good-natured fellow. We were all very fond of him.
He came in and examined my wound, and like the Federal surgeons, pronounced it fatal; as there were no bones broken he could do nothing. He
advised that I be kept perfectly quite and given cream at one half hour
intervals during the night. My cousin, he became very indignant and flew
into a terrible rage at his indifference as to my condition and lit into cursing him for it. I checked him and begged him to let the Doctor alone, as I
was satisfied he could do nothing more than he had done and this quieted
him down, and I knew the Doctor had a hard night's work ahead of him,
as there were several badly wounded men to see after.

Major General Fitzhugh Lee.
Library of Congress.

    I have since learned that our little squad of 800 cavalry men were pited against 3,500 Federal cavalry men commanded by 'General Averell' who was a classmate of Fitz Lee at West Point, and from a clipping I have taken from the *Youth's Companion Magazine,* and which I will, for a diversion, reproduce here.[8] It is headed: Returning a Visit. [Colley copied the article as follows.]

General Fitz Hugh Lee of the Confederate army had been a class mate at West Point with General Averell, the commander of the cavalry of the Army of the Potomac and the two men became personal friends. February 2 1863 General Lee attacked the Union out posts at Harwood Church and defeated them. On returning he left a surgeon behind in charge of the wounded and with him a note to General Averill which read something like this: Dear Averill I wish you would put up your sword leave my state and go home. You ride a good horse I ride a better, Yours can beat mine running. If you

won't go home return my visit and bring me a sack of coffee. Yours Fitz. Some
weeks afterwards General Averill obtained permission from General Hooker
then commanding the Army of the Potomac to return Lees visit. Averill had
expressed confidence in his ability to whip Lee on his own ground. If you do
replied Hooker there will be some dead cavalry men lying about. On March 17,
1863 the Union cavalry crossed the Rappahannock at Kelly's Ford and met
the enemy under Stuart and Lee. The forces were nearly equal about three
thousand and five hundred men and a battery of artillery on each side.
[Colley inserted the following observation: "This is untrue as to our side,
but true as to the Federals."] Previous to starting says Captain D. M. Gilmore
in Glimpses of the Nation Struggle, the men were instructed to have their
sabers sharpened and a field order directed the men to use sabre freely and
promised a victory. Charge and counter charge were in rapid succession. The
enemy were driven with in a mile of their winter camps at Brandy Station.
As the Union retired General Averill left with a field hospital part of a sack of
coffee and this answer to General Lees note: Dear Fitz, Here is your coffee.
How is your horse. Averill.

It is said by the same author that Mr. Lincoln obtained Lee's note to
General Averill from him and carried it in his pocket showing it frequently.
It was quite amusing to him, 'but Hell' to us who had to face the angers of
battlefields, with the long night vigils on the lone picket posts in rain and
sleet and mud, cold and hungry on the long marches, weary and aching
with stiffened limbs on the account of exposure night and day, and sleeping on the cold damp ground or on the soft side of a fence rail, or suffering
from wounds as I was at the time.[9]

6

I Came to the Conclusion "God" Could Not Smile upon This Kind of Thing

THERE WAS NOT much fun in all this, but I guess we had as much real enjoyment in our camp life and on the march as any set of men did that were ever banded together. If we had small rations we ate and enjoyed them, and if we had plenty it was the same. We believed our cause was just and that our Government was doing the best it could to support us. Now I must return to myself as I did not start out to write a history of the war. Before I proceed, I wish to demonstrate one theory practiced by our old doctor, that is bleeding would cure fever. As I stated, I had a severe attack of fever when I started out to the battlefield, but after the bleeding the Yankee bullet gave me I never had any more bleeding or fever; I was alive. Near morning, when Dr. Wilson visited me, he told my cousin to keep clothes wet with cold water on the wounds and continue to give me cream.

My brother Lewis [William Lewis Colley] came down from camp today. He was a member of the same company I belonged to. Colonel James M. Duke [James H. Drake] and Major W. A. Morgan [William Augustine Morgan] two of the officers of my regiment sent me a gallon jug of fine apple brandy and a half bushel of 'rice,' and their good wishes for my speedy recovery. I did not suffer any pain. I was too weak to help myself and lay with my hands crossed on my 'breast.' I knew everybody that came in to see me. I was too weak to talk any and I lay there on my pallet. Will Morrell had gotten a straw tick and filled it with straw, and with my Yankee blankets, I had a good bed. The family that lived here, worked as a tenant on Mr. Wheatley's farm. Their names were Brown. They were very kind and done the cooking for my nurses.[1] They brought their rations from camp.

My father came to me on the 3rd day after I was wounded, or as he left home, he thought he was coming after my remains. He was agreeably surprised to find me alive. Will Morrell had already written to my mother and sisters that I was alive. Father stayed with me until I was able to start home—twenty-five days after I was wounded. I gradually improved and done quite well until my appetite came to me and I began to crave solid food. The doctor and I had it hot and heavy for several days before he would agree for me to have bread and milk. I fixed up in my mind that I wanted an egg, a piece of cornbread, and a half glass of milk. I insisted until about the 12th day after I was wounded, before the doctor gave a reluctant consent for me to have what I craved. I had told them that morning I was going to have it despite of him, that I would crawl to the table at dinner time and get it if they would not bring it to me. I got my milk and egg and bread about 2 pm, and by 6 pm I had an awful spell of cramps—'colic'—and it lasted me until 4 am.[2] All the ease I could get was to sit up against my breast with my arms locked around them. Father and Dr. Wilson worried with me all night.

The doctor was afraid I would burst the wound out to bleeding again and insisted that I must be quiet, and I insisted that it was impossible for one to be quiet in a rack of pain, and so we had it all through the long hours of night. They had to send to camp for a syringe and gave me an injection before I could get any ease. I went to sleep as soon as I got eased and did not wake until 2 o'clock that evening. I was quite sore but quite free from pain. The doctor came in that evening but I agreed not to insist on eating anything he thought I ought not to have. I soon recovered my cheerful spirits and began to plan and think of home and the good times I would have when I got there.

One thing happened about this time, probably some 3 days after my bad spell of cramp colic. The house Mr. Brown lived in was right near the center of the field where we made our first charge on the morning of the 17th of March. I heard them speaking of the line of dead horses across the bottom and I had a great desire to see them, so one day, when they were all out in the dining room eating dinner, I thought I would go out and see. I held to the walls and made my way to the door and went out. I could not see anything from the door, so I made my way to the corner of the house, and still the yard fence and small out buildings obstructed my view. It was only a few paces from the corner of the house to the fence. As I had

The Wallach House. Library of Congress.

got along pretty good that far, I thought I could make the trip. The March wind was howling down the broad bottoms. I made two steps and down I went. I crawled back to the corner of the house and made my way back to my bunk and covered up snuggly before father or any of them returned from dinner. If it made me worse I had determined not to tell what I had done, but I did not get any worse from adventure.

I was not more than ½ mile from the river banks at Wheatley's Ford, where our pickets were stationed, and I began to get squirmish about being out there near our out posts and began to beg the Doctor to allow me to be moved back behind our camps. I got Will Morrell to hunt me a place in some private house. He found a place with Mrs. Douglas Wallach. Her husband was in Washington D.C., editor of the *Washington Star*.[3] About the 18th day, I was allowed to be moved up to her beautiful home. It stood on a hill just east of the Culpepper Court house. It was surrounded by a beautiful grove of 'Oaks.' The family consisted of Mrs. Wallach and two daughters. The old lady and one daughter were strong for the Union, the other daughter an uncompromising 'Rebel.'

Mrs. Wallach had paid a recent visit to Washington D.C. and brought back Yankee coffee, sugar, and rice, and that was quite scarce in Dixie. At that time, the family was extremely kind and good to father and myself. I had gotten so I could walk around and the balmy spring weather was invigorating and I improved rapidly. So, in a week or 10 days, the Doctor thought it would be safe for me to be brought home. Our kind hostess would not receive any pay for her trouble. Father promised to send her some 'salt' from the works in our county.[4] We tried in vain to get the Railroad to transport it but failed in our attempts. We bade her and her lovely daughters good-bye with many thanks for their kindness and generosity to us, and boarded the train for Lynchburg.

We moved on without any trouble until within some 24 miles of our home, when we came to a wash out in the road. A bridge had washed out east of Marion in (Smyth County) and we had to get private conveyance for some 8 or 9 miles. As there was but one engine on the west end of the road at that time, and it only made one trip a day, we had to lay over until the next day, as we failed to make connection with the train that left on this day. We arrived home amid great rejoicing with mother and sisters. The brother that had been mourned as dead was alive again. I soon gained some strength and began to feel like myself again. There was still soreness and occasional sharp pain in my left side, and my spine was affected to some extent. I could not stoop to lift anything, other wise, I was in a fair way to recovery.

After the Battle of Chancellorsville, I was requested and 'importuned' by a widow lady to go to Richmond and bring her son home. He had been wounded in the foot in that battle. He had a lovely sister that I had a hankering after at that time, and this was another incentive for me to act. The charms of the young lady had more weight than the widow's tens, towards influencing me to 'undertake' the arduous and fatiguing trip of 300 miles. Anyway, I decided to undertake it. I learned that three of my county men were engaged in the 'negro' trade at that time. A great many farmers in the Eastern Portion of the State had brought their slaves to Richmond and put them on the market for sale as the 'Union Forces' had over run their section of the county. These slaves were no longer 'profitable' or 'safe.'

These men bought them, and brought them out in the Southwest, and sold them or shipped them to Tennessee or Georgia.

They were good wholesouled men and I had a good time with them. I being reputed as being a fearless soldier—fighting for Southern rights as many called it at that time—that is about all a lot of us young hot headed fools knew about the war. Our homes were invaded by a ruthless foe. Our whole aim and ambition was to herd them back to their own barren hills and vales. Of course, all my expenses were paid by them so far as eating and drinking were concerned. Of course, I was not allowed to go to a hotel on our arrival in the city but was taken with them to 'Otey' Negro Market or prison.[5] It was a large brick building with grated windows and iron doors. Mr. Otey kept a bar and boarding house especially for 'buyers' and traders.

He had a Mulatto woman for manager or mistress. She did all the business relating to house hold affairs. Old Otey did nothing but drink whiskey and beer. He was drunk sitting in a high arm chair in the bar room when we went there, and when I left he was in the same condition. I went through the market from bottom to top. I saw the process of examining the various slaves, both rough farm hands, and delicate maids with a predominating proportion of white blood in their veins. I must confess that I was not favorably impressed with what I witnessed and heard in reference to this traffic in human flash. I came to the conclusion 'God' could not smile upon this kind of thing and my intense zeal for Southern rights was some what cooled for the time being.

The 2nd day after my arrival I went to Winder Hospital to find my wounded friend.[6] I had brought him some delicacies from home, which I delivered to him and had a long chat with him about the terrible Wilderness fight. He—being a member of the 4th Regiment Virginia Infantry, Stonewall Brigade—was in the hotest of the fight. The Surgeons of his ward said it was impossible for him to be moved at that time, so I had no other alternative but to leave him. As I was down here near the seat of war, and I learned my regiment was at Fredericksburg, I thought I would go up and see the boys, which I did and spent some two weeks very pleasantly with them. As I was not considered fit for field duty by our surgeons, I wished to get my horse and take him home with me, and as 'William Bailey and David Lynch' had died, their families wished their horses sent home.[7] A cousin of mine, Charles Morrell, was at home on sick furlough. He desired me to bring his horse for him.

I left my comrades and started on my long weary journey. Three of the horses were in the Valley of Virginia near Staunton and I had to make a long bend in my route towards home, but I took it slow and easy towards the Blue Ridge. There was no trouble to find friends on this side of the Blue Ridge. Every house was open to a Confederate Soldier. The last of my horses I found some 14 miles north west of Staunton. I was then something over 200 miles from home, quite weak yet from my wounds, with five head of old broken-down cavalry horses. I had to ride one and lead four. I got along pretty well with them until I got to Roanoke County. Then the time came to get somewhere to stay, and to procure feed for the horses. When I got tired I would stop and graze them along the roadside. I traveled 65 miles one day and night before I found any feed, and then only sheaf oats.

I crossed the Alleghany Mountain in the night and came to Christiansburg. There was no feed at the hotel. The proprietor advised me to go on out to Mr. Halls, who had a fine farm and plenty of corn and hay.[8] We had stopped at Mr. Halls place and camped in 1861, as our company was on its way to Richmond, and he would not allow his negro women to give us a little buttermilk on the strength of which the boys gave the old gentleman a 'serenade' and sang him our war song which went something like this. *You shant have any of our good whisky when your old whisky is gone and you shant have any of our good buttermilk when your old buttermilk is gone* [italics added], and so on, all through the good things a soldier could think of. Of course, I thought it a bad chance but it was in the direction of home and I moved out.

It was then near 11 o'clock at night. I remember coming in an ace of shooting into a fellow's door about two miles east of Christiansburg. I called at a house and hollered until the man came to the door. I requested permission to spend the rest of the night with him. He in a very abrupt manner said, "no you can't," and slammed the door in my face. I involuntarily threw my hand to my hip and drew my trusty revolver, pulled the hammer back and pointed it straight at the door, but in an instant my better nature asserted its self and concluded that dirty contemptible people like him was not fit to waste powder and lead on. To say I was mad is putting it mildly. The reader may know I was not in a pleasant mood when I came to Mr. Hall's fine brick residence surrounded with the cabins of his numerous negro servants. I rode up to the stile and hollered. There was a light in the house when I first hollered, but it was quickly extinguished and all was 'Dark as Egypt,' but I was determined not to be put off so easily and continued to hoop and yell until I raised an old negro man who came out to the stile to see what I wanted. I told him I had ridden all day and up until that time of night, and I wanted him to tell his master I wanted feed for my horses. He said, "Ole Massa is in bed don't like to be sturbed at this time of night." I said, "Ole Massa the Devil, damn you if you don't go get me something to feed these horses, I'll blow your damned Brains out." Drawing my pistol, at the same time letting him know I meant business, he said "Yes boss I will go and see Old Massa about it," and that is the last I saw of him.

I dismounted and tied my horses to the fence. After waiting some time for the old darkey to return I took my pistols and walked down to the front door and thumped on it with the butt of my pistol, hard enough to awaken a dead man. Then I went where I had seen the light when I first rode up and thumped. I could not raise any one. So, I walked around to some of the cabins and tried in vain to arouse someone, but all to no purpose. I went back to my poor hungry horses, judging them by myself. The large barns and cribs were on the opposite side of the road from the house and I went over there and searched all around for a place to get in where I could get some hay and oats or corn. The crib was lattice work built with heavy oak slats and striped on over studing with oak laths. I got a fence rail and tried to punch a hole through the slats but I was too weak for such work and had to abandon my efforts. I went back to the stile and took off my saddle and threw it on the plat form, and unbuckled my blankets and fixed my bed, and concluded I would stay there until morning.

I could not sleep. I was so hungry and 'wearied' by my long fast and long day and night ride and the thought of my poor hungry horses. The more I thought, the more determined I was to find something for my horses. I rested about an hour and saddled up again and moved on. I had gone about a mile when I saw a light in an old double log house. I stopped and gave a "Hello!" A soldier came to the door and I stated my case to him. He said he had just got off the train and came home. He had nothing at the house to feed on, but he had a stack of oats some distance from the house. As it was not long until morning, he said I could turn my horses into a clover lot below the road, and he would go a soon as daylight came and get some oats for them. I thought that was the best I could do.

He kindly helped unsaddle and turn my horses in the lot and I was soon in the house. The good woman wanted to prepare me something to eat but I would not allow her to do so. She gave me a glass of sweetmilk and a piece of cold cornbread. They insisted I should go to bed. I protested and insisted I should get my saddle for a pillow and my blankets for a bed and I would lay down on the floor, which I did, and slept soundly until next morning. The sun was high above the eastern horizon. After a good breakfast and my horses fed, I paid my kind host and thanked them for their kindness and started out on another long hot day's ride, and as it proved, until sometime up in the night again.

I had a tilt with a man on the night of this day, who had a table spread in his yard at least two hundred feet long and filled with every luxury both to eat and drink when we were on our way to Richmond in May 1861. I called on him some time after dark and asked if I could get feed for my horses. 'He hemed and hawed' until I got weary and I said to him, "Damn you, you could spread a luxurious table the first year of the war now you cannot keep a soldier all night." He said, "were you here then?" I said, "I was." "I reckon I'll have to keep you," he said. I said, "oh no I'll be damned if you do." I said, "Doctor Sawyers lives near here some where, they tell me his is a friend to the soldiers, tell me how to get there."[9] He gave me the directions and I soon found him and his house full of Kentucky Cavalry. He began to tell me his condition. I said, "Doc can you feed these horses?" He said, "oh yes." Well I said, "you can shove a pole out one of your 2nd story windows and let me roost on it." He laughed and said, "get down," and of course I did.

The servants came and took my horses. I had my saddle brought to the house and intended to use them for a bed as he was crowded and pressed for bedroom. He had me some supper prepared and I ate and fixed my bed and was soon in the 'Land of Dreams.' I was only some 40 miles from home now and was calculating on getting there the next night. I awoke greatly refreshed, and after a good breakfast, I fixed to start. I wanted to pay the good Old Doctor but he would not have anything. He said when he got so hard up that he would be compelled to charge Confederate Soldiers, he would quit taking them in and shut up shop. After many thanks and good wishes for his long life and prosperity, I started on my way feeling glad and good that there was yet some kindness and goodness of heart in the 'Land of flowers and fair women.'

I had not proceeded more than 10 miles before I met two of my county men in a two-horse wagon with the 'records of our county.' They were Mr. John Kreger, Deputy County Court Clerk, and Leonidas Baugh.[10] They gave me startling intelligance that the Yankees were on a raid up through East Tennessee. When they left Abingdon, the Yankees were reported to be somewhere between Kingsport and Bristol, some 25 miles away, and they had no doubt but that they were in Abingdon by this time.[11] They tried to persuade me to turn back, but my head was set for home and home I was going yanks or no yanks. So, I bid them farewell. Plodded on all through the day. I met parties from my home with wagons, negroes, horses and mules fleeing from the Yankee Raiders. I plodded along until I came to Colonel William Beatties near the line between the counties of Smyth and Washington. He had two sons that volunteered and went out with the same company I was in. One of them, Doctor Walter Beattie, a young physician, had died in 1861, and Fountain, who served with 'Mosby,' [John Singleton Mosby] was one of the first men from my company to go with Mosby, and he stayed with him until the end of the war.[12]

The old gentleman was down at the road side as I came up and said, "you are not going any further to night. Get down and I will have your horses put up and fed." I said, "I think I had better go on home." He was a little squirmish about the report of the Yankees raid. He said last reports they had not reached Bristol, and I told him if they were moving that slow, they would not come at this time. As I was tired and pretty well worn down, and with friends, I would stay. He called some of his negro men to come and take charge of my horses and feed them and he and I went up to the house, which was some 300 yards from the road. There was several young ladies there, with the teacher an old acquaintance of mine, and a woman of sterling Christian character and a great stay and help to me in after years in my infancy in the Christian life. Her name was Susanah T. Cox.[13] There was also a young lady boarding there and attending school with Mrs. Beattie and the family, who was an old school-mate of mine. I

Colonel John
Singleton Mosby.
Library of Congress.

spent a delightful evening. Of course, I had to tell them of the war and my recent wounding and narrow escape from death. After a good supper and refreshing sleep, I was ready for breakfast and by the way a good 'Toddy' as an appetizer—a thing a soldier never refused.

The Colonel insisted I turn my horses out on pasture and spend the day and another night with him, and by that time, we would get some 'definite' news from the front. But I told him I could not think of that. When he found he could not persuade me to stay longer, he had my horses brought out and I started again. I jogged along down to 'Captain Strathers' [James P. Strother] where I was to leave Jake Schwartz's horse. I was in 8 miles of home now and had not run into the yanks yet, altho rumors still aserted they were coming.

I arrived at home about mid day and fed my horses, and determined to deliver them that night. About 2 oclock pm I set out. I had to cross the county northwest from my home to get to Mr. Baileys. I arrived there about 3:pm and delivered his son's horse to him, and then I only had about half a mile to reach my uncle John Morrell's, where I delivered Charles's horse to him. I had one more, that was David Lynch's. His parents lived in Abingdon. Still, rumors said the yanks were coming. My uncle and family tried to disuade me from going to town that night, but I was so anxious to deliver all the horses and get them off my hands, I would not yield, and my cousin and comrade Charles Morrell said he would accompany me. So after we had taken supper, we started to Abingdon.

As we were in 3 miles of the place, we were not long in going there. When we entered the town, it was as dark and silent as a grave yard. We had no questions to ask of any one. We both knew where Mr. Lynch's residence was and we rode directly to it and called at the front door. Mrs. Lynch answered my call in person, and I told her I had David's horse and wished her to take charge of him, which she assented to and called a colored servant to come and get him. She insisted on us coming in but I told her it was too late and the Yankee Raiders might come on us. She said she would send the horse out in the country to a safe place so we bid her good night, and left to hunt up some one that could tell us about the movements of the raiders, but could not get any definite information. I came back home with my cousin and spent the night.

My grandmother Colley lived near my uncles and I had to visit that day and spent the day and night with her. She and an old Bachlor Brother lived together, 'Lewis Morrell.' My sister 'Bettie' lived with grandmother and uncle. Nothing of any importance happened to me during the summer. I visited around among my relatives and friends and had a good time with the 'girls.' On one occasion, I was invited to a quilting. I was the only male person present, and was invited to take the foot of the table at dinner, and if I had known before hand what was expected of me I would have politely declined or ran away—one or the other. When the ladies—some ten or twelve in number—were seated, I was requested to carve the chicken, a thing I knew nothing more about than a 'baby.' I could not back out or get out. I picked up the carving knife and commenced sawing on a wing. The knife was awful dull and I couldnt make an impression. Being young and backward and green in this kind of thing, I began to get red in the face and the girls, forgetting their decorum, commenced tittering at my awkwardness and embarrassment, and of course I grew worse embarrassed and finally got the chicken out of the dish on the table cloth. Our hostess seeing 'my predicament,' came to my 'rescue' and proposed to relieve me of my task. Of course, I was too anxious to be rid of my job to make any objection. This greatly marred my enjoyment for dinner and the company of the young ladies for the rest of the evening, and I thought at that time, ruined my matrimonial prospects in the community. [Here Colley, perhaps confused with the timing of events, recounts a story of the 'carving' incident, which he told of earlier in his journals.]

7

The Old Martial Fire Began
to Burn in My Chest

SOMETIME IN OCTOBER my old Captain, now 'Brigadier General' William E. Jones, was sent out from the Eastern Army to take command of the Department of South West Virginia and East Tennessee.[1] He was hurried off from there and came without any staff officers—except W. M. Hopkins [Warren Montgomery Hopkins] his Adjutant General—on his way to the front.[2] He came by my fathers and asked me if I could go with him and assist him until he could get up a staff. Of course, the old martial fire began to burn in my chest and I told him I would go as soon as I could get some rations cooked and get my rig fixed up. He said he would ride on and I could come on as soon as I was ready. Of course, I was not long in making my preparation. I mounted my horse and set out to over take my beloved commander. I thought I would over take him at Abingdon seven miles from my home. When I got there, I received the news that the enemy were at Blountville, Tennessee, and that a battle was in progress at that place; 'General,' on receiving the information, had pressed forward with all speed.[3] I had no other alternative but press on alone.

I did very well as long as I had daylight. I rode on, ever now and then meeting a courier or a panick stricken citizen saying the enemy was coming on towards Bristol. About dark I arrived at my aunts who lived in Bristol, only four miles east of Bristol, and stopped there and fed my horse and ate supper, as I expected to be on the move all night or until I found 'General Jones.' My aunt and cousins begged me to remain with them until morning but I said no, I must find my General to-night. So, I started out alone on the road to Bristol. This town was on the State line between

Virginia and Tennessee and only some nine miles from Blountville. I met a courier, or he claimed to be, some two miles from Bristol. He said our forces had been driven back and the enemy was advancing on Bristol and were probably there by that time. I knew Jones and our army was still down that way somewhere so I pulled on into town.

It was now 10: pm or probably later in the night. At last I ran up on a soldier that could give me some definite information. He told me we had no forces on the road from Bristol to Blountville except a picket line to watch the movements of the enemy. He said 'General Jones' had fallen back to 'Zollicoffer,' which was south of Blountville, and that I would find him by taking the road leading from Bristol to Zollicoffer. It was a place called 'Union' before the war. The Rebs did not like that name, and renamed it for the Lamented 'General Zollicoffer,' who lost his life early in the war at the Battle of Fishing Creek Kentucky in 1862.[4] It is now called 'Bluff City.'

I rode on alone on this road until I came onto the Paperville Road, and had proceeded down some distance when by the action of my horse I knew something unusual was near at hand, and I reined him up and stopped to listen. I heard the sound of horses' feet on the road, and as I was near a strip of woodland, I reined my horse to one side in the shadows of the trees until I could ascertain whether they were friends or foes. Before they got up to me I had recognized 'General Jones' by his old 'Clay Bank' mare and turned my horse out to move with the column. He recognized me and said, "Colley is that you?" I said, "Yes sir!" He said, "fall in here with me." We moved on the way. I had come down and come back to Bristol about day light and took the road towards Abingdon. We moved up about two miles about sun up, and halted to feed our horses and eat a snack of breakfast; 'The General' and I breakfasted off the rations I had brought from home. We halted here about one hour and then resumed our march.

The enemy moved up cautiously and came to Bristol that day. We moved on back to Abingdon and the General called out all the old men and boys, and prepared to give the yanks a warm reception. He chose his position on the east side of 'Beaver Creek,' a stream about one mile west of the town. He had the old men and boys throwing up breast works about one hundred yards from the creek and on the hills both north and south of the main road. He had his artillery posted. He established his headquarters in an old vacant house at the forks of the Bristol and Reedy Creek

Brigadier General
Alfred "Mudwall" Jackson.
Courtesy of findagrave.com.

Roads, on Esquire John L. Bradley's farm.[5] The only furniture we had was plank boards for a table, bedstead, and writing desk. Jasper Jones [Jasper Nathaniel Jones], a first cousin of the Generals and also a member of our old company, and Thomas W. Bailey [Thomas White Bailey] and R. M. Page [Reuben Murrell Page], two more of the old company, were at home on furlough. They came out and acted on the General's Staff and assisted in the establishing our line of defense.

By night of the 2nd day after our arrival everything was in readiness. While we were arranging the lines, 'General Mudwall Jackson'—as he was called—failed to obey an order General Jones had given him for placing his men in line.[6]

He ordered me to ride over there and tell him "damn him if he did not do what he told him he would put him under arrest." I started and he called me to halt before I proceeded far. He came on up to me and said, "I will go with you myself." We rode over there and found him on top of a high knob above 'Clapps Dam,' with his men all huddled up around him with no semblance of order or alignment. 'General Jones' asked for 'General Jackson.' A tall robust specimen of humanity stepped out and said, "I'm

General Jackson." He had on his head an old silk beaver hat that looked like a wagon had run over it and mashed it in on both sides. He probably used it for a pillow at night. It was what the country people generally called 'a Stove Pipe Hat.'

General Jones said to him "Why in the Hell didn't you obey my orders and place your men on the brow of the hill behind the fence where they would have some protection? If the enemy were to come and plant a battery on the hill across the dam there, forming at the same time to an 'eminence' west of the 'Mill Dam,' one shell well directed would kill every 'Damned' one of you." General Jackson commenced to say, "he thought," and that is as far as he got. Jones reported "Thought Hell, what right had you to think? Sir you place your men where I ordered you to or I will have you arrested at once." Jackson did not hesitate a moment. He gave the orders at once. Our lines being all perfected, we retired to head quarters.

Thomas Bailey [Thomas White Bailey] who was a mess mate of mine in our company mess, said he would go out home that night. I told him to bring me some rations next morning. Colonel Hopkins house was just north east of General Jones's headquarters, some ¼ of a mile. Jones and I both had pressing invitations to go there to get our meals but 'General Jones' would never go into any house for headquarters. He always made it a mile to feed his men. 'Colonel Hopkins' always brought him his meals, and on this particular morning, by that means was saved from what happened to the rest of us. Comrade Bailey returned early and brought a lot of nice biscuits and other things for our breakfast. We all placed our rations on the Broad Plank. Colonel Hopkins had already breakfasted at home and brought the General his meal.

Jasper Jones, Thomas Bailey, and I ate of the rations Bailey brought from home. As soon as we were done, we were hurried off to curry and saddle my horse. While I was at this I became awful thirsty with a burning sensation in my stomach, and I got my canteen and stepped across the road to a fine spring some 50 yards from our quarters. I filled it with water and drank it all. I was as thirsty as ever; I filled it again and drank that with the same result. I filled it the third time and drank that, and got the fourth one filled up and left the spring with it, drinking a little at a time as I walked toward headquarters. I thought something was wrong, but didn't know what. By the time I got back I had about emptied the fourth canteen. That was four quarts of water I had in me then. Colonel Hopkins had the mail pouch ready to carry to the Post Office up in town and he sent me to deliver it. It was one mile from our quarters to the Post Office. I rode on at a brisk trot and so arrived at the office. The Postmaster came to the door and I handed him the pouch and told him I would be back in a few minutes. I wanted more water.

I rode up to the drug store and asked if they had any water. Mr. Hickman the Druggist said, "plenty of it, get down and come in and help yourself."[7] I dismounted and went in the back room and drank 4 large glasses full of water. I said, "I am awful thirsty this morning. Do you know what can be the matter?" Hickman said, "being drunk last night I guess." I mounted my horse and rode down to the Post Office and rode on back to headquarters, and I carried the mail in the house and Colonel Hopkins emptied the contents out on our wide plank and he and I commenced sorting it out to the various regiments, batteries, and companies.

While I was engaged at this I was taken violently ill, became almost deathly sick at my stomach. I slid out the back door on the steps. I soon began to vomit and continued for ¾ of an hour. I imagine this gave me great relief but I was scared and squeamish about the stomach. I still did not know what was the matter with me. The third day after this, I met an uncle of mine who lived near Mr. Baileys residence. He asked me if I knew I had been 'poisoned.' In great astonishment, I said no. He told me Thomas Bailey and all the Bailey family were sick and under the 'Doctor.' The biscuits we had ate, and the family ate the same, were all made up with arsenic instead of soda, through a mistake as I learned later.

Thomas Bailey came home late that night. I had requested him to bring me some rations and he told the old colored cook, Aunt Angeline, he wanted her to bake up a lot of good biscuits for him to take with him next morning. Mrs. Bailey having died sometime in 1862, so there was no one to see after such things but 'young girls.' Angeline asked them for soda and they told her to look in a certain drawer in the side board and get it. Mr. Bailey had a lot of arsenic to poison ground squirrels and crows around his cornfield; both soda and arsenic were in the same drawer. 'Old Auntie' got the wrong package, which came near sending us all to our Long Home. 'Through the goodness and mercy of God' I was saved again from death. I accidently or apparently, I ought to say providentially, done the very thing I ought to have done—filled my stomach with cold water. Of course, that was all I done, not knowing what was the matter with me. The water neutralized the poison and caused me to vomit and relieved me from its deadly poison effects. Jasper Jones was taken violently ill and carried to the residence of 'Mr. Alex Findleys' [Alexander Findlay]. He and Tom Bailey were some three weeks recovering from the effects of their breakfast. I never lost a day, or hour I may say, from 'duty.' I will say just here that Mr. Bailey's family was poisoned for the second time before that deadly stuff was destroyed.

General Jones began to get restless as the enemy did not come on as he expected. He was anxious to find out what they were doing. He said to me on the third day "I wish you would ride down the Bristol Road. You will find Colonel Witcher [Lieutenant Colonel Vincent A. Witcher] some where on the road."[8] Tell him "to find out where the enemy is and what they are doing." I had heard a great deal of the terrible Colonel Witcher, but I had never met him. I had pictured him in my mind as a great burley headed six-footer that just chewed up every one that did not agree with him on the war question. I rode on musing on this and other topics. At last, some 7 miles below our quarters, I came on his reserve force and I inquired for the 'Colonel.' I was informed he had ridden out to his out posts and I would find him there. About one mile further on, I ran on some men in the road and inquired again for the 'Burley Colonel.' Someone pointed out a very diminutive looking little dirty man on a large Gray Horse.

I rode up and saluted him and said, "General Jones ordered me to say to you he wished you to find out what the enemy is doing and where they are at this time." He said, "By God Captain, there is the road pointing in the direction of the enemy." I said, "that is not my orders 'Colonel, but I am not afraid to go if you will give me some men." He said, "how many do you want?" I said, "ten will do." He turned to a sergeant and said, "detail ten men to go with the captain." When I had placed them in the road, his adjutant said, "Colonel I will go with the captain with your permission." He said, "go ahead," and we started off. We had to pass through a strip of woodland for some distance. When we got through that we came up on a high hill where we had a fair view of the country for at least a mile. Major Hamby's house on the road was in fair view, and just in front of it, mounted, were a squad of Yankee cavalry men: some 10 or 12.

I deployed my men on the right and left of the road. The adjutant and I kept in the road with revolvers in hand. When we came within three hundred yards I ordered a charge. The yanks broke and run down the road. Just as we came opposite the barn, one yank who had been asleep in it, ran out and we took him in and sent him to the rear. We continued on down the road rather cautiously as we had another body of woodland to pass through. I did not know but what they had a trap set but we passed on until we came out where we could see the smoke arising from all the bridges and trestles on the railroad as far as Bristol. I was occupied in looking forward. About a mile away, I saw them run a battery out on a hill unhindered for action. I do not know what the adjutant was doing any way.

Just as we came to a pole, that was laid across the road to turn the water off the road into a ditch at the side of the road, we were then just opposite 'Mr. Henry Preston's Residence.[9] We were confronted by some 20 yanks, stepping out from behind the yard fence and some large white oak trees at the road side. They brought their guns to bear on us and commanded us to halt; of course, we halted. The adjutant wheeled to the right and I to the left. As I wheeled, I drew my pistol down and fired. The adjutant lay flat down on his horse and run back up the road at full speed. I had no idea of going up the road, for as I had anticipated, the whole squad fired a volley right up the road after him. I ran out close to the yard fence and rode up to the corner of the yard. The fence was fortunately down at this point, and I rode in behind some out buildings and then up through the fields. 'Colonel Witcher' had followed us with a portion of his command. I rode up to him and we looked down on the yanks, with their horses loose in Mr. Preston's barnyard and meadows and the men laying idly around. I saw enough to satisfy me that they were falling back, as they were burning the bridges on the railroad. If Jones could have come on them at that time with all his forces we could have precipitated their flight and in all probability killed or captured a large portion of them.

That saved a many stampede during the war, the commander of one army not knowing what the other was doing at a particular time and place. Colonel Witcher, after viewing the mass of Blue Coats for a short time, said to me, "Captain you can stay here as long as you want to, I am going away from here, as the Yankees came near capturing me at this place yesterday." And off he went with all his men and left me alone. I

soon turned and rode on after him. I came back to Major Hambeys. Mrs.
Hambey was out in the yard and telling what the Yankees had done. They
had their artillery right in her yard, horses, guns, and all, and a Michigan
Regiment camped around the house and barn and had killed all her geese,
ducks, chickens, and pigs, and she was angry at the yanks and wished they
were all at home or in some other region.[10] I tried to console her the best I
could and she went on and brought me something to eat. They wished me
to get down and come in.

I knew there was nothing between me and the Yankees and I was too
old a cavalryman to get my horse in the face of the foe. I took my bread
and meat in my hand and ate it as I rode along. I got back to headquarters about sun down and reported to 'General Jones.' He immediately gave
orders for his command to move out in pursuit of the enemy. The cavalry moved out that night and next day. The General, William Hopkins,
and I moved out. The first stop we made was at Carter's Station on the
'Watauga River.' He had his tent put up and we had our cooking done
at a private house. He ordered a detail of a sergeant and ten men to be
made—from some Tennessee Regiment that were acquainted with the
country—as couriers. They soon arrived and made themselves at home
around the General's camp fire. They had their own rations cooked and
ate to themselves.

After dinner one day we were all with the General standing on a platform at the Depot when a courier dashed up and said, "Can any of you all
tell me where "Old bawly" is?" Of course, we all waited for the General to
speak. He said, "Who do you call 'Old bawly?'" "Why General Jones, thats
who," the courier said. "I am General Jones if that's who you are looking
for." The young man looked very much embarrassed and felt in his pocket
and pulled out a long yellow envelope and said "General, here is a dispatch
for you." After he had read it, the young man said, "General, I have an
aunt who lives a little way down the river, can I go down there and get my
horse fed and get something to eat?" In reply, General Jones put his hand
in his haversack and pulled out 3 ears of corn and said, "here young man
is 3 ears of corn give 2 of them to your horse and poach the other and eat
it. Old bawly might want you directly." That is all the rebuke he gave him.

One night about dark, he said to me, "feed your horse, I want you to ride
with me to night." I had no idea what to do, so I made ready. He took the

Sergeant and two men with us and we made our way towards Jonesboro, Tennessee. We arrived near the town some time past mid night. We concealed our horses in a clump of bushes some distance from the town, leaving the couriers as guards with our horses and equipment. With our trusty revolvers in hand the General, the Sergeant, and I cautiously made our way into the town. Sometimes we were in the fields and when we came to the suburbs of the town we made our way along dark and dusty alleys, and at last, crawled through a plank fence and came to the back of a house where the Sergeant—our guide—made a signal by rapping on the house. Presently, the back door opened and a man came out. He and the General had a long confidential chat, while the Sergeant and I stood guard.

After the General had gotten all the information he desired, we made our way back to our horses, mounted them, and moved off in the opposite direction from the one which we came in on. We pressed on all day. During the day, we met the remains of 'Colonel Botles' [Lieutenant Colonel J. L. Bottles] who had been killed some days before.[11] His friends were taking him to his old home for interment. Towards evening we came to a large white house. We called to get some water. The lady and her daughters found out we were Rebels and they insisted on the General getting down and having refreshments, but he declined. They brought us out some fine apples, which we ate as we rode along. We were now on the extreme right of our out posts near Kingsport, Tennessee. We crossed back over the Watauga River about sun down and soon came to Colonel Witcher's camp, where the General proposed to spend the night. The Colonel, wishing to put the best foot foremost, 'commenced sending out runners for eggs butter and chickens, and one came in with a fine turkey.' We had a real feast at supper and breakfast both.

The Colonel treated us in Royal style. After breakfast, we left our generous host and made our way south, back to the General's Headquarters. We arrived at General Ransom's [Major General Robert Ransom, Jr.] Headquarters. His brigade was near the center of our forces on the direct road from Blountville to Jonesboro. We took dinner with him and then moved on through the lanes and byways towards Carter's Station. The General and I were entirely alone on this evening's ride. It is the only time I ever heard him express himself on the subject of Religion. Since my miraculous escape from death at Kelly's Ford, I had been quite serious on that subject. Some how or other I had drawn him out on that line. I remember I asked him what he thought of Stonewall Jackson's religion, his answer made a deep impression on my mind. He said very solemnly, "I wish I was as good a Christian as I believe Stonewall Jackson to be."

That night, after we arrived at camp, the Inspector General for this department was the General's Guest for the night. They were old chums, both had both belonged to USA [Army]. He was an infidel, and after supper, we were all around the camp fire and he began spouting out some of his infidel talk. 'General Jones' cursed him and told him to stop. "Colonel," he said, "you shall not talk any such stuff as that before these young men," and made him hush right up. I found another thing I did not want to see, that was a letter from Major W. B. Richards, post marked Gordonsville, Virginia.[12] I had been assigned to his department for light duty under an act of 'Confederate Congress' requiring all able bodied men on detail in the various Departments to report to their commands for active duty and their places to be filled by disabled soldiers, and pronounced unfit for active duty in the ranks by their medical boards.[13] I had written Major Richards to transfer me to General Jones's command, and as I stated above, he had written me and said he had no power to transfer and I must report at once. I appealed to General Jones but he was stern and unflinching when it came to discipline. He knew if men were allowed to change or transfer when ever the fancy struck them, or they became offended at their officers, the 'Discipline' of the amry would have been destroyed.

The General saw how reluctant I was to leave him and the boys of our old company. When he was captain it always was thrown up to me that Jones was partial to me. He took a great interest in me, and I was very much attached to him. He was a soldier after my own heart, brave and generous hearted. I never knew him to ask a private to go anywhere he would not venture himself. To ease me off, he told me he was going to organize a Battery of Horse Artillery and that he would have me commissioned in it. But he did not live to carry out his plans. I left him and came on home to make arrangements for my new position in the Confederate Service.

8

I Did Not Volunteer to Curry Horses

ON THE 7TH OF NOVEMBER, I started on to Gordonsville. Just as I was leaving, the prisoners were coming to Abingdon that General Jones had captured near Rogersville, Tennessee. He had surprised Carter's Brigade, and captured, killed, wounded and dispersed his whole command, along with wagons, horses and mules.[1] It was one of the worst defeats the Yankees had ever experienced in East Tennessee, and at once brought Jones in prominent favor with his men. If he had apprised me of his intentions, he would have had some difficulty in getting me to leave him until after the 'fun war' was over. Nothing would have given me more pleasure than to have participated in that surprise 'and rout,' and especially because the command was composed of renegade Virginians and East Tennesseans. They had a particular hatred towards us and we had no kind feelings for them. At that time, we thought they were traitors to their state and they thought we were Rebels against the United States Government and ought to be shot, hanged or mutilated in some way.

I arrived at Gordonsville on the 10th day of November 1863, and reported to Major Richards. He was an old bank officer from Alexandria, Virginia. A financier who did not know anything about a soldier and was not at all in sympathy with them. He was a petulant quick-tempered business man, and all he knew was to get the best service he could out of such material as he had. Most of the men he had in his employ at that time were men who were willing to do anything rather than face 'bullets.' [Underlined in original.]

When I reported he sent me to 'Captain Forkner' [Captain E. Boyd Faulkner] who had charge of the horse and mule lots and stables, where all the horses, mules, and wagons that went to General Lee's army had to pass through, and all broken down horses, mules, and wagons were sent for exchange.[2] The Blacksmith and Wagon Shops were located at this point. There were some fifty Blacksmiths and a like number of Woodworkmen and Harness Makers. All corn straw and hay passed through this department. Captain Faulkner ordered me to report to the stable boss. He was a great looking, Scotch-Irish specimen of Humanity. He had been a negro overseer all his life and knew nothing but to drive, to order, and require obedience. I approached him and said, "Captain Faulkner ordered me to report to you." With out any further preliminarys he said, very abruptly, "get a curry comb," at the same time pointing to a lot of curry combs and brushes in the saddle and harness house. I looked him square in the eye and said "What?" He repeated his orders with great emphasis. I said "Look-a-here old man you don't know who you are taking to do you?" I said, "I volunteered in the Confederate army and I did not volunteer to curry horses and I would see you as far in Hell as a bird could fly in forty thousand years, before I will curry horses."

My father made me curry horses when I was a boy, and I got a distaste against that kind of thing. He said, "I will have to report you then." I said, "very well," and be damned, he trotted to Captain Faulkner's office at the gate and I soon saw the captain trotting out to report to Major Richards. I did not have long to wait. A little office boy soon came on a run and said, "Major Richards says for you to come to his office." I said, "very well my son, that is where I want to go." I followed the boy on and stepped into the office and saluted and said, "Major I am here." He looked up from his paper, on which he was busily writing, and said, "they say you refused to curry horses." I said, "I did," and then went on to tell him I was a volunteer in the army and if he had no other work for me to do, that I most assuredly would not do that, and more over I was sent there to perform 'Light Duty,' being disabled by reason of wounds received in battle from preforming field service. Currying horses was as hard work as one could be put to do. He ordered me to go around to my quarters, so I went.

Faulkner assigned me a room upstairs in a 4-roomed frame house; it had a fire place in it. I procured some plank and made me a good bunk, and I had my blankets with me. The Captain gave me a straw tick. I went to the feed house and filled it with straw and soon had me a good bed, and I drew my rations, and had a colored girl—who was employed as cook for the wagon bosses—to cook my rations for me and bring them to my room. I got some books and papers and spent my time reading and walking around making acquaintances with the employees and acquainting my self with the place generally. I helped cut and mix feed for the horses and mules, sometimes when I wanted to and no one meddled or interfered with me.

There was one of the 2nd Virginia Cavalry on light detail.[3] He was a wagon boss. There were two of the 8th Georgia Regiment there also.[4] They were badly wounded and disabled, and really not fit to do any kind of manual labor. 'They did not stay many weeks until Major Richards sent them to their homes in Georgia.' I had been at this kind of life some two weeks I guess, when one morning, I had orders to report to Major Richards's office. I had not seen him since my second interview with him and I could not imagine what was up, but I boldly walked into office and saluted him in true soldier style and awaited orders. As usual, he was busy writing. When he was through he turned to me and said, "I see by your papers you are a brick mason." "I said, "yes sir." He said, "I have some houses around there in the enclosures. I want chimneys built to them." I said, "all right sir. I am willing to do any thing I am able to do. If my back will stand it I will try it." He said he had a negro boy who knew something about laying bricks and I could have him to do the heavy work. He wanted stone foundations placed under them.

I went around to the yard and started to work on the chimneys. The colored boy was a bright, intelligent, good natured fellow, and we got along fine. Finally, on the 1st chimney, it was all brick. The next one was in the negro quarters. It was a long double fire place and he wanted it built up as high as the arch bars with stone. I worked at it all day, and my side and back began to pain me fearfully. I posted off down to the hospital at the depot, some four hundred yards from our quarters. I went in to the surgeon's office and waited my turn, as there was several patients ahead of me. When my turn came, I asked the doctor to please examine me, stating to him how I had been wounded and how I had been treated since I had been here. He had me to strip and allow him to examine me thoughly. After he was through he said, "you ought not to strain or exert yourself in anyway. It is true the wounds are healed in the outside but it is very tender through your body yet." I said, "I wish you would give me a certificate to that effect as it will be no use for me to tell Major Richards anything." So, he wrote out a certificate and went to the Major's office and laid the certificate on his desk. He picked it up and read it and handed it back to me and said, "Go around to your quarters." I went and stayed there several days again; one morning, he sent for me again.

I went around and he gave me a pass and transportation to Charlottesville to report to 'Captain Poindexter' who was in charge of a lot of broken down horses and mules.[5] He was feeding and recruiting them out in the country, some two miles from the town. I did not know what this new field would open up. When I arrived, I found Old Captain Poindexter, to be a big fat, jovial, whole souled old fellow. We were soon the best of friends and I spent my time very pleasantly with him. We had some 600 or 800 head of horses and mules in various stages of decay with Poul evil, Glanders, scratches, & Greasy heel.[6] The worst ones were condemned and sold to the highest bidder, and the best ones were driven to Lynchburg and turned over to Major Preston. At that place, he sent them out in the country to various points where hay and corn could be procured to feed them. I went with him on 2 trips. We had a wagon with us to haul our eats on, and our cooking utensils and ropes. He placed me in front of the cavalcade and another man with me, who's duty it was to stop at the crossroads and lanes to keep our stock from turning out of the road.

Our hands were all young men, too young for service, and two or three colored men. Those in the rear had a hard time with the weak horses and mules. They would slip and fall in the washes and gulleys and they would have to be lifted up and set on their feet again. Sometimes, they would step on them. On an old road near Nelson and Amherst Hills, the ropes would have to be brought out sometime and fastened to them [the weaker animals], and the wagon horses hitched to the other end to draw them back on the road. Sometimes three or four would be down at the same time and the procession would be stopped for an hour or two at a time. We were generally on the road a week or 10 days. We lived well. We could buy eggs, chickens, butter, or most anything we wanted along the road. Captain Poindexter generally put up at a private house. He was the best natured man I ever met. I never knew him to speak an unkind word to any of us. While I stayed with him he was always laughing. I saw him laugh a farmer into keeping him all night. He asked if he could stay, and the farmer refused, and he just set into laughing and never said another 'word' to him until the farmer became amused at him and told him he could stay.

If Preston had fresh horses, we had to take them back to Gordonsville and get another lot of invalids and carry them up to Albemarle County, and then go on up to Lynchburg. The last trip I made with him was about Christmas. We were in Lynchburg Christmas Eve. We had brought a lot of eggs on the road and prepared to have a big egg nog in Lynchburg. Captain Poindexter got us a room in the basement of the Orange House. He bought 2 gallons of 'Apple Brandy' and 20 pounds of sugar. We borrowed vessels to beat eggs in, and a clean wash tub to make the nog in. There was some ten or twelve of us in the crowd. We had to leave at 7:P.M. on the train for 'Gordonsville,' and we were up at 2 A.M. beating eggs and preparing for the nog. By 5:A.M. we had it ready and the Old Captain came down to our room and commenced drinking and laughing. We were all pretty 'boozy' by the time the next tub was emptied and our train was ready to pull out, and we kept jovial all day by recruiting with the raw material. We were all in fine Humor when we arrived in Gordonsville in time for our Christmas Dinner. All the employees were enjoying the holidays, both Black and white.

9

I Went Back

I HAD WRITTEN to General Jones about my reception and treatment in the Q.M. Department [Quartermaster Department]. As I learned afterward, he had stopped at Gordonsville on his way to Richmond on some official business, and had an interview with Major Richards, and I imagined he told him what kind of man and soldier I was. For immediately after the holidays, he sent for me to come around to the office. I expected some other disagreeable 'job,' but to my surprise he addressed me in a very kind manner and said, "Mr. Colley go around to the stables and select the best saddle horse you can find there and a good saddle and bridle, and bring him around to the office and hitch him to the rack, and then come in here." Of course, I was off in a jiffy.

I went and told my old friend the stable boss, that Major Richards said for him to furnish me the best saddle horse and rig there was in the stables, and he was so afraid of being sent to the army, he would have run his head in the fire if Major Richards had ordered it. He flew around and ordered a negro boy to curry a certain horse I had chosen, and he was in the saddle room laying out saddles for me to choose from. I selected the best 'McClelland' [McClellan saddle] there in the lot with a fine blanket. I was soon mounted and back at the office ready for further orders. The Major told me to come inside the railing and have a seat by the stove.

He handed me the Richmond papers and said, "you can read the news Mr. Colley, while I am getting ready for you." I was there probably an hour before he handed me a dispatch to carry to the telegraph office and to await an answer. As it was only some 300 yards, I walked down there and delivered the message and waited in the office for a reply, which was handed to me in some 25 or 30 minutes. I returned and delivered it, and took my seat by the stove, and read the papers. That is all I had to do before dinner. At dinner time, he told me to take my horse to the stable and have him fed. That was my occupation the balance of my time. I would have to go out to the saw mills sometimes and to the Convalescent Smallpox Camp, which was some 4 miles Southwest of Gordonsville. The mills were East in the 'Pine Swamps'.

When I returned at Christmas, I found a soldier who was a congenial 'Spirit,' James Aldridge. He was from Pocahontas Co., now West Virginia. He belonged to the 25th Virginia Infantry.[1] He was as high minded as a 'Game Cock.' He was suffering with, or rather from, the effects of white swelling. His thigh bone was effected, and some portions of it had come out. He was sent there for light duty. The first thing they put him at was making roads from the saw mills with heavy pine slabs. Of course, he could not stand that. He came in one night scarcely able to drag his lame leg. He was pitiful. I tried to persuade him to go down to the surgeon at the hospital and have him examine him, as he had done for me, and get a certificate. He would not hear to anything but that he was going to curse 'Old Major Richards,' and whip him if he could get him out from behind his lattice work.

In the morning, after he and I ate our breakfast, I had to go early to carry a dispatch to the Surgeon in charge of the Smallpox Camp. I told him [Aldridge] if he persisted in his course he would land in 'Castle Thunder,' a place in Richmond where they sent all the bad soldier boys.[2] He said he would surely not do that. When the hands started out to the Mills 'Jim' refused to go, and the boss reported him to Headquarters and the Major sent for him at once. Jim promptly reported. The Major said, "they say you won't work on the road anymore." 'Jim,' with an oath said he would not. 'Old Major' said, "what the hell will you do then?" Jim said, "I will whip you till Hell won't know you if you will come out here and take that Star off your collar." The Major of course did not want to be whipped, so he sent a messenger to the Provost Marshall, 'Old Captain Broyles,' to come at once and bring a guard with him.[3] Jim of course was still cursing and raging about treating a disabled soldier as he was being treated.

When I returned about 11:A.M., they told me what had happened and that Jim was down at the station in the Guard House. While my horse was eating, I ate my dinner, and as he [Jim] and I had messed together and slept together, I took a little bucket we had in our mess chest and packed him his portions of the rations and carried them down to him. I said, "Jim I am sorry old fellow, you let your temper get the better of you. The worst has not come yet. When the train comes down from Staunton this evening you will be put aboard of it and sent to Richmond and placed in 'Castle Thunder.'" He said, "surely they will not be so mean as to treat a poor maimed soldier in that way." I said, "all you have to do is wait. You cursed and threatened a superior and I do not know what the penalty will be." I had to leave him and be at my post, so I bade him good-bye and that was the last I saw of him until July of this year. When I lost my foot on the 28th of May, he was in the Hospital 'Stuart at Windsor Hospital' he found out I was at Jackson Hospital, and visited me everyday and brought me something to eat and drink.[4] I have never heard of him since.

After he left I was alone so far as soldiers was concerned. Jim wrote to his Colonel, I cannot recall his name. One day some, two weeks later Jim was sent off. A fine-looking man walked up from the depot with three Stars on his collar. He called for Major Richards, and of all the cursing and abuse a man ever got in his life, he gave him and invited him to come out of his hole and he would shoot it out with him. He said it was an out rage to treat a soldier as he had treated Jim Aldridge. He said Jim was one of the best soldiers in his Regiment and he had become disabled for field duty. It was an out rage to place men when the duties required of them demanded the strength of an ox. The Colonel found he could get no fight and all he could do was go to Richmond and procure Jim's release, which he did, and got him in the hospital service. It took the old Major several days to get over the fight. By this time, he had learned that disabled soldiers was the last thing needed to curry and feed horses and mules, lift heavy sacks of corn and bales of hay, or stack straw and Plank Slabs.

I had a lot of fun with the stout men who were detailed in the department. I had become well acquainted with them all. At night, I would get them together and tell them about the battles I had been in and how men, horses, and everything loose was torn and mangled and piled up together in one mass by shot and shells. I knew ever one of them were doing the most degrading drudgery than ever shouldered a musket. After Jim left me I was rather lonely. I took a big good-natured wagon boss in for a companion and mess mate. I liked him, he was good natured and liberal,

and both of us being out in the country, we could gather up eggs, butter, and other things for our mess tables. He was a Culpeper man named
James Emmons.[5] Altho I liked him, I could not help having some fun at
his expense.

I had acquired a habit of grinding my teeth or griting them together
after I laid down at night; especially if I was nervous from our exertion.
One night, after we had laid down on our bunk—I in front and he on the
back side—I was laying there gritting my teeth and studing. Jim commenced punching me with his elbow and inquiring what was the matter. I
wheeled over and threw myself on him and commenced biting him on his
arms breast and back. He was a powerful man, weighing something over
two hundred pounds. He scuffled and squirmed awful and finally tore
loose from me and ran to the head of the stairway and jumped off, and I
after him. He ran down and around the house to the front end where some
four or five other bosses roomed. He thumped and banged for admittance.
At last, they hearing the commotion, opened the door and he sprang in
over their heads. I made a last grab at him. He yelled to them not to let me
in. As I did not want to go in, I was not hard to keep out. I went back up
into our room and fell down and laughed until my sides were sore. I had
to work hard convincing him I wasn't 'deranged.' They got a report started
that my mind was affected by the sever wound I was recovering from, and
I had a chance to play the crazy game on them.

Sometime in February a very pompous Gentleman came down from
Amherst County and insisted on having a place assigned him as wagon
master. He annoyed Major Richards and Captain Faulkner day after day.
He was too good a man to be shot at, and was hunting a soft job to avoid
the Conscript Law.[6] Captain Faulkner, who had become a warm friend to
the men, sugested that I run him off from there. So, we made it up that I
should take one of my violent spells that night. They rehearsed to him how
I had bit Evans; he had taken great pains to show him the mark of my teeth
on himself. It was arranged that they get him into my room for a chat, and I
was to lay down and commence grating my teeth, and finally make a lunge
at him, which was all carried out to the letter. There were some two or three
that were in on the secret, so when I commenced gritting my teeth, some of
them ran to me pretending to hold me. Of course, I easily hurled them to
one side and made for him. He ran up in the corner, and as I aimed to throw
myself down and grab him by the legs and throw him on the floor and bite

him a few times, he sprang over my head like a frightened Buck, over the railing and down the stairs, and I after him. He run around to the front door but the wagon bosses were in on the secret and would not let him in. I ran him out in the stock yard and over the back fence into the Pines. I went back to my room and we laughed at his 'antic' until we were tired.

I learned next morning that he crawled into the negro quarters some-time in the night and begged them to let him stay till next morning. I went out to the stables to see about my horse and he was there, busily telling the old stable Boss about his narrow escape from death or serious bodily harm. I came up on him suddenly. He had immediate and urgent business on the other side of the stable. I went back to my room and procured an officers sword that some of the guys had there. I buckled it on and went out strutting around, as though I was determined to kill somebody. I took good care not to press him too close for fear he would faint from sure fright. I walked around the stable. When he saw me on his side he crossed over, and presently, I was around at last. He started toward the large front gate where Captain Faulkner's office was. I saw him enter there. As it was pretty near office hours, I had to eat my breakfast and be ready. I had the stable boy to have my horse ready, and I thought I would give him one final send off before I went to the office. I knew he was still in Faulkner's office. I came around so he could not see me, and was at the door. Captain Faulkner spoke to me and asked me to come in. I stepped in and around to the back of the office, and pretended as though I had not noticed his pres-ence, until he sprang up. Then I snatched the hilt of the sword and drew it from the scabbard. He sprang out the door and on toward the stables.

Faulkner and I laughed heartily. As I had ordered the boy to bring my horse to the gate for me, I left the sword in Faulkners's office and went about my duty. He [Colley's victim] went around to all the officers that day. He, and they to him, were in great sympathy with me. He urged that I be arrested and sent to the 'asylum' before I hurt some one; as he could not get any encouragement he concluded to go home on the evening train. I was down at the station when the train arrived and was walking around with an eye on him all the time. I got on the opposite side from the plat-form and I could watch him under the coaches, and moved along until he mounted the steps opposite me. I sprang up meeting him, and as he went into the door I grabbed him. Of course, I did not attempt to try to hold him. He appealed to the guard on the train not to let me on the train. I laughed and shook my head at the Guard. I told him I did not want on, I could not have gotten on without a pass. Major Richards laughed heartily when he found out the trick I had worked on one of his would be bosses.

I had a hard trial to content myself at this place as my whole company had been sent home to spend the Winter and recruit their horses. From time to time I would receive letters from home telling me what a time the boys were having; plays, receptions and dances and so on. I would be almost wild to get home and be with them, but there was no way to get there but run off and that was one thing I would not do, either from danger of for the sake of pleasure. I had to tough it out. I had two strange experiences while at this place that I never have been able to account for or understand. My cousin W. W. Morrell was shot and instantly killed at a point some where between Shepherdstown and Charlestown. He and Joseph Pendleton were both killed there, and Colonel James H. Drake of the 1st was killed at the same time.[7]

As I have stated, my cousin, and Thomas W. Bailey [Thomas White Bailey], and I were bosom companions and as dear friends as men can be. Another mess mate, and the next in affection and comradeship, and as void of fear as either of us, was killed the day the company started back to their place in the Regiment. On both of these occasions I had a dream or vision. I saw them and had fixed an impression on my mind that they were 'dead,' some time before I got the news by letter. I have never had any such impression before or since. I was told a similar experience by a Colonel—who was in the Confederate Army and a prominent Lawyer after the war—Colonel Abraham Fulkerson, of a remarkable experience he had in reference to a class mate of his at the University of Virginia. He said he taught school the 1st winter after he left the University. His class mate was preparing himself for the ministry, and went home to Augusta County. When he left the University, they corresponded with each other. He said he had received a letter from his home that his classmate was very low with fever. He said he had to walk two miles from his school house to the post office, and he generally walked over at play time. The pathway was through the woods most of the way. On one of these trips he met his classmate in the woods and they sat down on a log and had a long conversation as to the colonel's spiritual welfare. He said in a few days that he received a letter from the young man's Father, that he had died the day, and in the house that he had met him. Col. Fulkerson was a brave

Colonel James Drake.
Courtesy of Fold3.com.

generous hearted man. 'He is now dead, 1902.' He was one of the 600 officers sent to Morris Island.[8]

I had written to my Captain C. T. Litchfield [Connally Trigg Litchfield]
and asked to be sent back to my company, while I was mad about the horses
currying and chimney building. My application had to go the rounds of all
the Departments, through the Army, and War, and Medical Department.
Of course, this took some 3 or 4 months. It did not reach Major Richards
until April 1864. He called me into his private office one morning and said
he had received my transfer and commenced begging me to let him send
it back. He had become very much attached to me. He had found out that
if he sent me out after anything or to ascertain any information I had rendered him some good service during the winter, in keeping him informed
about the movements of the Yankees. They had gone up into Albemarle
County on a road, some 10 or 12 miles north of Gordonsville. They ran on
Captain Breathed's Battery up there, and he and his men gave them such
a reception that they went back farther than they came.[9] There is where
it was reported that 'Breathed' whipped the Yankees with rocks and fence
rails. Something frightened them so they did not visit our place.[10]

As I started, he begged and pled with me and put my papers back in his
desk drawer, but I was stubborn as a mule and would not yield. My friends
all said I was a fool to leave a good safe place and go back and put myself
up for a target to be shot at, but let that be as it will. I went back.

10

That Is the Last I Knew until My Foot Was Off

I LEFT GORDONSVILLE on the 5th day of April. I see by the pass given me by Major Richards, my Regiment was down near Orange Court House, a little north, on the Madison Farm. I had to stay there 10 or 12 days before I could get a furlough to go home for a horse.[1] I got one about the 20th of April for 30 days, and boarded the train for home. Things had begun to look quite gloomy for our cause. By this time Confederate money had depreciated so it took about $25.00 to get a square meal at a hotel. The enemy had over run and devasted a great portion of Virginia and inflicted the whole of the States forming the Confederacy. A great portion of our men were in northern prisons and we had no place to recruit from. The most of us who volunteered at the commencement of the struggle were determined to fight it out to the bitter end.

I procured me a beautiful Bay Mare. She was heavily built and could stand any amount of hardships. I left my mother, sisters, father, and friends. 'At the time I left home the Battle of Wytheville and Cloyds Mountain had been fought.'[2] The Yankees were all along the road around Pulaski and New River. A comrade, Newton Roe [Newton Edward Roe], who had been transferred from 37th Virginia Infantry was with me. We were advised to turn off the main road at or near Fort Chiswell and cross New River at a private ford and get on top of the Blue Ridge and make our way by a bridle path. We traveled for some 2 days on top of the mountain. We had some fun out of a lot of Refugee negroes we ran upon on in the mountains one day. I told them we were Yankees; they almost went wild with joy. They hugged our legs and jumped and skipped around like monkeys. They preferred to show us wagons, horses, mules, and everything if we wished. Friend, we told them, we were only the advance and must be moving on. The main army would soon be on and left them to await with impatience for their friends in Blue.

We plodded on in this way and did not come down until we were near Rocky Mount in Franklin County. We arrived there at night and put up with one Mr. Turnbull.[3] He turned [charged] us to the tune of $75.00 next morning for our nights lodging—us and three horses. I was leading a horse for one of my comrades who wished to spend a few more days at home and then go down on the train. We arrived at Appomattox Court House the next night. We were sleeping on the floor in the reception room at the hotel. We were aroused in the night by the jailor requesting us to go to the jail with him. The prisoners had fled the jail, and the jail was on fire, but not to any dangerous extent. It had been discovered, in time to put out the blaze before it had much head way, by an old colored man who slept in the jail. After the fire was out we went up stairs where a burley negro was confined in an iron cage. He was under sentence to be hung for killing a white man. There was no other prisoners with him except a young negro lad. The old negro had made him crawl out of the cage through a small place where one of the bars had been broke out. It made a space about 8x12 inches. The jailer made him crawl back through that small place. He was the one who was starting the fires. He had to go outside of the cage to get to the stove. We went back after the excitement was over and slept until morning.

We made our way over to the James River. We found our command out north of Richmond in Hanover County. We were on the move now all the time. Now the vast army under 'General Grant,' like a great serpent, was gradually folding its huge masses around the Doomed Capital of the Confederacy. The little squad of half starved, rugged Confederates had to be on the move all the time to meet an advance, first on the right and then on the left, and next day in the center. Of course, the cavalry was expected to keep our Chieftain informed of every move made by his adversary.

We arrived on the 22nd day of May, some 12 days after the death of our Great Cavalry Leader 'J. E. B. Stuart.'[4] He was greatly lamented by his Brave Troopers that had followed him from 1861 to 1864. On the 25th, General 'Fitz Lee,' being informed that some 800 negroes were manning a fort at

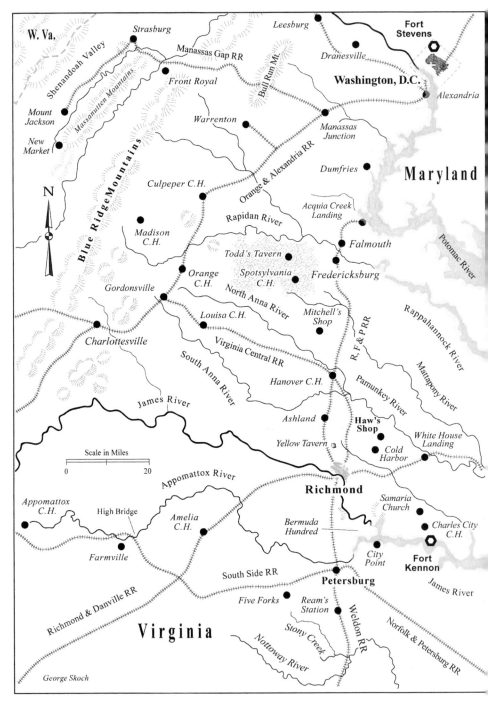

Northern Virginia, Maryland, and Washington, D.C., 1864, showing location of two engagements, Ft. Kennon and Haw's Shop, which Colley participated in.

Wilson's Wharf [Fort Kennon], he planned to surprise and capture them. The enemy, by some means, were informed of the move and had reinforced it by the white troops from Bermuda hundreds. The river was full of gun boats and transports. We made three unsuccessful assaults on the works and had to withdraw our forces. We had some 82 or 83 killed and wounded on the ground and made our way back to our position north of Richmond.[5]

On the 27th we moved rapidly forward towards Haw's Shop, where we went in to line on the extreme left of our line. Dismounted as sharpshooters, it fell to the lot of every 4th man to hold horses. In my lot of fours, my cousin Charles Morrell was the 4th man and I was still weak and suffering from my wound and could not stand very long on my foot.[6] My cousin begged me to let him take my place. I could not think of such a thing as that or anything that would show the least sign of cowardice, and then I would not have any one to risk their life to screen me. I have thought how I would have felt had I yielded to his entreaties and he had gone forward in the line of battle and have lost his life or limb as I had done. I feel now that it would have been a source of regret deep and lasting as eternity 'itself.'

As I stated, our Brigade went in on the extreme left of our line, and our company, being in front, came in directly in line and closed upon them as we came in through a dense thicket of bushes and vines. We could not see or be seen until we came right up to the line, which was formed at a fence or rather two fences with a small space between them—hardly big enough for a hog or sheep to pass along between them. As we came in some 10 paces of the fences two Yankee sharpshooters rose up from between these two fences and said, "Don't shoot us we are your men," and our officers and men commenced howling to the men not to shoot. We stood in that position some 2 or 3 seconds when they both raised their carbines and fired into our ranks. One ball striking Newton Roe near the heart and killing him almost instantly. They both sprang over the fence as we all fired at them, and disappeared in the dense forest and bushes. One of them left his saber and belt on the fence as he went over. I do not know whether his belt was cut off by some of our bullets or whether he had it loose in his hand and dropped it.

As there was a dense line of Infantry some 40 paces in our front, lying down in line we had all we could do to attend to them and keep them there all day until the shades of night began to settle down over the earth. We were all ordered to move up to the fence. They were only six of us who

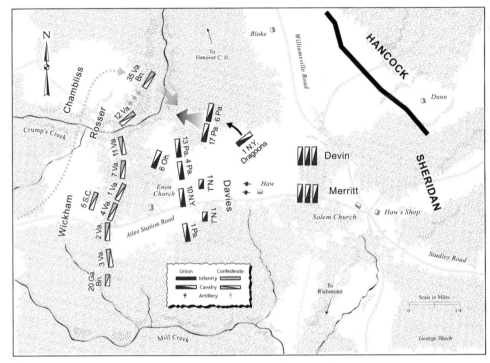

Battle of Haw's Shop, May 28, 1864. The wound to Colley's foot
during this engagement resulted in amputation.

obeyed the order. At the right of our line 1st Sergeant M. M. S. Ireson,
[Michael M. S. Ireson], Y. R. Pendleton, John G. R. Davis, S. D. Saunders
[Stephen Drake Sanders], G. L. Clark [Isaac Lewis Clarke], and myself.
I had been appointed 'Corporal' a few days previous to this.[7] The rest of
the company got behind tree stumps or anything that would shield them
from the sheet of Balls that were constantly fired at us. As we were so close
together, their balls went over our heads. We who went up to the fence
were laying down flat on the earth with our carbines poked through the
fence; as they were Breech loaders, we did not have to withdraw them to
load.

I suppose we had been in this position one or probably two hours when
some of my companions behind me fired a shot that came near hitting
me in the back of the head. I turned my head and yelled to them to quit

shooting over me. It was no time hardly until another ball struck the end of a rail and threw dust and splinters all over my face. I turned again and asked them not to shoot over me. It was not many seconds until another ball struck me ½ inch in front of my boot heel and passed through the sole and up to the ankle bone on the outside and ran around the joint lodging against the ankle bone on the inside, completely shattering the joint. As the shock deadened my limb I did not feel any immediate pain. As we had just received a fresh supply of cartridges, I just tore the wrappers from the package and laid them on the ground where they were handy to get at, and just went on with my shooting.

I began to feel a stinging sensation on my ankle bone and the blood was running up my boot leg. I had fired away all my cartridges. I thought I would get up and see whether I could walk or not. When I rose and attempted to put my weight on it, the bones crushed and I would have fallen to the ground had not two of my companions John G. White [John Greenway White] and H. C. Butt [Henry Clay Butt] ran to me and caught me. They carried me up a slope of some 10 paces where the Yankee bullets had a fair sweep at us. How we all escaped without farther damage I cannot conceive, it cannot be accounted for in any other way, only the unseen hand of 'The Great God' who cared for us in our infancy.

As we crossed the little ridge and came down on the opposite side, there was a stream of water. By this time I was burning up with thirst and I begged them to let me down so I could get some water, which they did, and I just laid down flat in the water and drank until I was satisfied. By this time one of the soldiers, who was packing ammunition in to our men on horse back, was coming out with a horse and my comrades got him to put me on his horse and carry me until I was back where I could be put in an ambulance, which we found some ¾ of a mile back. I was brought back to our field hospital in old Mr. Haw's yard.[8] I was put out there in front of the house under the shade of a large Walnut tree. It had been blown down in 1896 when I visited the place. Here our surgeons placed me under the 'influence of Chloroform.' The last thing I remember was trying to free myself from two great big ambulance drivers who had my arms stretched out and had them pinned to the ground. I pulled them up to me and by a quick movement of my arms hurled them away from me and made a pass at the Doctor who was holding the sponge to my nose. He was too quick for me. Before I could hit him he threw himself forward on me and called out to the assistants not to let me get up. That is the last I knew until my foot was off.[9]

Our Chaplain was giving me some whiskey in a glass tumbler. I was put in an ambulance and hurried off to Atlee Station, and some 40 of us, all wounded, were packed in a 'horse car' and sent down to Richmond that night. As it was quite late, we could not be removed that night and were shut up in there and left without food or water. It was the most awful experience I ever had in all my life. Forty poor wretches shut up in a 'Box Car' with no air; the cries for water that long night could not be exceeded by vast murmurs in the Infernal Regions. About nine a.m., they came down and opened our prison doors and hustled us out into ambulances and to our various places of destination. I was taken up Broad Street over the cobble stones. The jarring caused me such intense pain that I begged the 'colored boy' who was driving the ambulance to stop, and of course, he had orders to keep in line. I could not endure it any longer, and begging would not avail anything, so I drew my old army pistol, which I still retained in my scabbard and cocked it and presented it at his head and said, "Now Damn You, if you don't stop I'll send a pistol Ball through your 'wooly scull.'" He stopped.

My pain got easy. I told him to move on. He did not get far until I brought him to a halt again and I told him to get off that street and on to one that was smoother. He turned off on to Grace and down to Main Street. I was taken out to Jackson Hospital.[10] It was a temporary Hospital put up out of planks and covered with boards. It was located on General Winfield Scott's Farm.[11] I arrived there on the 29th day of May and stayed there until the 25th day of July. My father came and spent a week with me. I was quite low for some three weeks. I do not know anything that went on around me. I had a violent fever. I was insensible to pain, attributed my condition to the deadly effects of the Chloroform. It may have been exposure and the want of attention.

The first night and the next day till noon, I improved quite rapidly and became quite lively although I suffered agonizing pain. The amputation was a very bad job. My foot was unjointed, the ligament that held the socket bone in place was twisted off, and was there like a hard piece of leather string until some 3 years after the amputation. I procured some

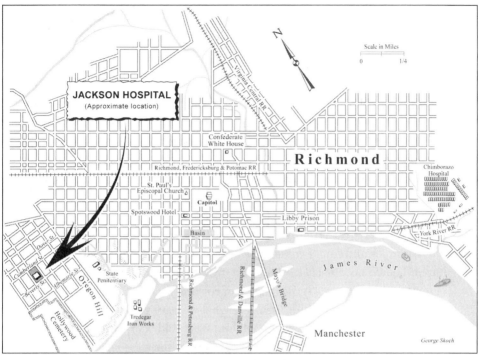

Street View of Richmond, indicating approximate location of the Jackson Hospital, where Colley received treatment after his wound at Haw's Shop.

Alum Mass, and it ate it out of the flap over the end of the stump, sloughed off, and left the bones exposed. Doctor Boggs who had charge of the ward was in cursed as a funeral the first time he examined me, and said, "The doctor who performed the amputation was either drunk or a fool."[12] I guess it was the former, as we always accused the doctor of drinking the whiskey and rubbing the bottles on us; of course, this was only jestingly, as a general thing. The Confederate Surgeons were all devoted and as self-sacrificing body of men as ever lived. They did the best they could do with the medicines and materials they had to do with.

A comrade that was brought up with me in the same ambulance, one of the 4th Virginia Cavalry, was shot in the forehead. He was placed on the bunk beside me. Poor fellow, he had a mortal wound and did not live but a few days. His brother stayed by him till he died. There were but few

Virginians in this hospital. It was a South Carolina and Georgia Hospital. There was one of the old 8th Georgia Regiment in the ward; he and I were both there with our third wound. He was full of life and mischief like myself. We had a lot of fun with the weak-kneed fellows. There was one in particular we teased unmercifully. He had been a detailed man for the first three years of the war. There was an act of Confederate Congress exempting men who had as many as fifteen negro farm hands to raise grain and supplies for the Government.[13] His time had come, and he had been sent to Petersburg, Virginia, and put in the trenches. He had taken the measles and was quite low when he was first brought in our ward. When he became convalescent, that's when the fun began.

We could hear the boom of cannon from Drewry's Bluff and Petersburg all day long and on up into the night at times.[14] He would begin to cry and whimper and say, "I would give every nigger and every foot of land I have if I could only be back home with my family." Then we would let in to cursing him and calling him all kinds of cowardly names, and hold up our wounded limbs and tell him, "see here what we have got," and tell him "he had not got a taste yet." We would tell him we would bet he was an original secessionist and urged all his poor neighbors in the army for a sixty days frolic, and the frolic lasted a little longer than you expected and now your time has come. We would hear the Boom Boom of the guns and call his attention to them and tell him we hoped one of them big shells would hit him and tear him into fragments, and he would shudder and cry at the very thoughts of his precious carcass being torn to shreds. We teased him until he begged Doctor Boggs to take him out of our ward.

It is truly said by the Poet, 'The coward dies a thousand Deaths. The Brave man dies but once.'[15] Soldiers who had volunteered in 1861, and had gone through all the hardships and trials up to this time in 1864, had but little patience with a coward and 'especially' one that was a fire eating rampant 'secessionist.' As the great bulk of Virginia soldiers were Union men in 1861, up to the time Mr. Lincoln called on Virginia for her quota of men to cover her Sister Southern States that had with drawn from the Union.[16]

Of course, my great desire was to get home to my family and friends. It was several weeks before the doctor consented for me to make the trip. I see by my date of my furlough I left Richmond on the 13th day of July

1864. My brother had obtained a 30-day furlough, and he came to the hospital to accompany me home. We got along very well until we passed Lynchburg. We had to get off the train and hire private conveyance to carry us to the town of Liberty in Bedford County, Virginia, as there had been a cloud burst or heavy rain storm, and washed away the two bridges at 'Big and Little Otter.'[17] It was a trip of some twelve miles over hills, rocks, and gullies. If I had not been going home I could not have stood the Jolting and Jostling I got on that ride.

There was some 8 or 10 of us badly wounded men in a 4-mule wagon with myself and brother, and as there was but one engine and three box cars on the western end of the road, they only made one trip every 4 days out to my home. We were pushing with all our might and aim to make connections but we 'failed.' At last, just as we got insight of the place, our train was pulling out so we were compelled to go to the wayside hospital and wait patiently until they could make another trip. I came near meeting with a serious mishap as I entered the hospital. I had to decend a flight of steps, about 6 in number. I think I had never went up or down stairsteps on crutches and did not know or think. I aimed to put my sound foot foremost in decending and of course I could not reach the step below me with my crutch still on the step above it, so that threw me up in the air with nothing to support me but my crutches. I either had to fall forward, down 6 steps, or fall back on the floor. My stump was then very much swollen and I had it swung by a bandage over my shoulder, and my leg resting on a pillow between the 'bandage.' The attendants and my brother caught me and did not let me fall with all my weight. The end of the stump came in contact with the floor hard enough to knock the piece of heel bone loose, which the doctor had left. It caused me considerable pain at the time and was the cause of numerous risings in it after months and even years, and small fragments of bones working out. It was seven years before I was entirely rid of this kind of pain and trouble.

After the young surgeons in charge of this hospital had dressed my stump, I was comparatively easy and rested up by the time the train came back. Some 30 sick and wounded placed in an old box car and we were brought to Central Depot, and there we had to lay over all night.[18] All that was able went out of the box car and found some place to stay all night. My brother and I had our blankets and we stayed in the old box car all night, as I did not wish to take any more risks on stairways and steps. We had plenty to eat. The fireman on the engine was an old friend of mine and he tried to get the mail agent to give me room in his car, but he was afraid it would cause him to lose his job; 'John Littral' was the fireman. He had been in the army some two years and had some sympathy for a soldier.[19]

We pulled out next day early and arrived at our station before sun-down. We had only two miles to go from there home, so the old mother's heart was gladdened again. It was made twice glad this time; both her boys had returned this time, one to stay. My brother had been wounded at Funkstown, Maryland, in the fall of 1863.[20] He had a pretty serious wound in the foot. He had recovered and taken his place in the ranks again. When he came with me he was on a 30-day furlough for a fresh horse. His stay at home was short. These were sad days when we parted. There were about 10 chances to one 'that we would never meet in life again.'

11

Men and Women Went about Softly . . . Waiting and Dreading the End

I HAD TO REPORT at Emory Hospital every 30 days, as my furlough indicated by the renewals on back of it.[1] Of course I could do nothing but read the daily papers and keep posted on the daily movements of my comrades in arms, east and west. My friends and neighbors visited me and brought me the comforts of their friendly greetings and what leisures they had at hand in these days. Of security and gloom in my hours of loneliness, my thoughts were constantly of my comrades and bleeding country. I had laid my all on her attention, and had been taken on a mean wreck. All I could do was weep and wail. The Great Strength of our Dear Lord was daily being taken, and I helpless, both physically and financially unable to do anything. I read in the papers how our heroic women were taking off their jewelry, and giving up their silver plates to the Government to aid in carrying on the contest to the bitter end. If I had a Million Dollars at that time, I would have laid down the last dollar to help on the Cause Dear to My Heart.

Sometime in the month of December 1864, a large force of cavalry was organized at Cumberland Gap under Generals Stoneman, Burbridge, and Carter, for the purpose of raiding East Tennessee and Southwest Virginia, and destroying the Saltworks and the Lead Mines, as our small force had been withdrawn from this section and sent to the Valley of Virginia.[2] They had but little opposition and came on to Abingdon and burned the courthouse and jail and some private property.[3] I was more uneasy about my piece of a carcass during the raid. I had heard so much about the East Tennesseans in the Federal Service, and Burbridge's negroes, that they

Brigadier General Stephen
Gano Burbridge. Courtesy of
*The Photographic History of
the Civil War*, vol. 20, p. 207.

Major General
George H. Stoneman.
Library of Congress.

were brutal and unscruplus about what they done to Rebels.[4] Naturally I felt a great dread of falling into their hands.

At that time, my father occupied the residence of the Rev. T. K. Catlett near the Village of Cedarville, 8 miles east of Abingdon.[5] All day long rumors of their coming were spread. My father and other neighbors had taken their horses and mules to secluded places in the mountains for security. My mother, and two sisters, and I were left alone with an old colored woman servant of the Rev. Catlett who lived in a cabin in the yard. I did not know what she would do when it came to the test. I had my bed moved upstairs in a room. I had a good army pistol, two carbines, and a good Dirk Knife. I had plenty of ammunition and had resolved to save my life as near as possible if they found me.

We were eating our evening meal. The window of the dining room faced to the west. I was telling mother and sisters how they would advance with a line of skirmishers. Just at this moment, I threw my eyes up to the window and saw the skirmish line some fifty yards from the house. The garden fence was at that point. I slipped upstairs some how; I do not know how I went without crutches or assistance from anyone. I had hardly got in my room when I heard some of the soldiers speaking to my mother and asking her if there was any damned Rebels there. They did not enter the house or molest anything. After they passed, on I crept to the window and looked out. I saw a squad of negro Cavalry with a white officer pass through the yard.[6] I got back to my room and close to my 'arsenal.' They passed on.

Some time after this I heard some one speaking to my mother and inquiring if there was not some brandy or whiskey in the house. Mother had told him there was not, but he had been informed by some one of our neighbors [of whiskey]. It was there he told mother he was a surgeon and was compelled to have the brandy, and pledged his word; we were not molested any more at that time. The columns were moving on the main road. Our residence was ¼ mile south of the road on their return from the Lead Mines. They had a pretty severe engagement at Marion, Virginia.[7] They destroyed the furnaces at the Salt works and tried to fill up the wells.

At this time, they came back to Cedarville, that is, a part of the force, about 400 who were cut off in the fight at Marion. They were trying to make their way to East Tennessee but were over taken by a courier and ordered back to Saltville as everything was quiet. Father had brought the horses back home and he had gone to Abingdon that day. They came on us all unaware and got two of our horses. One was a great favorite. My sisters could catch him anywhere and bridle, and saddle, and ride him or drive him anywhere. They begged and pleaded with the soldiers who had them, to leave them that one horse. I had crawled to the window where I could see them and hear the conversation. How I wished I was able to mount a horse and clean them up. I had my carbine in hand and was tempted to raise the window and fire on them, but I did not know how many there were near by and had to refrain. I knew if I killed one or wounded one of them our house would be burned. One time I had to back out and let them pass on. We were not molested any more.

Captain James L. Cole got up a little squad of men and come on them at day light resting, and gave them an awful fight.[8] They ran in every direction, leaving horses guns and amunition. There was only some 8 or 10 in Captain Cole's squad and they were soon encumbered with prisoners and had to give up the pursuit. They carried their Prisoners to the river hills south of the Middle Fork of the Holston River, and kept them there till our forces returned.

There had been a long spell of wet weather, and at this time, I think about the 20th of December 1864, the North Fork of the Holston River was very much swollen, so much so that the Federals had to swim it on horseback. They got their boots full of water and their rear guard was constantly being harassed and driven in by our men. Witcher's Battalion, and Giltner's and Vaughn's Brigades of Cavalry were hovering around them on ever side.[9] The night after the yanks swam the North Fork it turned intensely cold, so that the men's boots froze on their feet, and I was told since the war, by Captain Harry Ford of Pikeville, Kentucky, that they lost one half their command; some 2,000 men killed, prisoners, or frozen.[10] He said they were under fire from the time they entered 'Lee County,' Virginia, through Cumberland Gap, until they passed out of Virginia in Wise County through Pound Gap. He said if a man straggled out of ranks his doom was sealed.

After the raid was over everything in the Southwest settled down quietly. There was not much to 'Excite or Create Commotion.' But every true Patriot who had intelligence enough to know anything, knew about the weakness of our armies, and the terrible straights they were driven to on the account of food and clothing. Hundreds of them were barefooted through this Long Dreary Winter, without clothing and many without blankets. Those in the Eastern Army under the 'Fearless' General Robert E. Lee, were lying in trenches filled with water and mud a great portion of the time. There never was an army of men bonded together who suffered all the privations with such cheerfulness, and if the alarm was given that the enemy was threatening any point along the line of entrenchments, they were ready to move at a moment's warning to the right or left. And not only those who were in ranks suffered, but also our brave men who were confined in the various prisons. Throughout the North and Northwest, hundreds of them were starved or frozen during this awful period from November 1864 to April 1865. These noble men were offered freedom if they would take the 'Oath of Allegiance' to the United States Government; but few of them availed themselves of the privilege, and none of them were respected by friends or foe. The yanks called them 'Galvanized Yanks.'[11]

So, for any man or set of men to say that the Southern Soldiers were just a set of 'Rebellious Children,' not fighting for a noble principle, and that too a 'principle' as deep and lasting as any ever given to man by his 'Creator,' well, that is the right of self government. We were over powered by numbers and the great mass of them hired missionaries from every nation under the sun. No true Confederate soldier has anything to be ashamed of, but through the blessings and mercies of God 'he has many things to be proud of and grateful for.'

I cannot compare these last few months of the great struggle, at least to me. I could do nothing but sit and listen for the end. It was more to me like sitting or standing around the bedside of a very dear friend, after the attending physician had said all hope was gone and the glared eye, and the death damp on the brow told the awful story to all around, that the end was near.

Men and women went about softly and with 'hated breath,' waiting and dreading the end. From what we had seen and heard of the brutality of some of the officers and men composing the Armies operating in the South, we could look for or expect no mercy from men of such characters as they had shown themselves to be. When armed resistance ceased on our part, nothing but death, arson, and ruin stared us in the face. For my part, I expected to be 'hung, burned, shot, or torn all to pieces' by some infernal machine invented by the yanks to torture. But their greed for blood appeared to be saturated by the execution of our poor foreigner Captain 'Wirz,' and a poor woman Mrs. Surratt [Andersonville Prison head Henry Wirz, and accused accomplice in the Lincoln assassination Mary Surratt], and puting shackles on our Noble Leader 'Jefferson Davis.'[12] The only humiliation I was subjected, was cutting the buttons off my uniform. 'I surrendered them to a fair young Virginia Girl.'[13] I told her she could cut them off, but no yank should ever lay his hands on them. The next thing was taking the 'Oath of Allegiance,' then the next was having to walk up and vote beside a negro, and next the Reconstruction Period—District No. 1 until 1869. All these things were galling to a true Southerner, but we lived through it.[14]

12

Blessed Be the Name of the Lord

I WENT SOUTH with horses and mules in the spring of 1866, and that fall I visited Laurel County, Kentucky, where my father had purchased a farm in 1859. It had been confiscated and sold and purchased by the original owner; he, being a loyal man to the U.S. Government. I made 2 trips there before the suit was finally settled. In February 1870, I went to Baltimore, Maryland, and took a course in penmanship and bookkeeping. I had a severe spell of sickness while I was there. I had escaped the mumps in childhood, and my companions in the war had them, and I never took them till now. A young clerk who roomed with me had the mumps, and of course, I had no thought of taking them from him. I had a slight hurting under my left ear on Saturday morning but thought nothing of it, as that was a leisure day. I wished to see the sights of the city and rambled around all day in a drenching rain. Next morning, I had mumps all over, from the top of my head to the end of my great toe, and I had them for some 3 weeks. They left me weak and prostrate and with the hot summer weather coming on I could not gain weight and strength. I weighed 220 pounds when I went to Baltimore, and weighed 156 pounds when I left the 5th day of August.

After I recuperated I took a trip down to East Tennessee. I was playing 'Fruit Tree Agent.' I soon learned I was not cut out for that business. I went as far as Cock County, 'to my Uncle Charles Morrells.' I stayed there some 2 or 3 weeks and rested up and then came back; my cousin James R. Morrell accompanying me. We came home about Christmas and enjoyed the Christmas Holidays. An old comrade of mine, J. D. Cosby [John Dabney Cosby] 'having been elected Sheriff under our reconstructed State

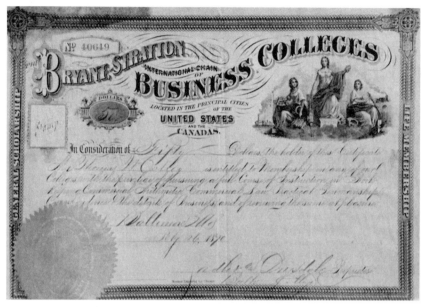

Colley's College Certificate. Thomas W. Colley Collection, Ms2003-017,
Special Collections, Virginia Tech, Blacksburg, Va.

Laws,' offered me the Deputys place under him and I accepted it and was
sworn in 4th Monday in January 1871, and served in that capacity until
May 1875.[1] I had no thrilling experiences during my term except with a
negro named Champ Ferguson from Russell County, who had shot two or
three women and had finally killed a young man in that county.[2] He came
over into Washington County and was hiding out in the mountains adja-
cent to the Poor Valley. I was told by some of my friends he had threatened
to kill me.

I was riding along down the Poor Valley road one evening, when I met
him in the road with two big pistols on his belt and a white woman following him. As soon as I saw him, I slipped my hand in my saddle pockets
and secured my pistol and cocked it. I knew he was a desperate character
and if he showed fight I would have something to do, but he passed me. I
spoke to him and he to me. I kept my eye back to the rear until he was a
respectable distance from me. I never had a warrant for his arrest in my
hands.

The other thrilling experience was with a white man named 'Furn.'
He had a reputation. After court adjourned one evening, I went to the

Colonade Stable to get my horse. As I mounted, and was riding along a back 'alley,' I came on Furn and another man trying to make old man Dowell—who was very drunk—give them some money. I heard the man with Furn say to him, "There is Mr. Colley he will arrest you." Furn said, "G_ _ D_ _ _ Mr. Colley or any other man. There is not enough men in this damn town to arrest me." He had an army pistol in his hand. As soon as I heard what he said, I wheeled my horse around and told him to come up to me and give up his pistols. He commenced telling me not to push him and presented his pistol at me. I had a large Hickory Cane in my hand and tried to push my horse on him so I could strike him with my cane, but he kept himself right in front of my horse. If I turned him to the right, he would move that way.

He and I see sawed some 50 feet back and forth until he came to a pile of brick and debris where an old chimney had fallen down. At this stage, 'Daniel Trigg' came along near where I was and I called to him to come and help me arrest this man.[3] Furn turned on Mr. Trigg and told him not to push on him and presented his pistol at him. Mr. Trigg picked up a brick bat and threw it at him. At this instant, Theo Dunn, who was town sergeant at that time, came up and we began to close in on him and it got too hot for him and he leaped off the brick pile and ran down the alley.[4] There was a wagon coming up the alley and he dodged by it and shut off our pursuit. He ran to the railroad and at that time the 'Material Train' was at the tank taking on water. He ran under the cars and I was calling to the hands on the flats to "catch that man." He went out the Knob Road at a two forty speed. He fired his pistol just as he came from under the flats. He did not come back to Abingdon for two years. I was so intent on hitting him with my cane that I entirely forgot I had a pistol in my saddle pockets, and it was well for him. I have thought many times since, if I had drawn my pistol and he with a cocked pistol in his hand, I have no doubt but what I would have shot him. I am glad it was as it is, no Blood on my hands from that poor man.

In April 1872, I took a step that changed my whole after life. The friends of Temperance organized a council in the county, which soon spread almost all over the county at every school house. In April, there was one organized in my neighborhood and almost the entire community joined it and took the Solemn Pledge not to drink any Spiritual Liquors, wine, or cider. The drink habit had begun to grow on me and I had become alarmed and determined to rid myself of it. God being my helper, and by His help, I have been able to keep my pledge to this good hour, now almost 31 years. As I had promised 'God' to seek him when I was stricken down on the battle field at 'Kelly's Ford,' I could not rid myself of that Solemn Pledge. And now, upwards of nine years from that time, I had taken the first step in the right direction.

I am satisfied that there is but little hope for anyone to turn to 'God' as long as the 'Devil' can persuade him to pour that 'Accursed Liquid Fire' down his throat, 'to fire his brain' and drown his conscience. No one can see that until he or she cuts loose from it. I tried for years to taper off and only take a little now and then, when I thought I needed a little to drive out cold or when water was bad, or I felt bad, or as an old comrade used to say 'he never drank any unless he was by himself or with somebody.' Oh the 'horrible curse.' How thankful I feel to my Dear Lord that with all my other short comings and misdoings, I have been all these long and weary years kept free from the Deadly Cup, and my heart's prayer to God is that I may never have any use for it.

As one good thing follows another, about the 12th of September 1872, at Revival Meeting at 'Washington Chapel,' I was soundly 'converted' and cleansed from all my past sins. I was made to feel and know that 'God,' for Christ's sake, has power to cleanse a sinner's heart, and that he can feel and know it for himself. If I stumble and fall away and go down to the 'Bottomless Pit,' I am satisfied I will still retain the knowledge that I was one, clean and free from sin's 'Domain,' and meant for the Master's use.

For some three years I enjoyed the blessed evidence of my Master's presence. His spirit bearing lively evidence with my spirit, that I was his beloved follower. In the same meeting my intended wife was converted, along with some 45 others. It was a time of great rejoicing on the old Camping Ground. I think it would be proper to state what brought about the great stirring up of the dry bones. I had from my infancy been taught to Love and fear God. And when I was some 14 years old, under the Preaching of the Gospel by our beloved W. G. E. Cunningham—before he sailed for China—I was deeply convicted, and if I had yielded to my convictions and given my young life to 'God,' what I might have been, of course, I am unable to say. But I know enough now to satisfy me.[5]

Colley and his wife, Ann Eliza. Private Collection.

My life would have been quite different from what it was, and my soul would not have been marred by so many sins, and instead of tearing down and destroying, I would have been aiding in building up my 'Masters Kingdom.' I started to tell what started the revivial. My wife's Uncle George Ryan—a wild rolicking, drinking fellow—was accidently shot; the ball entering his groin and lodging internally caused his death in some 9 days after the accident.[6] His wife was a good Christian woman, and she fell to praying and talking to him, and he was converted and commenced to all who came to see him. The nearer he drew to 'Deaths Dark Door,' the more earnest were his exhortations. When he got hold of one that had drank and caroused with him, he never let him go until he exacted a promise of him or her; a promise that they would seek the 'Lord' and find Him precious to their souls. And nearly everyone kept their promise. As soon as he was laid to rest, a prayer meeting was started and the Spirit pervaded from the commencement to the end. One preacher came out for this revival, Rev. David McCracken of the Holston Conference, M.E.C. South. A loyal Preacher who worked in this revival from first to last.[7]

On the 25th of December 1872, I was happily united in marriage to Ann Eliza Ryan in the house in which we now live, by the Rev. James L. McCulloch. Our first great sorrow came in December 1873, when our first child was born to us. He was only spared to us 30 days, until the Lord took him back to Himself.[8] I had solemnly dedicated him to God in earnest humble Prayer. It was hard to give him up, but I could only say the Lord gave and the Lord has taken away, 'blessed be the name of the Lord.'

13

I Have Wondered Up and Down in This Old World

NOVEMBER 1874 our second son was born.[1] My wife made her home with her father as I was away most of my time attending to my duties, until May 1875 when I quit and went to Meadowview, Virginia. I bought a lot from Wm C. Edmondson Esquire and built a dwelling and Store house, and he and I went into partnership in the goods business.[2] Neither of us had any capital. We bought some $4,000.00 worth of goods on credit, and both commenced drawing on them to satisfy our creditors at home, to the neglect of those from whom we purchased our goods. The consequences was a busted concern, and I being the 'weaker Partner,' was squeezed out of house and home in two years. This was a great trial to Faith in the Christian Life. Mr. Edmondson and I, of course, came to law. He had asked for a dissolution of the partnership and I granted it, and then he asked for a deed of trust to secure himself and he got that. My brother and I had 6,000 acres of mountain land in Johnson County, Tennessee, and that all went into the smash.

After all that, he enjoined me from collecting any debts due the firm. He had an apportionment inventory made of the stock by 'Leonidas Baugh,' and we met one day in the circuit court clerk's office to take depositions; Mr. Edmondson with his council C. F. Trigg, L. T. Cosby, and Clerk L. Banghand, and I on my own part.[3] Mr. Cosby was proceeding to take Mr. Baugh's deposition. The question was asked him, if he had taken an inventory of our goods. He was proceeding to answer in the affirmative when I stopped him and told him 'positively and emphatically,' he knew he had never taken an inventory, and he should not swear a falsehood. At that,

Mr. Edmondson called me a liar and I made a dive at him, he dodged behind Mr. Cosby's desk. Mr. Trigg and Mr. Cosby ran between us and stopped me from hitting him. I told him I would get him. That stopped the depositions and they stand today just at that point.

I was determined, as I thought, to follow Mr. Edmondson up the road as he went home that night and maim him until satisfied. I waited in town until almost dark for him to start out, but I found he was not going as long as I stayed in town. As we both went the same road for some 2 miles or more, I concluded to start on and wait for him. I went out a mile and waited for him to pass me, and then took out after him. I was still very angry as I rode on behind him. My better nature began to work, and my 'Good Angel' began to whisper to me, 'suppose you follow that poor old man and strike him a fatal blow in your anger and you kill him or maim him for life, how then will you feel?' By the time I had gotten to my turning off place, I had decided to let him go on his way. As the test came to me 'Vengeance is mine and I will repay sayeth the Lord,' and I let the Lord have his way, and I was glad I did for in a short time the 'Lord' laid His hand on him and took him away. He and I were friendly when he died.

We had another son born to us in 1876, October 5th, and we moved our little effects to my fathers in laws, and I could not find anything to do so I took three 'patent rights,' and started to West Virginia to sell county rights.[4] I had a long and 'wearisome' trip and sold nothing. I met a kind friend who helped me out in my last extremity, Mr. Thomas Lively, near Union in Monroe County.[5] I stayed with him some 14 days and traded him my spring wagon and watch for a two-year-old filly and a few dollars in money. One night on this trip, I was out of money; had just 50¢ left. It was raining and quite cool. I was studying and praying. Did not know what I would do when I came to a Large farm house on one side of the road, and a fine barn and stables on the opposite side. I drove up under the shed to get out of the rain, when a gentleman at the gate in front of the house accosted me to know what I was doing there. I said, "I am getting in the dry and I am going to stay here until morning." He said he guessed not, and by that time he had walked across the road to where I was, and I told him my condition. He said, "get out of your jersey and we will see what can be done for you." I said, "feed my mare and I will crawl up in the hay mew and sleep there."[6] He said, "no you won't, I have beds in the house to sleep in and you will have to have something to eat of course." I yielded to all of his suggestions, feeling quite humble and willing to do anything in reason. His wife was a kind, good woman and of course I faired well and was sent on my way rejoicing—'My God Bless them.'

I have wondered up and down in this old world in many places and have always found 'friends' when I needed them very bad. The patent right venture proved to be an entire failure. It only learned me a 'lesson;' not to fool my time away with some other fellow's 'tricks.' The man that 'invents' and sells State rights gets all there is in it.

I concluded in 1879 to offer [run] for Superintendent of the Poor; they were chosen by the Board of Supervisors for the county. It was composed of 7 members, one for each district in the county. I received the support of 4 out of the 7, and was elected and entered upon the duties of the office 1st July 1879, and served 8 years, and was earnestly solicited to continue in charge of the 'Alms House' by the board, but declined to do so. I had many things to try my faith while in charge of the paupers. I am glad to know that many of the paupers were converted and brought to 'Christ' during my term in office. I tried in every way to inculcate moral and religious principles into them. The most of them were of the lowest and worst degraded characters to be found when I went in to office. I found them in a wretched condition, their quarters were old log cabins filled with vermin of all kinds.

I went to work with the Board to remedy this, and succeeded, before my term of office expired, in seeing them placed in comfortable brick cottages with new bed steds, new bedding, and a new home in ever respect. I had the pleasure of being with them in their new quarters the last 14 months of my term. I had some minister to preach to them as often as I could get them. Brother J. J. Lloyd made regular visits once a week, and I had an old colored brother, Landon King, to preach to the colored people once a month.[7] Uncle Landon, as we called him, was a noble Christian man and a pretty fair preacher. I always attended his services when I was not away attending my own church services, and assisted him the same as I did Brother 'Lloyd.'

During this last 14 months, I was terribly scourged by sickness in my own family and among the paupers; the Whooping Cough, Roseola and Scarlet Fever. We had at that time 3 boys and 4 girls of our own family.

The 3 boys were not so severely effected as the 'girls.' At one time, all four of them were so low that we could not tell which would pass away first. But after weeks of uncertainty, two passed away from earth's sorrows and trials 'to enter eternal life with Jesus' and their other loved ones. Sallie Henrietta, died first on the 23rd day of May, and Ella Ryan on the 13th day of June. It was hard to give up these precious ones who had only been with us long enough to entwine themselves around the tendrils of our hearts. Sallie was the younger of the two, and she was the most loving and affectionate child to me of all my children.[8] I thought of the awful struggle that must have went on in the inmost recess of the heart of 'Old Father Abraham,' when God told him to take his only son 'Isaac' and offer him as a sacrifice. That long sad journey to 'Mount Moriah,' when the grief was so intense that he could not reveal it to his wife, son, or servant, when hope had fled and there was no light from any quarter. Like him of old, I just placed everything in the hands of 'God,' and trusted Him for the final result. When the end came, and all was done that 'human's love' and human hands devise, the grave was closed. Then came peace and joy amid tears and sorrow, and like David could say it 'is well with the child,' so it is with all who trust 'God' implicitly. Put your trust in me the Master has truly said, and I will comfort and bless you. After weeks of watchfulness and care my other two little 'girls,' Mary L. and Barbara C. were spared to me; then another son came to rejoice our hearts, John M.[9]

As the Great Boom had struck our part of state in 1888, I went into prospecting for minerals. My principal search was for hungriness. My partner and I thought we had struck it rich in the Little Valley in Tazewell County, Virginia. We took options on a large boundry of land, and negotiated it to a Mr. Cross in East Saginaw, Michigan, for $20,000; he paid us $1,000.00 down and furnished $4,000.00 to develop it.[10] We spent some 6 months working, sinking shafts, and tunneling in the mountains. Of course, we encountered a great deal of opposition on every hand, and at last, we allowed Mr. Cross to ship a car load of Manganese to Pittsburg, to Mr. Carnegie's [Andrew Carnegie] steel works. They pronounced it no good, and the bottom fell out of our boom, and all my fond anticipation vanished like thin air, and I became poor again. So it is with all worldly ambitions and worldly desires—if we had it all we would want some more.

I was appointed sealer of weight and measures by the county clerk of Washington County and the Corporation Court of the City of Bristol, and was secretary of the Democratic County Committee in 1894 & 1895; it was quite a bitter campaign. The Democrats were split in two factions. The regulars called indivision by the independants, 'the Watermelon and Corn Liquor Party.' I belonged to the regular organization, and we succeded in electing our ticket over the Independants and Republicans both.

I had a bitter and another sad experience at this stage in my 'life.' I had, with other friends and brothers in our church, helped place a Kentucky soldier in charge of the 'Alms House.' He was a praying member and we all thought a worthy man, but he soon got to drinking, and as the proof was shown during an Impeachment trial, he was maltreating the poor. In every way, he was a desperate man and almost everyone in the community feared him. It was difficult to get anyone to tackle him. As I had just preceded him [in office], all eyes were turned to me and I was urged to undertake to defeat him. He had the whole Board of Supervisors under his thumb by some 'Mysterious spell,' with the exception of one Mr. J. C. Porterfield.[11] When the election came on I was working and toiling, and praying. He [candidate] brought a drunken man with him. He had circulated an eye on me and Mr. Jeff Caldwell, a former Confederate soldier we were trying to defeat him with.[12] I had spoken to the gentleman; was telling him what he had said was quite a different statement altogether from what he had told.

I went along to hear what was said, and he commenced to apologize and say he was mistaken. When I became so disgusted with his hellish hypocrisy and lying that I said, "You infernal old lying scamp, you tell lies all over the county and then try to get out of it by saying you were mistaken. Why did you not know the fact before you made the statement?" At this he commenced walking off from me and saying he did not want anything more to do with me. He had a pen knife open in his hand at the time. I was walking after him and telling him I did not want anything more to do with him, only that he should quit lying on me. At this point, his son-in-law run up in my face and asked me very abruptly, "Who is a bigger liar than you are?" I made no reply but let drive with my right fist from the shoulder. 'I aimed to hit him in the mouth but he turned his head slightly,' and I struck him on the cheek bone with one of my knuckles and slit a gash over his left ear, and knocked him down against the legs of the men who had gathered around to witness the fun. If it had not been for them, he would have fallen over a wall at the west end of the Court House, some 3 feet high, and probably broke his neck.

I could have kicked him with my 'wooden leg' while he was down, but I did not wish to hurt him, as his brothers had been my mess mates in the army and I loved them as dear as life. Two stout men grabbed me and were holding me when he recovered from the shock and run at me again and tried to collar me. As he was a small man I did not pay much attention to him. A friend of mine grabbed him and jerked him loose from me. He wrenched himself loose again and rushed at me and tried to grasp my throat. I reached down and caught his waist and placed his two front fingers in my mouth and commenced shuting down on them. The bones had begun to crack when my friend caught him again and wrenched him back, tearing off the tip ends of his fingers. I spit out the blood and skin. By that time, I was beginning to get my blood up a little and had determined to kick him in the stomach with my wooden leg. He had torn himself loose from my friend and was coming at me again with his own cane drawn to strike me. I was just in the act of freeing my arm from the man who was holding it, to ward the blow from my head and at the same instant kick him in the stomach with all the vim I could put in it. My friend grabbed him in time to ward the blow and in all probability saved his life.

By this time the old Kentuck had returned. He had gone to Mr. C. F. Trigg's office to get his overcoat and pistol. He came out with his hand in his pocket. I kept as close to him as possible so I could knock the pistol up or down if he drew it. I was as calm and unconcerned during all this melee as a May morning. This took place just before the Board of Supervisors met to hold the 'election.' They went in the Court House to proceed with the election and of course all hands went in to witness the contest. They balloted several times without any results. J. S. Smith, and J. C. Porterfield voting for Caldwell; Preston, Talbert, and Hawthorne for Kentuck; Buck Beny not voting at all. This continued until the dinner hour when I whispered to Mr. Porterfield to move an adjournment, 'which he did.' I wished to get Caldwell and Buck together and try to defeat them in that way. We were thwarted in that, as Kentuck's friends took charge of Counts and wined and dined him and brought him under a special escort.

So, on the first ballot after the dinner hour, Kentuck got 4 votes, which elected him. He had under the law to be confirmed by the County Court. We still had a chance to file affidavits as to his conduct and defeat him there of course. As I had been forced by circumstances to make the first fight before the Board of Supervisors, it dissolved on me to continue the fight. The Commonwealths Attorney John C. Summers sent for me to come to town, and he and I, and Mr. James Buck had a conversation on the Subject.[13] I was sent out to hunt up the witnesses and procure their affidavits. I procured some 5 or 6, which was thought sufficient to cause the Court to refuse to confirm the appointment, which he hid, and threw the election back before the Board of Supervisors. They in the face of all this, and in direct contempt of the Court, reappointed Old 'Kentuck,' and held a one sided Mock Court composed of their own members, of four of them at least. I doubted it the 'Sanhedrin.' I was summoned to appear before that body but had pressing business in another 'quarter' that day, and it was well I did. There was some very hard criticisms passed on me I learned afterwards, which might have caused me to resent them in a rough manner had I been there in person.

I called one of the gentleman, Mr. Jonas S. Kelly, to law about his remarks on that occasion, through a mutual friend of ours, Mr. D. M. Stuart.[14] Mr. Kelly wrote me a long letter of apology, stating he had been led into a false attitude by the party directly concerned. The case came back before Judge George W. Ward for confirmation.[15] As he had passed on it once, he could do nothing but empanel a Special Grand Jury to enquire into the matter. The Grand Jury was composed mostly of the best men in the county: Wm M. Gray, Foremans Major D. A. Jones, Jere Mongle, Wiley E. Avens, Jacob H. Rhea, George Graham, and Thomas Lester. Captain Graham asked to be excused, which they granted. Wm M. Gray being sick on Friday, the day set for the investigation, the jury adjourned over until the following Monday. On Saturday, Old Kentuck and a bosom companion of his, with a jug of Bug Juice, went to the house of Mr. Thomas Lester and whiskied him and stuffed him with a pack of lies to prejudice him in his favor, and against any statement I or any witness made that came before them.

On Monday, when the 'Grand Jury' met, I was sent to them by the 'Commonwealths Attorney.' Mr. Lester assailed me at once, and 'intimated' that I was prosecuting the case against his friend on the account of

'Personal Prejudice,' which I at once emphatically disclaimed and denied as a 'lie.' I asked him if he was sitting as council for the defendant, or as an unprejudiced Juror. He said he was sitting as a Juror. I said, "well I will procede to make my statement," which the other five Jurors assented to. If the world was filled with men like Mr. Lester, a man could take a Jug of Liquor and get anything he wanted right or wrong, which ever way the party with the Jug wanted him to go. Alas! Alas!

Will the day ever come, when men will all act from principle and not through 'eyes and ears blurred by the Juice of the Jug?' The investigation proceeded with out any serious hindrance. The only thing that called me to act again was a report that one of Kentuck's Council, a poor drunken wretch, was meddling with one of the witnesses for the prosecution; that he had her in a room in the Court House. I immediately went up to the room designated and found him. There, I caught a word as I entered the door that aroused my blood. He said to her, "You know the defendant is a gentleman and he will kill you if you swear what you are reported to have stated." At that time, I stepped in to the room and said to him, "You have no right to be here meddling and trying to intimidate this witness, and you know you have stated a falsehood to this witness." I said, "you get out of here," and that quick he said to me, "you ought to stop this thing." I said, "alright, I'll stop when I get to the end and not before."

He had sent this man to me some days before to bribe me, and he and I had some harsh words. He made him drunk, and hissed him on me to raise a row with me, and I had proven him the 'lie,' and would have kicked him with my 'peg leg,' but one of the town sergeants was close at hand and caught him and held him back from advancing on me. I told him then, I said, "this is the third time you have approached me in reference to the man you represent and I want it to be the last time. You was a Confederate soldier and so was I, and I do not want to hurt you and especially in the condition you are in now. I'm always 'sober,' and if you persist in annoying me in this way I will certainly hurt you." He said, "Tom I will not trouble you anymore on this matter," and he never did.

The jury of enquiry, as they could not get Lester to agree to bring in indictments against the defendant, reported him from the evidence before them, as being unfitted for the position, which is a matter of record in the County Court Clerk's office. The Board of Supervisors, seeing it useless to persist in a course that was becoming more obvious to the citizens of the county every day, met and elected Jeff Caldwell, which the court 'confirmed,' and old Kentuck became more enraged when he saw he was downed and swore vengeance against the Judge, Clerks, Jury, and me especially. He attacked one of the Grand Jury, Mayor D. A. Jones, one day when he was on a drunk.[16] Some one caught him and kept him from doing the Mayor any violence. He told the Mayor that day, he intended to do [kill] all the Grand Jury and me especially. He said he had the thing in his pocket to do the job with.

The first time I went to town after that, the Mayor took me to one side and said to me "Tom are you armed?" I said, "Yes I have two arm's God gave me." "Ah!" he said, "you know what I mean, have you got a pistol?" I said, "no and I do not want any now." He said, "you ought to have one by all means. That man swore he intended to kill you." "Well," I said, "I will be at the killing I reckon, look out for yourself, I will take care of myself, God being my helper." I said, "He has been killing me ever day and night for the past 4 months and the job is not finished yet." Some how, with all the terrible stories I knew of and had heard of the man, I did not have any fear of him, and as our farms joined, I had to come in contact with him on the roads as I went about my business and he about his.

On one occasion, some other would be 'Friend' had reported to me some of his vile threats of kill, slay, and eat. I was some 80 or 90 yards from where our lands joined fences one morning, with my squirrel rifle in my hands, when he came along the road. There had been a hard rain and washed the 'chinking' out from under his fence and made a hole that hogs could get through into his field. He lit off on his horse and started to my fence, as I imagined, to get a rail to stop the place in his fence. I set the triggers on my gun and pulled the hammer back. When his good angle, or mine, intervened and stopped him in four or five feet of the fence. He wheeled around and went to his own fence and got a rail and stopped the place in his fence and went on, unaware how near death's door he had been. I had fully determined if he took a rail from my fence to say to him 'you old thieving scoundrel, what are you stealing my rails for?' I expected an insulting reply, and then, with out further notice, planned to pull down on him with as true a rifle as a man ever loaded, to send a ball into his anatomy, some where above the belt.

I was glad he was turned away and thankful that 'God' had intervened in some mysterious way to keep me from having my hands stained with human gore. I had enough of that as a soldier. Nothing but the Judgment Day will reveal to me the number of poor wretched men my trusty carbine and pistol sent into 'eternity.' They were invaders of my beloved state. My conscience does not hurt me on that score. While I am truly sorry, I was forced by their acts of invasion to put as many of them out of the way as lay in my power. I am off again on the war; in this mood I was not following in my Master's footsteps, and I resolved to turn about and ask forgiveness for 'sins.' After some twelve or fifteen months, the peace and Joy I once had known came back to me and I was pardoned, and my heart filled with the 'Love of God,' and then I had love for my fellow men—enemies and all.

Old Kentuck was the first one I thought of, and I told my wife I was going to be reconciled to him altho he was still riding around with his pistol swearing he would kill me on sight. That did not daunt me in the least, so I saddled up my horse and rode over to his home. My wife tried to keep me from going, she said he would only insult me or shoot me. I laughed at her 'fems' [feminine response] and went. I found him mounted on his horse, and a neighbor, Captain Pratt there. He was changing saddles with Kentuck's wife. They were going to Abingdon on some business. He was on his horse, and had him standing square across the 'road,' which was quite narrow at that point. He would have forced me into the ditch at the road side, if I had been going to pass him, as heretofore he was looking his savagest. I rode up and turned my horse square up to his side and threw my hand out to him, at the same time addressing him in that old familiar way that I had always done in by gone days, when we were friends and brothers. I said, "Give me your hand old fellow, all animosity and spite has gone out of my bosom and my heart is all right towards you and all mankind." He began to cry and extended his hand to me and I grasped it. I exhorted him to turn about and seek forgiveness, and be able again to rejoice, and the Love of God shall abound in his heart. He said he would try. I said, "that will not do, say you will do it." I could not get him to give me a positive answer. I turned to his wife and the children and spoke to them. He insisted they all come and give me their hands, which they all did. Before this, he would not allow them to speak to me at all; two of them would always speak to me, unless he was with them when they passed me. We were friendly from that time up until his death.

Soon after this, I was appointed one of the real estate assessors for 1895 in the upper end of the county. Associated with me was Charles W. Steel, C. W. Allerson, and John S. Mullen.[17] Our assessment gave entire satisfaction as there was not an appeal to the County Court for any correction or relief from erroneous assessments. In 1897, April 23rd, I with my family, my brothers-in-law, and John J. Clark and his family, along with some 10 other families moved to Enoree, South Carolina, to work at the Cotton Mills at that place.[18] We arrived there just as the bell on the mill tower was sounding the hour of 12 midnight on the 24th. We were all huddled into an old mail coach attached to a freight train at Spartanburg, and taken down to Enoree, 28 miles. There was not sitting room and hardly standing room for us all. It was a desperate rainy time, had been raining for a solid month or more, and 'the old mica mud' was up to the horses or mule's knees all around the depot and all over the streets and grounds at the mill. There was no hotel accomodations at the mill and we were all packed in a wagon, or rather each family was put in a separate wagon. It was as dark as 'Egypt.'

We were then taken to the houses allotted to us and dumped out in the dirt and filth left by former occupants, and told to make out the best we could until morning. It was quite damp and cool for my wife's step mother—quite an old lady—the three small children of our two daughters, a neice of my wifes, and two sons. One of the stable bosses loaned me his lantern or we would have been left entirely in the dark. My eldest son and I procured an ax and cut some wood and got a fire started, and ate some cold grub we had brought with us from home. I had been used to this kind of thing as a soldier and I could bear it better than my wife and children. Of course, they, being accustomed to pretty comfortable quarters all their lives, this was hard on them, and my wife fell to crying and saying the children would catch their death of colds and all die, and finally wound up saying "she would give a thousand dollars if she was back at home." I said, "My Dear Wife, if we had a thousand dollars we would not be here, not while it lasted at any rate."

I tried all my life to never anticipate sickness or trouble of any kind; it was enough to bear when it came. We all piled down on the hearth in the dirt, and tried to get a little, much needed sleep. I with one little boy in my arms and my wife with the youngest in her arms. We all got some two hours sleep. Next morning, I went out and got a woman near by to make us a pot of coffee, for which she charged me 25 cents. We still had plenty of cold rations. As soon as breakfast was over I went to the company office and got an order for something to housekeep with, until our furniture we had shipped by freight arrived, which by the way was some 14 days on the road. I had a cook stove and some mattresses and rations. We got our stove brought over and set up, and the dirt cleaned up and mattresses put down on the floor. Fortunately, it was not very cold and we got on tolerable well.

The children all went to work in a few days after we got there, and soon learned up in the various floor or departments to which they were assigned by the Superintendent of the mills. I soon learned that their mode of doing business was not in keeping with my ways of thinking. The employees from all walks in life, and from various states, for the most part were wild and reckless; drinking, especially Saturday night and Sundays. 'Dancing and carousing, some was shot or cut every Saturday night nearly.' The company had erected a nice brick Church; none of the boss men took much interest in the church or church matters. They were principally concerned about the 'Almighty Dollar.' They were charitable in a sense, when appealed to for help.

The M.E. Church South, to which I and family belonged, had a pastor and parsonage located at the mill.[19] The Missionary Baptist also had a pastor, and the Presbyterians also had a pastor. The two latter did not reside at the place, but filled their monthly appointment. They had a Union Sabbath School when I went there. After the first year I was there, we decided, as the Union Literature did not set forth the Doctrine taught by either denomination represented there, we would each organize a Sunday School and use our own literature, which we did. The Methodists met at 9:A.M., the Baptists at 2:PM, and the Presbyterians at 4:PM. I worked in all the Sunday Schools, assisted a teacher in the Bible Classes, and acted as superintendent when the regular Supt. was not on hand. We had a weekly prayer meeting composed of all denominations that wished to take part in them. There were some devout men and women in all the denominations, and we tried to serve God the best we knew how.

While the Devil was going on with his work outside; some few times he invaded the 'half Sanctuary' with his emissaries in the shape of Drunken men. The laws were quite severe on such characters in the Palmetto State, and an officer was most always present. We were seldom troubled by any of the riotous Characters. Another thing that disturbed me was working the machinist and section hands in the mill all night Saturday night and Sunday, and Sunday night. This was the time set apart to cut and tighten up the belts or looms, pickers, card, and spindles, and repair all machinery needing repairs from wear and breakage. I protested from first to last about this violation of the 'Lord's Day,' but to no purpose. I am sorry to record here that I was opposed by some of the leading members of my own, and the other denominations. They could see no great wrong in it. They argued if the repairs were not done on the 'Sabbath,' that 800 hands would be idle one day at least out of every week. The great thing I think with them was, when I pinned them down to the stocking point, was that if they did not do what the company wanted them to do they would lose their job. As they expressed it, and the officers of the mill were in the same predicament, if they did not push on the work and make cloth sufficient to satisfy the greed of the 'Stock Holders,' they would be turned down and lose their jobs.

I had quite a tussle for the P.O. at this place. The incumbent, Jno. W. Bishop, was drug clerk in the company store and ran a livery stable and a Dept. of Private Entertainment at the depot.[20] I asked Mr. Coffin, the President of the mill, if he had any objection to my having the office.[21] I was assured by him he had none, and at once I circulated a petition among the patrons for the office. But I soon found the officers, with a few honorable exceptions, would not give me any support in obtaining it. Mr. Bishop, being a 'South Carolinian,' a native of the county, he called me a 'Farmer,' and said, "I had come down there and was trying to scrounge a native out of his office." Bishop worked Sunday, and everyday, and kept a petition at the delivery window in the P.O. to catch all the country people that came in for the mail. I got some 300 names on my petition and sent them up to Washington, as we were both Democratic, there was no notice taken to my application, as a Republican Administration cared nothing about one Democrat more than another.[22] The officers of the mill would not tend either [candidate] any assistance, so they proclaimed to the public, but I am satisfied in my own mind that they lent towards Bishop, as the P.O. helped to augment his salary as drug clerk and saved the company paying $600.00 a year that they would have had to pay a clerk in that department.

Bishop got very angry with me for some 12 months before I left there. His conduct became so obnoxious he was discharged soon after. He was a 'Liberalist,' he was a church member too, a nominal one, who paid his assessments and went on with his drunkness. He threatened to shoot me, I was told by several men. I did not pay any attention to that. I had been shot and threatened to be shot so much I had got used to it.

In 1897, by the assistance of W. A. Hill who lived near the mill, we organized a camp of U.C.V. [United Confederate Veterans], No 905, with some 50 charter members, of which he was elected 'commander and I adjutant.'[23] I served as such until I returned to Virginia in November 1899. I represented the camp at Nashville in 1897, and at Atlanta in 98, and Charleston in 99. We have a very good time in our meetings. Our camp was named for Captain Chichester, one of the principal officers who defended the city of Charleston so faithfully during the long seige that was kept up against her defenses.[24] He was also a minister of the Gospel, and preached to the Sailors from all nations that visited the City of Charleston. He was quite a learned man, could preach or converse in five different languages. He and his excellent wife visited Enoree soon after our organization. She had our camp badges made in Charleston, and brought them up, and pinned them on each officer and member—as their names were called—with her own hands. Many of the men had belonged to her husband's company. She gave each one some kind word as she pinned on his badge; some were deeply affected. We had a fine picnic on this occasion and a speech from Captain Chichchester in the evening. He preached to the veterans on the following day, which was Sunday. The good old man passed to his final reward soon after his return to Charleston. I called on his widow in 1898 during the reunion held there in that year. She was quite glad to meet me again and had lunch prepared for me. She was a true Christian and Southern woman.

All though I was janitor for the church the last year I was in 'Enoree,' I had to fire the furnace and fill and light the lamps at night. I came up from the basement blacked with coal dust and had to lead in Prayer, or conduct the Sunday School. I enjoyed the 'Love of God,' amid all my other drawbacks in October 1898. We had the sad trial of parting with our baby boy 'Charles Westley,' he of course being the youngest was the pet and idol of the family, and of course, it was a hard trial to give him up. He was stricken with that fearful malady so destructive to the young children of that climate 'Bloody Flux;' he lingered along for several weeks.[25] Dr. J. H. Allen, my kind friend and physician, done all that humane skill and medicine could do.[26] But it is one of the mysteries only known to our Heavenly Father, why the Idolized child must be wrenched from the loving embrace of parents and brother and sisters. As we can not solve the mystery, we can only bow our heads and hearts in humble submission to His holy will and say, the Lord has given and the Lord has taken away. On the 16th day of October we laid his little body in the ground; with Brother Gray, the Presbyterian Pastor performing the Burial Service. We placed head and foot stones at his little grave and bid him farewell until the Judgment Day. His sweet little cousin, Ella Clark, was placed by his side some twelve months afterwards. She died of Typhoid Malaria. Today, I can say sleep on dear child I know you are in safe hands, you are with Jesus our 'Saviour.' God has been good to us, as He has taken four of our children up to this time and left us eight at this writing. May God Bless the living and help them to make their calling and election sure, and meet the Dear ones on high.

We came back to Virginia in December 1899. In 1900, I was elected Commander, Wm. E. Jones Camp U.C.V. 709 in Abingdon, Va.

I had assisted in organizing it in 95. We were first represented at the reunion in Richmond, Virginia. 1896 I went to Louisville, Ky. I was again elected commander 1901, and served until 1902. I represented my camp at Memphis 1901, and Dallas 1902. I love my old comrades and hope to do so as long as life and love lasts.

I was elected Superintendent of 'Washington Chapel Sunday School,' when Miss Susanah T. Cox moved from the neighborhood[.][27] She had for several years been teacher of Day and Sunday School both. She was a saintly Christian woman, converted at 12 years of age. She conducted a young womens' Prayer Meeting at the age of 14 years. She commenced teaching school at her 15th year, and spent her life in that noble work. She was a great stay to me in my first Christian experience, or in my babyhood and childhood in Christ. She and my Father-in-law James Ryan were the only two members that prayed in public for several years after the close of the war.[28] In fact, up to 1872 in September, at that date of the revival already alluded to in these manuscripts, and I owe a great deal to them in getting my feet firmly planted on the Rock of eternal ages.

Colley and other members of Abingdon's W. E. Jones SCV Camp.
Private Collection. Colley second from left.

Right here I will say for the benefit of old church members, a great responsibility rests on us in reference to young converts—'Babes in Christ,' as Paul expresses it—in not exhorting, admonishing, but instructing and encouraging them in the New Life. I fear hundreds and thousands drift away on this account, all soon swallowed up in the fashions and allurement of the world, lost to the 'Church Militant,' and I fear lost to the church triumphant. Away with the foolish doctrine of once in 'Grace always in Grace.' I remarked to the Baptist brother Acken at Enoree, S.C., on one occasion—after we had a gracious revival and their church had received and baptized some 40 young members–"Brother what are you going to do with all these young people, just baptize them and turn them loose?" I said, "You have but one member here who walks up rightly, and he is too timid for a leader."[29] He hung his head and looked quite sad and bewildered for a moment and then said, "Brother Colley, I fear so."

I started to tell of my strugles as Supt. of Sunday School—a poor weak sinful wretch—as I thought of trying to take the place of that saintly woman. I prayed earnestly for help from above and received many blessings.

The spirit would come upon me in great power and Sister Woodside [Frances W. Woodside], a good Sister, assisted me and I got on tolerable well, but never to my own 'satisfaction.' I was appointed 'Steward' at my Church, and served in that office for some 8 years and was elected Trustee. My wife and I deeded two acres of land to the church, and boarded the hands while they were erecting the 'New Church'–'Washington Chapel'– and I paid, as poor as I am, some $200.00 in erecting the same, and some $75.00 worth of worthless subscriptions died on my hands, which I had to make good to the contractors.[30] I have no regrets about this. I feel now and have always felt in my inmost soul 'that I owed all I had and all I ever will have to God, who for Christ Sake forgave all my Sins.' The only and great regret is that I have not done more for Him and His Holy Cause.

I was a delegate to almost all the District Conferences after I had been a member of the church long enough. I had been there so much, that brethren said the Conference looked lonely with out me while I was away in South Carolina. I have been a delegate twice since my return. I was twice elected by the District Conference, a Delegate to the Annual Conference. God and the Brethern have been good to me, more than I deserve, because I feel the Battle is still going on. 'The World,' the 'Flesh,' and the Devil, are contending for the Mastery, and will until I overcome the Last Enemy which is death. I am looking up to Him who is able to keep me and who has promised that I shall not be tempted above what I am able to bear. And that He will, with the temptation, also make a way to escape, that I may be able to bear it. For 30 long years, amid sunshine and sorrow, I have been trusting Him, Who is able to save the uttermost.

I am Superintendent of the Sunday School; at this time on my second year. I am versed and tormented about the carelessness and indifference of my brothers and sisters in this community, in reference to attendance and encouragement in the Sunday School Work. It is ground work for the church, 'the foundation stone for coming Generations.' May the Good Lord awaken all parents everywhere to a lively interest in this Great Work.

In July 1903, being in hard luck and pressed with poverty and no viable way of making a support, I decided, after consulting some of my most intimate friends, to run for the office of Commissioner of the Revenue in the 1st District of Washington County, Virginia. I had 3 very strong opponents in the 'Democratic Party;' one a brother Methodist. The party

An older Colley poses
with two of his sons,
both WWI soldiers.
Private Collection.

decided to hold a mass meeting at August Court, and appoint a Delegate
to a convention to be held on the 5th of September. After much prayer
and placing everything with God, I received a Great Blessing and that
decided my course. I submitted my name to the convention; contrary to
the advice of many of my best friends. It was currently reported that I
had but 2 Delegates in the convention out of 45, still I went in, calm and
collected, to win or lose as the 'Lord Willed.' Contrary to all, I received 15
votes on the 1st ballot, and 19 on the 2nd, and 28 on the 3rd, which gave
me the nomination.

The Republicans then held a convention and placed J. C. Sisk, one of
the strongest men they had in their party, in opposition to me.[31] I canvased
the county as well as my limited time would allow, and would admit, was

Thomas W. Colley. Courtesy American Civil War Museum,
Richmond, Virginia.

kindly received by my county men of All parties, for which I am Truly Grateful. My parents used every scheme of strategy imaginable, and by the help of God I came out victorious over all opposition—both the sore hands of my own political brethern and my Republican opponents. I received 1,767 votes while my opponent received 1,588, which gave me 179 majority. Henry C. Stuart of Russell County furnished me a horse to ride during the canvas. C. F. Keller, an old Confederate comrade, rendered me good service in my canvas, for which I am very grateful, and hope that God will bless him and all others who assisted me.[32] I have no unkind feeling towards those who opposed me. That is their right and privilege.

My old comrades, irrespective of party lines, stood by me almost solidly. My God, in His infinite Wisdom and goodness, assisted me in the discharge of my duties, incumbent upon me on the 28th of December 1903. I was sworn into office, and Mr. George Stuart, J. L. Litton, and W. F. Minnick served as my bondsmen. By the help of God, I served my term of four years and at the expriation of four years, I was reappointed by Judge F. B. Hutton for the 2nd term of 4 years on the Last day of December 1911.[33] I served out my 8 years as Commissioner. The duties of Commissioner became too burdensome for me, both physically and mentally. The awful strain on both body and mind was almost unbearable. At this date, 1915, I am now almost at the end of the 78 years of my Earthly Exhistance. George Stuart and William H. Aston were my bondsmen for my last four years as Commissioner of Revenue. George Stuart, and his father and family, have been staunch friends of mine.

End of Thomas W. Colley's life history.

Regimental History and Biographical Roster Sketch Contained in Colley's Journal[1]

Washington Mounted Rifles

A Historical Roster of the Washington Mounted Rifles 'The 1st Cavalry Co.,' organized in Washington County, Va. in April 1861 by Captain Wm. E. Jones. It was afterwards Co. L, until the reorganization April 1862, when it was known as Co. D. 1st Virginia Cavalry A.N.V. and served with the Regiment, until the close of the struggle at Appomatox C.H. April 9, 1865. This Roster is made principally from memory and by inquiring of other members who are yet living, now 38 years since we laid down our trusty Carbines, Pistols, and sabers.

To our foes who out numbered us 5 to 1, we were over powered but not conquerd. The indomitable spirit which had sustained us through the four long years of hardships incident to a soldier's life was not dimmed in the least. As time has proven, men returned to their desolated and wasted homesteads and threw their old cavalry saddles under the porch or shed—made an improvised jenny of some sort or other—and went to work to make bread for themselves and their loved ones and to build up the waste places.[2]

The first letter I received from one of my beloved commanders a 'Major General' at the close of the war,—'Fitzhugh Lee.' He told me how he had thrown his old cavalry saddle under the portico at his home, and had fixed up a set of plow gears and was plowing corn. Men who suffer for a principle can not be over come and cast down 'but they will rise again.' Of such material as this were the men whose names called here, or at least the great majority of them.[3]

Roster of Companies [L] & D., 1st Rgt. Va. Cavalry. Wm E. Jones, Captain, a native of Washington County and a Graduate of West Point; a Lieut. of cavalry in the U.S. Army when the 1st Brigade of Cavalry was formed in the summer of 1861. Our Col. J. E. B. Stuart was promoted to 'Brig Gen.' and Wm. E. Jones became Col. of the 1st and remained so until 1862 when he was sent to the Valley of Virginia

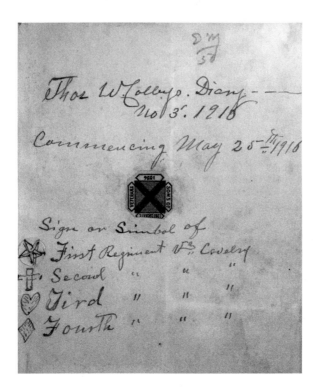

Regiment Symbols
as drawn by Colley
in front of one his
diaries. Private
Collection.

and assigned to the command of the 7th Regt. Virginia Cavalry. He was there until the winter of 1863, when he was promoted to Brig. Gen. of cavalry in the fall of 1863. His Brigade saved the defeat and utter rout of Stuart's Cavalry Corps at Brandy Station.[4] In October of that year, he was sent out to take command of the Department of South West Virginia and East Tennessee; in his short stay in this Department he done the enemy more damage than all the officers who had preceded him. In June 1864, he was ordered with all his command that could be spared, from the South West to make a forced march to the Valley of Virginia to meet the notorious 'General Hunter,' [Major General David Hunter] who was burning barns and mills and in some instances dwelling houses; placing that beautiful and fruitful land in a condition that a crow passing over it would have to carry its rations, that is said to have been his 'Language.'[5]

General Jones arrived at Staunton late on the night of the 4th of June and moved out towards Mt. Crawford and across to New Hope or Piedmont, where he scarcely had time to form his lines when he was attacked by the Union Forces. I am informed by General Imboden [Brigadier General John Daniel Imboden] and

Major General David Hunter.
Library of Congress.

W. M. Hopkins [Warren Montgomery Hopkins], Jones's Adjutant General, that from an 'eminence,' which they occupied, they could see the rear of Hunter's army and that the utmost confusion prevailed there. His wagon trains and ambulances were moving off down the Valley. At this critical moment, some of Jones's men had given away and [Jones] rushed down in their midst to rally them and was instantly killed, when victory was almost perching on his banner. The news of his death spread like wild fire and all became confusion and rout. So, on that fatal field, and on the 5th day of June 1864, the life and light went out of as brave and patriotic spirit as ever drew a Sword in the Defense of the Lost Cause.[6]

The 1st Lieutenant W. W. Blackford [William Willis] is still living. He was a fine Horseman and expert swordsman. I owe my 1st lessons in Saber exercises to him; I loved him. The men as a whole did not take kindly to him as he was a man of rather cold exterior, and as they thought rather proud, and held himself rather high from the rank and file. He was a brave kind-hearted man. He was defeated for captain at the reorganization. He was on General Stuart's staff for some time and was Lieutenant Colonel in the Engineer Corps at the close of the struggle. He is now dead. [It is likely Colley made this last entry after Blackford passed in 1905.]

(2) Lieut. Rees B. Edmondson: was a brave man and a generous whole souled fellow, he was twice wounded and died in Washington D.C. on February 13, 1901, where he resided. For several years he was 1st Lieutenant, from March 1862 to the end.

(3) Lieutenant George V. [Victor] Litchfield, became 2nd Lieutenant in 1862. 'Vick' as the boys called him, was a good soldier and always ready for fun or a fight. He was twice wounded. Lieut. Litchfield died October 1904; his health had not been good for several years.

(4) Lieutenant Thomas B. Edmondson, a cousin of Captain Jones, was elected 3rd Lieut. at the reorganization. He was rather a reckless, brave man, a genial whole souled fellow liked by everybody. He was killed at Spotsylvania in 1863, [as he] moved forward in front of the company and [was] shot down by sharpshooters. He was orderly sergeant under Litchfield.

First orderly Sergeant James King. He had been in the regular army and could learn in many things about caring for our health, and other camp manners. He was a brave generous man and a rigid disciplinarian. He became offended because Captain Blackford was promoted over him, and left our company in 1861 and joined the 37th Infantry, and was killed at Kernstown in 1862; buried in Bluefield.[7]

2nd Sergeant Conally [Connally] T. [Trigg] Litchfield; yet alive. He was orderly sergeant after James King was elected captain in March 1862 and remained such until the end. He was thrice wounded and carried one ball in his face or head for several years; it came out on its own accord after 34 years. He was also severely wounded in his arm at another time. He was a whole souled generous hearted man, his men all loved him. They all called him 'Captain' or mostly 'Con.' He died August 6, 1909. [Again, Colley seems to have updated his initial entry after Litchfield's death.]

3rd Sergeant Thomas B. Edmondson I have already given a note of him as 3rd Lieutenant.

4th Sergeant J. M. [James] Byars; he died since the war. He was a good kind man and a very good soldier. His health failed and he obtained a discharge in 1862, being over 40 years of age.

W. M. Hopkins [Warren Montgomery] was appointed Color Sergeant to carry the company colors. He was afterwards made a sergeant and then adjutant of the

1st Regiment under Colonel Jones and then was 'Adjutant General,' which he commanded until the end of the war. He died 1877. He was a cool brave man and a kind officer.

1st Corporal James K. Rambo died in 1902. He was made captain under General Jones. He did not remain with us long.

2nd Corporal John A. P. [Alexander Preston] Baker; he is now dead. He was deposed by Captain Jones, he was wanting in 'grit.' He was a physician and was assistant surgeon of our regiment in the latter part of the war.

3rd Corporal Dr. Gilbert C. [Christian] Greenway: yet living; Gil was a good soldier and a Liberal hearted companionable man; he left our command with James King. I cannot trace him through the war; I wrote him for information, received no reply.

Jacob L. Fields, was appointed to superceed Dr. Baker: he died in 1862. He was a good, quiet man, always ready for duty.

M. M. [Michael S.] Ireson: alive at this writing. He was appointed bugler by 'Col. Jones,' and afterwards became 1st Sergeant, and acting orderly at the surrender. He was one of the old stand byes. He was a fearless soldier and a good man.

P. C. [Paul Carrington] Landrum: was appointed Sergeant in 1862: he is now dead. He was severely wounded at Gettysburg, Pennsylvania, in 1863: He was a truly brave cool deliberate man, a fine shot, and died in Abingdon, Va.

P. C. [Putnam] Miles, [served as] 3rd Sergeant when he was killed in 1864. He was a native of Lee County, Virginia. Pat was a good one in camp or on the firing line; killed at Spotsylvania 1864.

C. H. [Charles] Dulaney is alive. His home is in Madison County, near the line of Culpepper County. He was a noble soldier, he was only 16 years old when he volunteered in 1861. He was appointed corporal, by Captain Litchfield and arose to 3rd Sergeant on the death of Pat Miles. He was severely wounded at Spotsylvania, came near losing his leg.

D. A. [David] Fields: won the Corporal Stripes by hard fighting. He was 1st Corporal at the death of Pat Miles and of course went up to 4th Sergeant. Poor old David, he went through all the close places from '61 to '65, and at last succumbed to Texas Fever some years after the war.

Thomas W. [Wallace] Colley: was appointed Corporal in 1864 and at the end was 1st Corporal. He was three times wounded in 1862–1863–1864, lost a foot in 1864. He is the writer of these lines. Let some one else speak for him.

C. M. Waldron: was 2nd Corporal, he was a young man from Campbell County, Virginia. He is highly spoken of by Captain Litchfield.

These are all the non-commissioned officers I can find any record of. I obtained these facts from Comrade Ireson.

S. J. McChestney [Samuel Jefferson McChesney]: was Ordnance Sergeant until he was severely wounded and lost part of his hand in 1863. He died since the war, he was a young M.D. when he volunteered. Sam was a good boy any place you put him.

B. [Benjamin] Gildersleeve [Jr.]: was appointed Ordnance Sergeant and was acting as such up to the end of the war. He is yet alive, through all the fearful things he was called upon to pass through during the fearful 4 years of war. Ben is a good man.

Privates:

Beattie, R. F. [Robert]: Cloud cap, he is yet alive, he was wounded. He is now dead. [another postscript from Colley]

Beattie, Walter: he was a young M.D., he died in 1861 of fever.

Beattie, Fountain: he is alive, good jovial Old Fount, he was transfered to Mosby's Bat. and made Lieut. in one of the companies.

Bailey, Thomas W. [White]: dead in 1864, he was a victom to his love for fun. He was teasing one of the conscript guard of this county—one Tom Palmer—when Palmer shot him in the stomach, from which would he died in a few hours. He was a noble man and soldier, and a messmate of this writer.

Bailey, O. S. [Oscar Shaver]: Alive. He was wounded, he was a good boy, and quite young. When the war broke out he was also a mess mate of this writer. He died at his home in Steele, Mo., Feb. 6, 1919 [another postscript from Colley]. Born in Washington County, Va. Feb. 17, 1844, a true solder, a good citizen of his adopted State.

Bailey, James A. Jr.: Alive. He was a good all-around soldier.

Baker, Joe [Joseph] H.: Killed May 7, 1864. He was a good soldier. After the first few skirmishes and battles we passed through, he died; lamented by the whole company.

Butt, John W.: Killed in 1864 by a fall from his horse; he was a good true man, a little wild and reckless.

Buchanan, Randolph: Died since the war. 'Old Ran' was in for anything the boys proposed and sometimes came round with his own accord.

Barker, W. D. [William]: Alive. Billy was not afraid of anything. He says one of Stuart's Staff, a young officer, one time in a very hot place, rode up to him and told him to press the enemy. Bily told him to dismount and try it. At the same time offering him his carbine and saying he was not a good hand [shot]. About that time, a shower of bullets came hissing and zinging around the corner. Our staff officer let out at full speed; he had as much pressing as he wanted. He was transfered to the 63rd Virginia Infantry and was taken prisoner and confined in Camp Douglas till after the surrender.[8]

Buskell, Alex [Alexander]: never transferred he served in Co. D. to the end; he was severely wounded in 1864.

Buskell, Richard/Richland: Killed at Fredericksburg in 1863. He was also transferred to Pelham's Battery. He was a noble soldier; was promoted to sergeant for gallantry before he was killed.

Barr, David: Alive, he is an Episcopal Minister in Washington D.C. He was transferred to a company from Alabama; do not know his record as a soldier. He was at last in Captain Barr's Battery (his brother).[9]

Catron, A. P. R. [Andrew]: Died of consumption since the war. He was a good soldier and made a noble young man. He graduated at E&H [Emory & Henry] College in 1872; died after he finished his course.[10]

Clark, Wm. R. [William Riley]: Was shot on Picket Post in 1861 and died from his wounds. His horse was shot at same time. He was a true man and always ready for duty. Died Oct. 1861. [November 2, 1861]

Clark, W. F. P. [William Franklin Page]: Accidently shot in camp and died from wounds in Nov. 1861. He was a kind-hearted gentleman and one of great promise as a soldier and citizen. He was greatly lamented by both his officers and men. He was a mess mate of this writer.

Cole, Thomas V. [Van Buren]: He died in Mo. since the war. He was one of those genial whole souled rolickin fellows. He received a severe wound, and was taken prisoner on the retreat from Gettysburg and kept until the close of the war.

Cole, D. C. [David]: Another one of the young boy soldiers. He was always at the fore front. He was killed by a premature explosion of a dynamite blast in Colorado since the war.

Cassell, Rufus R.: Alive. He was severly wounded at Union in Loudon County in November 1862. He was a good average soldier; he was transferred from our company and did not serve with us till the end. He was transferred to 51st Va. infantry and was captured at Waynesboro, Va, and sent to Fort Delaware, where he remained a prisoner until June 1865. Died July 31, 1911.

Colley, T. L. [Thomas]: Died since the war in Mo. He was a good soldier.

Crawford, Ben C. [Benjamin]: He is alive and lives in Texas. He is a dentist. He was severely wounded in 1863; was a good soldier and a genial companion, the boys all loved him. He died March 26, 1903 in Georgetown, Texas. I learned from a letter to his sister, Mrs. Thompson, that Ben was a member of the ME Church South and died in the full triumphs of a living faith.

Crawford, Thomas C. [E.]: He is alive in Texas. He was a good frolicking boy, always in for fun. He was wounded in 1863. He stayed to the bitter end.

Cook, J. F. [John Frank]: He is alive I learned, [living] in New Mexico. He was another of the boy soldiers. He was rather wild and reckless, but a good sharpshooter.

Crockett, A. M.: Died in Corsicana, Texas since the war; he was a native of Lee County Virginia. He and Pat Miles came together. He was a noble man and a zealous defender of Southern rights.

Davis, John G. R.: Alive. Old Griff was always steady and true as steel. He was transfered to Capt. Fred Gray's Co. 23rd Cavalry; was Lieut. Died January 1905. [postscript from Colley.]

Dunn, Dr. W. L. [William Logan]: Alive. He was transferred to the Medical Dept. He and Jon A. P. Baker [John Alexander Preston Baker] captured 3 yanks at a farm house in 1861. One of them was a sergeant, who afterwards became a guard officer. General Hospital: Dr. Dunn served in this hospital in Richmond; he afterwards became surgeon of Mosby's Bat. and served with him up to 1865.

Deyerle, John B.: Whereabouts unknown. He was a native of Roanoke County. He was no good as a soldier.

Edmondson, M. V. [Martin Van Buren]: Alive. Von was a good general fellow. He was a good soldier. He did serve with King's Bat.[11]

Euk, Frank J. [Enk, Francis A.]: He was a young Frenchman, whom General W. E. Jones brought from France. He obtained a discharge, do not know what became of him. He made a good deal of fun for us with his English French.

Findlay, Frank S. [Smith]: Alive. He served some time on General Stuart's Staff; was wounded. He raised a company and was captain of it.

Fields, Charles B. [Baker]: Alive in Yuba City, Calif. He was severely wounded in 1864. He was one of my original mess mates. He was a fearless fighter.

Fulkerson, Frank R. [Robert Frank]: He is alive. He was not a native of Washington County. Frank was a noble man. He was a sufferer from bronchial trouble. He would march all day in the rain and mud, and suffer all night. I have known his mess mates to work with him all night to keep breath in him. He was told if he did not get out of camp life he would die, but that did not dampen his ardor for the Southern cause.

Gildersleeve, Ben Jr. [Benjamin]: Alive. Ben was an educated high-toned gentleman. As I have stated else where, he was ordnance sergeant. He was the soul of honor.

Gray, Fred T. [Frederick]: died since the war. He served with us until 1862, when he received a discharge being over age. He organized a company in 1863, and was captain of it until the end of the war. He was a solid, good man. If there was hard fighting the boys always liked to see 'Uncle Fred' around.[12]

Gray, R. E. [Robert Emmett]: Died in 1901. Emit was captured and made his escape from Point Lookout; he and two others. He was quite a shifty soldier.

Gray, D. C. [David]: He is alive in Mo. Poor Dave, he made lots of fun for the company. He had a knack for getting into some trouble. He thought he was a fine judge of horse flesh. General Stuart came on him sitting down on his post once and ordered him to get up and walk his beat. It made David furiously mad, he threatened to resign and go home.

Gollihin, J. A. [Gollehon, James Alexander]: He was courier to General Stuart for a while; he hired a substitute in 1862 and came home. He is alive.

Gammon, Melvin [William Melvin]: His is alive in Georgia. Mel was a good fellow, he accidently shot himself in the spring of 1862. He came from Tennessee with Fulkerson and Russell. He did not return to the company after he was wounded.

Hockett, John: He is alive at Merit, Texas. John was a true man, always in place. I have been beside him in many occasions. He was courier to General Stuart for some time. John Hockett died at his home in Texas January 1905. [postscript from Colley]

Hockett, William: Alive. Laughing Bill, he would laugh if the balls were as thick as hail. He said he did not like war much, but he managed to get as much fun out of it as any man I ever met.

Hubble, Thomas [G.]: He was stricken down with Typhoid Fever soon after the 1st Battle of Manassas, and he is lost sight of since that time. He is a native of Smyth County, Virginia.

Jones, Jasper [Nathaniel]: He died in South America since the war. He was a cousin of General Wm. E. Jones and had served on the Texas frontier. He was a true type of Southern soldier. He was at home in the Strife. He was transferred to Mosby's Battalion and was twice wounded. He was one of the men who made name and fame for Col. J. S. Mosby.

Jones, Henry S.: Died in Orange County, Idaho, July 27, 1900. Pete was a cousin of General Jones. He was a noble boy, he was full of life and fun and always ready for duty. He was severely wounded in 1863; he recovered and returned and was at the final wind up [surrender].

Larimore, John [Larimer, John M.]: He was quite young when he enlisted. He was always ready for duty. He drove the ordnance wagons for some time. He is alive and lives in MO.

Lynch, David [David Campbell]: He died early in the war. He had taken a course at V.M.I. [Virginia Military Institute] and was one of our drill masters. He was one of my original mess mates. I loved him. He was a liberal hearted boy.

Loggin, John: He was one of those poor unfortunate fellows who loved the alcohol too well. He told Mrs. McGuock at Fort Chiswell a lie to get a bottle of wine, and Captain Jones ordered him to leave the company, which he did, and his whereabouts are unknown.

Meek, S. D. [Stephen]: He died in Texas since the war: He was ruptured and was discharged in 1862. Old Steve was a jovial fellow and full of fun.

Montgomery, Wm. F. [William]: He is alive. William was as hard as a pine knot. He was severely wounded. He hates the Yankees, yet he says they never whipped him.

Morrell, W. W. [William W.]: He was killed near Shepherdstown July 1863. He was one of the truly brave and the most generous hearted man I ever met. I have known him to give his rations to some of the boys who complained of being hungry and do without himself. He was my mess mate and bosom companion. I loved him above all my comrades. He was perfectly void of fear, a man after my own heart, a soldier in ever sense of the word. It was a sad day to the company when he was stricken down in death.

Morrell, David H.: Killed at Saltville October 1864. He and his horse 'Billy Peacock,' afforded a good deal of amusement for us on the march. He was a true Southerner.

Morrell, Charles M.: Died in 1899. He was a loyal soldier of the South. He was slightly wounded with a piece of shell. Had a severe spell of Typhoid Fever in 1861 and was made prisoner in 1862; was exchanged and served to the end. He was a cousin and mess mate of mine.

McNew, Leander: Died in MO. 1901. Lee was quite a dolt. He reported to Captain Jones once that Lieut. Edmondson, who was on the outpost, said they are shooting their cavalry, infantry, and artillery all at us.

McNew, Tobias S.: Toby lost his health and was discharged in 1862. He was quite a good fellow. He had all the elements of a good soldier.

McReynolds, James M.: Do not know his whereabouts. He drove an ambulance most of the time. He finally drifted away, deserted.

McReynolds, Wm. [William]: He was just the reverse of his brother to all appearance. He did not fear death any more than he would a cup of Yankee coffee. He was killed in the City of Richmond in 1863 by some unknown person. Body was found in Bacon's Quarter Branch in the suburbs of the city.

Mahaffey, W. A. [William]: He is dead. He was the hardest man in our company to discipline. He gave General Jones a good deal of trouble. He had to walk almost all the way to Richmond because of his insubordination. He was transferred to Pelham's Battery.

Mosby, John S. [Singleton]: He is alive in the employ of the U.S. Government; he was not with us much. He was employed by General Stuart as a scout, and then organized a battery which is known to history. [Mosby organized the 43rd Battalion Virginia Partisan Rangers.]

Moore, David: I cannot remember anything of him, do not think any such man ever belonged to our company. [One of] M. S. Ireson's boys.

Ornduff, John [D.]: Poor old 'Honest John.' He has long since gone to his reward. He was company quartermaster. I can hear his sonorous voice now, "boys come and get your corn." John was good anywhere you put him.

Orr, C. M. [M. C.]: Alive. He was discharged on the account of deafness in 1862.

Page, R. M. [Reuben Murrell]: He is alive. He was a boy soldier. He was one that helped to make the reputation of the 'Old First.' He was wounded severely in 1864. He was one of my original mess mates. He always done his part in camp or on the field. Died in 1914. [Another postscript from Colley]

Pendleton, M. N. [Morgan M.]: he is dead, was drowned in the far west in Snake River. He was a native of Wythe County, Va. He was one of those characters what we seldom met. He did not care any more for killing a man than he did a chicken. He was twice wounded. He was appointed corporal and rose to the rank of 2nd sergeant. He would have been orderly sergeant, being in the educated class. He could not fill the office and resigned and went back to the ranks.

Price, Dr. W. H. [William Humberson]: He was an educated man and a noble, good fellow. He went to the Valley of Virginia with Col. Jones and was not with us after the reorganization in 1862. He is now a minister in the M.E. Church South.

Roberts, John H.: He died of fever at Appomattox in 1861. He was a good man and had at that early day shown his soldierly qualities.

Rambo, A. F. [Andrew]: He is alive, not withstanding everybody predicted his death in a very short time. He was the sickliest looking boy in our company. Captain Jones tried to persuade him to go home, but he would not do it and he tried to get him to stay in Richmond after we arrived there and go to school, offering to pay his board and tuition. But he declined the offer, said he had volunteered to make a soldier and nothing else would satisfy him. He soon became amended to camp life and his health improved. He was a calm and dedicated soldier.

Riddle, James W. [S.]: He died from brain fever in 1861. He could not stand the whine of bullets.

Rush, Jerry C. [Jeremiah]: Alive. Jerry was a good soldier, always ready for service. He stuck to the bitter end. Now dead. [Another postscript from Colley]

Russell, John [R.]: Killed in 1863; he was not a native of Virginia, he came from Rogersville, Tennessee. He and Frank Fulkerson were mess mates and inseparable companions. He was an ardent lover of the Southern cause and laid down his life in her defense. He was a true friend to his friends. His dust rests in Culpepper County, Va.

Robertson, Frank S. [Francis Smith]: Alive. He is a noble hearted true Southerner and is still as bitter as ever. He served on General Stuart's staff and was Lieutenant of Co. B, 48th Virginia Regt. at the end of the war. Frank says he belongs to all the branches in Confederate Service.

Rodeffer, J. Alex [Joseph Alexander]: He was not much on soldiering. He was with the ambulance train most of the time. He was transfered to the 45th Va. Infantry and served with it till the end of the war.

Sanders, R. J. [Robert]: Died since the war. He was not a coward by any means. He received several balls through his clothes at Waterloo Bridge in 1862. His health failed and he was discharged. He was one of my original mess mates.

Sanders, J. W. S. [John William Summerfield]: Alive, He was a good soldier, was severely wounded in 1862. He was transfered to Mosby's Bat. Came back to the old company and was wounded the 2nd time, May 8, 1864.

Sandoe, D. P. [David Prince]: Died since the war. He was another small, diminutive little boy. He made a good soldier, was a great favorite with the captain and all the men: we called him 'Bulley.'

Scott, Wm. E. [William]: He was quite young when he volunteered. He was a good true man to hitch to in a close place. He died some years after the close of the war.

Smith, Wm. Buck [William J. "Buck"]: He did not remain with us long. He was discharged by being over age. He is now dead.

Smith, Thos. Col. Stigens [Thomas]: he is yet alive; he was a fiddler and could sing anything. He was a perfect mimic and droll. He was the life of the camp. He told Captain Jones, plain and square out, he could not stand the singing and zigging of the bullets, to please give him something else to do. Jones put him in charge of our pack mules and he stuck to them until he was transferred to the 45th Virginia Regiment. He served with that regiment until the close of the war. The men all loved and respected him.

Smith, Wm. [William]: He is alive. He was a good, steady going fellow and managed to keep up his side of the single tree. He deserted.

Snodgrass, Wm. [William L.]: he was a good all-around soldier. He is yet alive.

Shepherd, Thomas [J.]: He was quite a good jovial fellow. He was a victim of Typhoid fever. He died in 1861.

Vaughan, Wm. W. [William]: Billy was a good easy going fellow. He was wounded early in the war in 1863 and drifted away some where. He never returned to the company.

White, Wm. B. [William]: He is dead; died since the war. He was a noble, generous gentlemanly man, polite and affable to all. He served on to the end. He was a faithful true soldier.

Williams, Rufus C. [Chapman]: Killed May 8, 1864 at Spotsylvania CH. We dubbed him 'Captain.' He was a fine soldier, he loved a soldier's life. Had he lived he would have made his mark in the world. He was full of energy and vim and had the courage to take hold of anything, hit or miss.

Wright, T. D. [Thomas]: I am informed by Sergeant M. M. S. Ireson, [Wright] should be on the role of the original company in 1861. He was discharged for some physical reason.

There were two negroes with our company in 1861, which I think deserve notice as they were faithful and true in performance of the duties asigned them.

John Revels: We dubbed him 'Rebbs.' He was a free man before the war. Captain Jones employed him as his hostler.[13] He afterwards served Captain Litchfield to the end of the war. I am informed he died in Ohio a few years ago.

Frank Trigg: was Dr. Gilbert C. Greenway's servant. They were both at the wagon train most of the time. They always had something to eat and have relieved the gnawing of the stomach of the writer. They are both dead.

A Roster of Recruits enlisted in Company D. 1st Virginia Volunteer Cavalry from 1862 to 1865. [Editor's Note: not all entries appear in alphabetical order.]

(1)   Arnette, J. A. [Arnett, James F., Jr.]: dead. He was found dead, supposed to have been killed by the accidental discharge of his gun. He was a fine marksman with a rifle. He asked permission of Captain Litchfield at one time to allow him to try his marksmanship on a "Yankee Artillery" officer who was using great exertion to keep his men to their guns, as Major Pelham was making it rather hot for him. It was quite a long shot. At the report of the rifle, he threw up his hands and fell backwards from his horse. Nothing pleased him better than to have an opportunity to try his hand at a sling shot. He was a prisoner for some time at Point Lookout.[14]

(2)   Asbury, Mansfield: He died since the war; he was a fine soldier. He captured the colors of the 5th U.S. Regular Cavalry in a hand to hand fight in 1863. 'Mans' was a good, steady soldier and citizen.

(3)   Asbury, Wm. [William L.]: He did not like the music of the balls and shells [when he served] with 37th Regiment.

(4)   Asbury, L. D. [Lorenzo]: He is alive, he was another of our boy soldiers. He was a good soldier, knew no fear, was always ready and anxious for the fray. Now dead, 1913. [Another postscript from Colley]

(5)   Allison, Abbram [Abram]: Died in January 1862. He was not a robust man in health, but always filled his place in ranks.

(6)   Bailey, Walter W. [Waller Warren]: He was killed in Maryland, near Funkstown, in 1863. He was in Memphis, Tenn., when the war broke out. He came to the company in 1862. He was a noble, zealous soldier. At the time of his death, he was courier to General Stuart; he was a mess mate of mine.

(7)   Bailey, Wm. [William]: He died of fever in 1863. He was quite a young boy, the youngest of the four brothers that belonged to Co. D. He was a noble-hearted boy and would have made a fine soldier if his life had been spared.

(8)   Bailey, Floyd: He was quite young, he took the fever in two or three weeks and died.

(9)   Bearden, Wm. [William M.]: He was not a native of this section, came from some of the Eastern Counties.

(10)   Butt, Henry C. [Clay]: He died since the war. He was an exceptional man, a fine soldier and a true Christian. He carried his religion with him in camp. He was for a number of years a minister of the Gospel in the M.P. [Methodist Protestant] Church, the first Chaplain of Wm. E. Jones Camp, U.C.V. The world is always made better by the lives of such men.

(11)   Buchanan, Wm. [William]: He is alive at this time but quite deaf. He was a good steady soldier and is now a good citizen.

(12)   Bradley, James H.: He was a good man, and died since the war.

(13)   Black, W. D. [William D. W.]: He is alive, he could not stand the racket and managed to get a discharge soon after his enlistment. He tried to play deaf at first. We laughed him out of that, and then he lost the use of one of his arms and won.

(14)   Black, Sam D. [Samuel]: He is alive. He was a fair soldier. He was a prisoner at Point Lookout for some time.

(15)   Byars, A. H. [Henderson]: 'Old Dad.' He is yet alive. 'Dad' was a fine soldier, a good companionable man, and is a good citizen.

(16)   Bryant, John W.: He is yet alive. He was severely wounded in 1862 in the Pope Campaign [Major General John Pope]. He was quite young. His father was a strong Union man, and through his advice, John deserted and was caught and placed in 'Castle Thunder.' I did not, and do not now, think any disgrace ought to rest on him for this act.

(17)   Campbell, John: 'Uncle John' as we called him, he was a true patriot and a volunteer in truth. He was an old white-headed man. He died of fever in 1863.

(18)   Carmack, D. C. [David]: He died since the war. He was a passable soldier. He was deputy sheriff for four years and constable for several years. He was transferred from 4th Tennessee in 1864.

(19)   Catron, Frank M. [Francis M.]: Died since the war with consumption. He was a great liberal, jovial boy. Droll and awkard. The boys had a good deal of innocent fun at his expense. He was a good average soldier, one of the poor unfortunates whose rations were never sufficent to satisfy the cravings of his appetite.

(20)   Clark, James H.: 'Squaty' the boys dubbed him. He was another one of the good, jovial boy soldiers. He was always full of life and fun and always ready for a fight. He died with Typhoid fever in 1900.

(21)   Clark, W. D. [William Dixon]: He is yet alive. He was one of the boys that got tired of infantry and came to the cavalry to find an easy place. He was originally a member of the 37th Va. Infantry. He was a good steady soldier. He had a particular love for a soldier's life.

(22)   Clark, G. L. [Isaac Lewis]: Alive at this time. He was severely wounded in both hands in 1864. He was a good average soldier. He was one of 6 that went with me to the fence on the 28th of May 1864 at Haw's Shop. He is now dead. [Another postscript from Colley]

(23)   Clapp, Theo M. [Theophilus Mitchell]: He is alive at this time. He was quite a boy. He was wounded at or near Shepherdstown in July 1863. He was by some means brought to notice in General Orders by Gen. J. E. B. Stuart. None of the company has ever been able to tell how, or for what. Nine-tenths of the men composing the company performed as heroic acts as he, of which there was no notice taken. It stands as a matter of history that he, of all the brave men composing that company of heroes, is the only one ever brought to notice by a General Order.[15]

(24)   Colley, W. L. M. [William Lewis]: Alive. He was as truly a brave man as any who donned the gray. He was wounded at Funkstown, Md. in 1863, and again at Winchester, Va. 1864. He is the only brother of this writer. He was with Gen. Floyd [Brigadier General John B. Floyd] in 1861, came to [Company] 'D' in 1862.

(25)   Cosby, Lewis T. [Thompson]: He is alive. He was a mere boy when he joined the company. He was a good soldier, always in line.

(26)   Cosby, John D. [Dabney]: He is alive. He was with the 37th Va. Infantry until 1863, he had the fever and it settled in his leg and he was not physically able to march in the infantry, and was transferred to cavalry. He was a jovial, whole souled fellow.

(27)   Cubine, Wm. [William H. N.]: He is alive. He was transferred from the 4th Tenn. Infantry in 1864. He was quite young. I do not know much of his record as a soldier. I met him at Dallas in 1902; his home is in Texas. He was a noble soldier, and led the last charge of Appomattox.

(28)   Davis, John M.: He died in Texas since the war. He was a genial gentleman, and fought from principle. He was with me on the 28th of May 1864, one of the 6 that went forward to the fence, where the company was ordered to form in line on the extreme left of our line.

(29)   Davidson, Thomas [C.]: He was a victim to camp fever. He did not get to remain long enough to prove his soldierly qualities. He was a gentleman and a companionable man, and I have no doubt he would have made an excellent soldier.

(30)   DeBusk, David: Alive. He was a good, quite boy, always ready with the rest of the young recruits to go forward. Now dead. Died in 1913.

(31)   DeBusk, Samuel: He is alive. He is brother to David and equally as good.

(32)   Duff, Thomas B.: He was another young boy soldier. He was killed at the Battle of Strawsburg in 1863.[16]

(33) Duff, J. M.[James]: 'Chippy,' he is alive in Texas, I saw him at Dallas. He is quite a jovial Texan. He was a good soldier.

(34) Edmondson, John B.: Died since the war. He was a good Presbyterian brother. He thought it quite a sin to steal citizens' chickens and pigs; he soon learned better. The boys got him to steal a lady's pepper off the table, and that cooled him. He was a good soldier and a good companion, he messed with me a long time.

(35) Edmondson, Strong: Do not know his whereabouts. He was a good all-around man. He is a Railroad Engineer.

(36) Findley, Thomas K.: Died since the war. He was wounded in 1863. He was transferred to Co. D. from Price's Army [Major General Sterling Price] in Mo. in 1862. Tom had a kind heart in him and he was not a coward by any means. He belonged to Bledsoe's famous battery.[17]

(37) Fulkerson, Charles H.: He is alive. His home is in Lee County, Va. He was of fighting stock. His father, Arch Fulkerson, "would not let a Yankee darken his door," if he knew it. Charles was a good soldier.

(38) Fulcher, Samuel: He died of fever in 1862. He was in Texas when the war broke out. He came home and joined Co. D. in 1862; did not live long. He enjoyed a soldier's life and would have made his mark as a fighter. He messed with this writer.

(39) Fleenor, Jacob: I do not know his whereabouts, I am told by [William] Cubine that he came with him from the 4th Tennessee.

(40) Foster, Charles: He is alive I learn. Sergeant [Charles] Dulaney says he was a good soldier. He was quite young. He was transferred from 4th Tenn.

(41) French, J. L. M. [John]: He is now dead. He became a minister in the M.E. Church South after the war. He was quite young. He came to the company in 1864 and served to the end.

(42) Greenway, W. T. [William]: He died since the war. He was a captain in the 48th Virginia Infantry and resigned to join the cavalry. He was a kind-hearted man.

(43) Gray, Charles P.: He is alive. He is another boy soldier. Charles was a good one.

(44) Gray, James [James Craig]: He is now dead. He was a good all-around soldier and a strong Southern man. Afterwards, transferred to Capt. Gray's Co. 21st Virginia Cavalry.

(45) Grant, Robert [E.]: He was a dentist. He did not remain with the company long; was detailed in the medical service.[18]

(46) Hall, Wm. A. [William H.]: Died since the war. He was a brave true man. He was shot by Johnson County [TN] bush whackers soon after the surrender.

They came to rob his dwelling and they found him at home and prepared for the fray, wounded as he was he continued to shoot. He plugged one of them.

(47) Hall, John D.: He is now dead. John was a Northern man who married a Virginia woman and when the time came around for him to enter the service he came to Co. D. and took up his abode with the boys on the line. He hired a substitute and went home in 1864.

(48) Harris, A. Findley [Alexander]: He was another wee boy soldier. He is quite proud today of his record of Co. D. Now dead, 1914 [Another postscript from Colley]

(49) Hockett, Samuel: Now dead. He was quite young and his health was not good. He was always ready for duty.

(50) Hickman, R. M. [Robert]: Now dead. Bob was a good genial, fun making man. He always tried to keep his place in ranks.

(51) Hewlett, George: Do not know his whereabouts. He was quite a good soldier, he was not a resident of this section of the state.

(52) Horn, Basil [Horne, Basil L.]: He was another victim to the deadly camp fever. He was a good young man, and much liked by his comrades.

(53) Jones, Robert [G.]: Was killed at Funkstown, Maryland in 1863. He was a cousin of General William Jones. Bob was a noble true soldier. He was quite young. He was always ready and willing to do his part.

(54) Jones, David [L.]: He was hanged by order of General [George Armstrong] Custer in 1864. He was transferred to Col. Mosby's Bat. in 1863. He was a noble spirited youth. He was always ready to kill or be killed. He was a brother of Jasper and Robert. He was greatly lamented by our company and the battalion. His name is carried in marble as one of the Mosby men hung by the cruel order of a Federal officer, for which 14 poor Federals had to answer with their lives by order of Col. Mosby. Such is war.[19]

(55) Keesling, M. G.: He died in Bristol, Tenn. in 1910. He was another boy soldier and a good one. He was a native of Wythe County, Virginia. I learned from M. G. Keesling that John Keesling was his brother and was quite young when he enlisted. He died in Missouri some 4 years ago.

(56) Keller, Robert [J.]: He lived through the war but died soon after its close. He was quite a small little fellow but as brave and true as steel. He was a great favorite with the officers and men.

(57) King, H. W. [Harvey Winton]: He is alive. He is another boy recruit from Wythe County, Virginia. He was true and loyal and I am told is a good man today.

(58) Keesling, John: He is alive; I do not know anything concerning his record.

(59) Keesling, Emory [S.]: He is alive in Wythe County, Virginia. They both came to the company very late in the war. [Colley likely references John and Emory when stating "both."]

(60) Latham, M. H. [Moses Hugh]: Now dead. He was an honest true soldier and one that would stick as close as a brother. He is an uncompromising Rebel yet. He messed with the writer a long time, and I became quite intimate with him, and our undying friendship still lasts.

(61) Latham, L. W. [Leonidas]: He died since the war. He was a quiet man but always ready to obey orders.

(62) Legon, Ben D. [Ligon, Benjamin D.]: He died since the war. He was plumb full of fun, he did not care what come or went. He was bound to have his fun, and something in his haversack. All the boys loved him. If they grew despondent or hungry, they hunted up Ben. A comrade told me Ben was wounded at Five Forks. He said he done some tall cussing, he cursed the whole Yankee nation, from Abraham Lincoln down to a wagon driver. He was full of wit and humor and loved his "Toddy."

(63) Lowry, David: He is alive. He was another boy soldier. David was true till the end. He had been detailed a few months before the surrender to carry the battle flag. 'When he learned that General Lee had surrendered, he tore the colors from the staff and concealed them and brought them home.' Has them in his possesion now.[20] David was the true blue, even if he is small in statue. He carried the colors from November 22, 1864 till the end.

(64) Lewark, D. K. H. [David]: He is now dead, a victim of strong drink. He did not join the company until late in the war, sometime in 1864.

(65) Littleford, John [H.] and Willis [L.]: They are entirely lost sight of. They were transferred from 4th Tennessee with Cubine. They are Tennessee natives. They were good soldiers.

(66) Meek, James R.: He is alive. He was quite young when he came to the company. He was a good soldier.

(67) Montgomery, Lilburn [B.]: He is alive. He was a good, jovial, companionable man.

(68) Morrison, John L. [Jonathan Logan]: He is alive so far as I know. He moved to Lee County, Virginia, soon after the close of the war. 'Johnnie' was another favorite with the company. He was always full of life and vim. I am informed he went from Lee County to South America.

(69) McNew, George [W.]: He was alive at last reports. His home is in Mo. He was quite a boy. When he joined our company, like all the young soldiers, he was always ready to obey orders.

(70) McChesney, Wallace [Thomas Wallace]: I learned recently that he died at Hanover Junction in 1864 of camp fever. He was a noble true man.

Colley with the battle flag Lowry carried home. Courtesy of the American Civil War Museum, Richmond, Virginia.

(71) Meadows, M. T. [Miles H.]: ——————————— [Colley obviously had no information on Meadows.][21]

(72) McConnell, Thomas [Jefferson]: Another boy soldier. He was killed at Brandy Station in 1864. Did not get to serve but a short time after enlistment.

(73) Munday, J. W.: He was a native of Greenwell County.[22] He was a good soldier. Now dead.

(74) Murray, J. H. [John Harvey]: He is alive in Crockett, in Wythe County, Virginia.

(75) McCall, Samuel: He is alive. He was another boy soldier, he was always on his place.

(76) Mead, William [William Henry "Harry"]: He was killed in 1863 in the Valley of Virginia. He was with Col. Wm. Jones. He was a great favorite of General Jones. I think he must have been the youngest soldier in our

company. He ran off from his mother. In 1861, when our company was on a scout somewhere near Georgetown, D.C., Captain Jones tried to get him to return but he refused to do so. He was bent on being a soldier. Captain Jones used him as a spy or scout. He dressed him like a barefooted country boy, with eggs and chickens, and sent him inside the Yankee lines to see what he could learn. Nothing pleased him better than a fight. He was a bright intelligent boy. I loved him as dear as if he had been my brother. He was as calm and deliberate as if he had been out to the playground, under the most murderous fire of shot and shells.

(77)   Page, James H. [Henry]: Died since the war. He was a brother of R. M. Page. He was a reckless cavalryman. The most that distressed him—his rations were too short to meet the demands of his appetite.

(78)   Page, John W.: No record after transfer from 4th Tennessee with Cubine.

(79)   Page, Robert: No record after transfer from 4th Tennessee with Cubine.

(80)   Painter, Wm. M. [William]: He died of Camp Fever in 1863. He was a brave boy. The boys put up a job on him soon after he came to the company. He was gracefully insulted by a member of the ambulance train, and they told him he must challenge him to mortal combat. The other fellow was let in on the secret, that the pistols were to be loaded with blank cartridges. The boys said he stood the test as firm as a rock. It gave him a great lift with the whole company. He was a first cousin of mine. He died, soon after I was wounded at Kelly's Ford in 1863.

(81)   Pendleton, H. G. [Hiram]: He was killed in the Wilderness fight on May 7 1864. He was as calm and deliberate as if death was nowhere near. He was from Wythe County, Virginia.

(82)   Pendleton, Joseph [H.]: He was killed at Shepherdstown in July 1863, on return from Gettysburg. He and W. W. Morrell was both buried in the same grave. They were the only two companions near me when I was shot through the body at Kelly's Ford. There never was a truer man, living or dead, than Joe Pendleton. He was a native of Wythe County, Virginia.

(83)   Preston, R. B. [Reuben]: He was always ready for duty and is now a good citizen. He is alive; he was another boy soldier.

(84)   Preston, Thomas [M.]: He is alive. He was a brother of R. B.; still younger than him. He did not get in until near the close of the struggle.

(85)   Roe, Newton Edward: He was killed at Haw's Shop May 28, 1864; he and I went from home together. He was just transferred from the 37th Infantry. He was a good companion. From our short acquaintance, I thought a great deal of him. He had been wounded and disabled for infantry duty.

(86)   Roe, S. E. [S. J.]: Do not know anything about him.

(87)   Ritchie, James L. [Lafayette]: He is alive. He was a noble, true soldier, full of life and fun. He is a good man, raised a large family of some 13 children, and is a church worker. Now dead 1914. [Another postscript from Colley.]

(88)   Rosenbalm, A. D. [Andrew]: He died since the war. He was a good all-around soldier and a good citizen. Peace to his ashes.

(89)   Roe, W. M. [William]: Mike Ireson does not know anything about him.[23]

(90)   Ryburn, David [Beattie]: He was killed at Union in Loudon County in 1862. He was a noble, free hearted, brave young man. He was greatly beloved by all the company. He came to the company in April 1862. Ben Gildersleeve was detailed to bury him when he died.

(91)   Roe, Newton Edward: He was killed at Haw's Shop May 28, 1864. He and I went from home together. He was just transferred from the 37th Infantry. He was a good companion. From our short acquaintance, I thought a great deal of him. He had been wounded and disabled for infantry duty.[Colley repeated his entry for Roe.]

(92)   Richards, John B.: He is yet alive. He is, and has been all his life, a weakly man in subject to hemorrhages of the lungs. He was a mere boy when he came to the company in 1863. Now dead, 1912. [Another postscript from Colley.]

(93)   Sanders, S. D. [Stephen Drake]: Alive. He was a good true soldier. He was one of the 6 that went to the fence with me at Haw's Shop May the 28th. Like myself, he has been a failure financially. May the Good Lord Bless him in his latter days, and may he go down to the grave and rest in peace. Died 1913. [Another postscript from Colley.]

(94)   Swartz, Jacob J. [Schwartz, John Jacob]: He is now dead. He professed Christ before his departure and died in the full triumphs of a living faith. He was a German, and had not been in the U.S. six months when he substituted for J. A. Gollehon. 'Jake' was twice wounded and once a prisoner at Fort Delaware. The boys all loved him. He was a natural born soldier, at home in camp, on the march, or in the line of duty[.] Wounded the 7th of May 1864 at Gettysburg, Pennsylvania.[24]

(95)   Smith, John L.: He is alive. He joined the company in 1862. John was a good soldier, a good Christian man.

(96)   Strother, W. Trigg [William]: He is yet alive; he was another boy soldier. There is no one I had rather have for a backer in a tight place. 'Old Trigg' always stuck. He lost an arm in the Great Negro Riot in New Orleans in 1869 [1866].[25] He was a good one.

(97)   Trigg, Thomas K. [King]: He is alive. He has been adjutant of Wm. E. Jones Camp since its organization 1893. He was another 37th Virginia boy. He tried the Jackson foot cavalry for some two years, and then got a transfer to the horse cavalry because of a lame leg. After a long spell of sickness, he said he did not find a soft 'place' in Old Company D's Sharpshooters, Yankee spurs. [The meaning of Yankee spurs in this sentence remains unclear.] He died of heart failure Nov. 3, 1915, at his home in Abingdon, Va. [Another postscript from Colley.]

(98)   Trigg, Conley F. [Connally Findlay]: He is alive now. He says he was the baby recruit of Company D. He is quite enthusiastic on the war theme yet. He gave old D. a reunion at his home some years ago. His home, for some time, has been in Washington, D.C. He is attorney for Wm. Trigg Shipbuilding Co.

(99)   White, Wm. [William]: He is alive and a successful practicing physcian. He is another 37th Infantryman that tried the foot cavalry some two years and then got a transfer to the regular horse cavalry. [Colley seems to have added the following after the doctor passed.] Dr. White, Wm. died Oct 1904, he was kind to the poor. His office was always crowded with poor people. He gave them medicine and good advice. He was a true friend and a bitter enemy. He was a man of his own convictions and stood square to them.

(100)   White, John G. [Greenway]: He is alive. He is quite an enthusiast on the war question. He was just in the rear of me at Haw's Shop when I was wounded in the foot, when I got up and tried to walk and fell. He and H. C. Butt ran to me and helped to carry me from the field.

(101)   Webb, A. H. [Augustus]: He is alive. He was wounded severely on the Rappahannock in Aug 1862, came near losing his arm; he did not return to the company. Afterwards, I learned he deserted and went to the enemy. A. H. Webb is now drawing a pension from the U.S. Government, 1913.

(102)   Wright, T. D. [Thomas]: This name is transferred to original company roll by advice of Sergeant M. Ireson.

(103)   Wampler, E. W. [Edward]: He is alive. His home is in Wythe County, Virginia. He was a good soldier.

In addition to the names already stated I find from a roster published in an 'Extra' of the *Abingdon Democrat* of Friday April the 26th 1861, the day Miss Lizzie Harden, a teacher at Martha Washington College, presented a flag to our company. It was a beautiful silk banner. It was left in Richmond, Virginia, with other useless luggage, and destroyed by fire in the city armory.

The Names are as follows:

1)   Dickerson, J. W. P

2)   Mchaffey, F. C.

3)   Grant, J. T. [James Taliaferro]

4) Cato, J. L.
5) Skinner, Danl.
6) Beattie, R. L.
7) Johnson, J. H.
8) Dorsey, Elias
9) Bowers, J. B.
10) Hunt, Stephen
11) Clark, Thomas W.

The last name was discharged by request of his father, on the account of his sleeping disease. The others all went off with other regiments. Some of them were students from Emory & Henry College, and were so afraid that Captain Jones would not get there until the war ended. They rushed off with the 1st company or regiment that passed our place, but there are none of us today but what are satisfied we got there soon enough to take an active part in the melee. Our zeal for Southern Rights had ample time to call before the end came.

1916 Feby 22nd

A Roster of Co "D. 1st Va Cavelry
Army of Northern Virginia
Corrected and revised by "
M S Freson Orderly Sergent 1863
Thos. W Colley 1st Corporal 1863
A. F. Rambo Private one of the origina
David Lowery Color Bearer Battle Flag
L. D. Asbury Private Recruit 1862
L J Cosby " " 1863.
Thos "K" Trigg Private Transfer from 3
Va Infantry 2 Brigad Stonewall Division
after some 25 years of search and
Consultation with different "parties we
Composed this Company" I have honest
tried to give a sketch; of the record
of Each member of this famous Comp
any whose deeds of "Valor" are matter
of History in inseperable connexion
with the achievements accomplished by
the Cavalry; of the Army of Northern V
from 1861 to 5

Thos W Colley
Late Corporal Co D. 1st Va Cavalry

Page from Colley's Roster. Private Collection.

APPENDIX 2

Regimental History and Biographical Roster Sketch Written as a Separate Journal

1916 Feby 22nd

A roster of Company D. 1st Va Cavalry Army of Northern Virginia, corrected and revised by M. S. Ireson, Orderly Sergeant 1863; Thos. W. Colley 1st Corporal 1865; A. F. Rambo, private, one of the original; David Lowry, color bearer, battle flag; L. D. Asbury, private recruit, 1862; L. T. Cosby, private recruit, 1863; and Thos K. Trigg, private transfer from 37 Va Infantry, 2 Brigade, Stonewall Division.

After some 25 years of search and consultation with different 'parties who composed this company,' I have honestly tried to give a sketch of the record of each member of this famous company, whose deeds of 'Valor' are matters of history, in inseparable commission with the achievements accomplished by the cavalry of the Army of Northern Va., from 1861 to 65.

> Thos W. Colley
> Late Corporal, Co. D., 1st Va Cavalry

This company was organized in the town of Abingdon in April 1861, by Capt. Wm. E. Jones, and thoroughly drilled—mounted and dismounted—as skirmishers & sharpshooters. This company was named the 'Washington Mounted Rifles' in 'honor' of the company he [Jones] held commission in as 1st Lieutenant in the U.S. Army up to 1855, when he resigned & visited several of the European Nations. This company was composed of men of the best and most influential families in the town and county.

This company was perfectly drilled in all the maneuvers known to the science of war, as set forth in *Hardees Tactics*.[1] We left the town of Abingdon the last of May, and arrived in the City of Richmond about the 1st of June, & was sent to camp in what was known as the 'New' Fair Grounds, some two miles west of the city, where we were armed with Sharps Rifles [they actually received carbines], sabers,

and was tendered a uniform made of 'coarse gray cloth,' said to have been man-
ufactured in the state prison, which the proud mountaineers refused to accept,
until forced to do so by the positive command of their leader, who stood fearless and undaunted in the presence of 'about' 95 angry resolute men. His coolness
and undaunted courage, as he stood, pistol in hand and ordered James King O.S.
[orderly sergeant] to call the roll, & said the first man who refuses to take up his
uniform when his name is called I will shoot him down. When the last name was
called, the stack of uniforms was gone; quiet prevailed. Most of the men threw
them away, preferring their old jeans and hunting shirts that they were uniformed
with at home.[2]

There was never in the annals of history a more brave, determined body of men,
banded together to defend a cause which every soul from captain down to the lowest private believed to be a just cause. After a week or ten days spent in our camp
at this place, we were sent to Ashland, the cavalry camp of instruction.[3] Here, on
the race track, we were drilled in saber exercise and target practice. After a few
days spent at this place, we were ordered to the 'Valley' of Virginia, at Winchester,
where General Joseph E. Johnston was in command.

We were assigned to the 1st Regiment of Virginia Cavalry, designated as Co.
L which letter it retained until April 1862, when it was changed to 'D,' and was
known as Company D until the 'End April 9, 1865.' History gives an account of the
heroic deeds of valor performed by its dauntless body of men, with its commanders J. E. B. Stuart, the 1st colonel; then Wm. E. Jones, the second colonel; and then
the generous & kind-hearted Fitzhugh Lee; then Wickham; Drake; Carter, who
was detested, and finally removed or cashiered; and W. A. Morgan, as noble and
brave and generous a soul as ever drew sword in just cause. They have all crossed
the river & are resting under the shade of the trees.

Wm. E. Jones, Captain, was promoted to Colonel of the 1st Regiment Va. Cavalry
in the fall of 1861, and continued in that capacity until 1862, at which time he was
sent to the 'Valley' to take command of the 7th regiment of Va Cavalry; 'Colonel'
Ashby's [Turner Ashby] old command. In the Winter of 62–3, he was promoted
to brigader general, and commanded a brigade of cavalry in the Army of Northern
Virginia. In June of 1863, his untiring vigilance and forethought saved the surprise
and utter rout of the cavalry 'corps' at Brandy Station. There was a jealousy or an
ill feeling that existed between him and General Stuart. In October 1863, he was
removed from command in the East and assigned to command of all the forces in
South West Virginia and 'East Tennessee,' where he had ample power to display
his wonderful genius as a cavalry commander. He did the enemy more damage in
the few months in this department than all the officers that preceded him in the
previous 2 years.

About the last of May or the 1st June 1864, the notorious General Hunter [Major General David Hunter] was moving up the Valley of Virginia with a band of vandals burning and destroying mills, barns, and dwelling houses, driving off and destroying stock of all kinds. General Jones was ordered to Staunton with all available forces to meet this force. He arrived at Stanton on the night of the 4th of June, and moved out towards Mt. Crawford and across to New Hope or Piedmont. He scarcely had time to form his lines before he was attacked. I am informed by Gen Imboden [Brigadier General John Daniel Imboden] and W. M. Hopkins, his adjutant general, that Hunter was whipped & had began to move his ambulances & wagon trains back down the Valley. At that critical moment, one of Jones's regiments at the ford of the river gave way, and he rushed down to rally them when he was shot and fell from his horse dead; all became confusion and rout. The master spirit, the commanding voice, and fearless body, which was always in front in the hottest part of the conflict, lay stark and cold in the agonies of death and in the hands of his victorious enemy. But the unconquerable spirit had taken its flight back to the God who gave it. This battle was fought on the 5th of June 1864. Jones was a strict discipline man; when off duty, he was a kind generous hearted man and looked after the welfare and comfort of his men.

First Lieutenant W. W. Blackford, he is now dead, died at Lin Haven, his house. He was educated as a civil engineer. He was a fine horseman and an expert with the 'saber.' I had my first lessons from him in saber drill. He was a brave, high toned 'gentleman.' I was very much attached to him. He was defeated for captain of the company at the reorganization in April 1862. He served on General Stuart's staff for a short time, and was assigned to the Engineer Corps with the rank of 'Lieutenant Colonel.' I had neglected to state that he was captain of the company, by serving after Captain Jones was promoted to colonel in 1861, and he served as such until April 1862.

Second Lieutenant Rees B. Edmondson, 'Rees,' as the men usually called him. When on duty in camp he was a brave, generous hearted, whole souled, companionable man. He studied law after the war and was at one time Commonwealths Attorney of Washington County. He finally settled in the City of Washington, D.C., and died there Feby 13, 1901. He became first lieutenant at the reorganization in March 1862, and held that rank until the end; wounded 2 times.

George V. Litchfield, third lieutenant until the reorganization in 1862, when he was elected second lieutenant, and remained in that rank until the close of the war. In camp, the boys called him 'Vick.' He was a jovial, good hearted, kind man, always ready to divide rations with a hungry comrade and always at the post of duty. Was twice wounded, survived the war and died at his home in the Town of Abingdon in October 1904. [October 28, 1903]

M. S. Ireson informed me that Warren M. Hopkins was elected first lieutenant at the reorganization in 1862, but never served as such. Colonel Jones took him with him when he was sent to the Valley, he afterwards became General Jones's 'Adjutant General,' and remained with him until Jones was killed. He was made colonel of the 25th Virginia Cavalry and served as such until the close of the struggle. He was 'color bearer' of the company flag presented to us by Miss Lizzie Harden in 1861, until it was left in the City of Richmond with our shot guns and squirrel rifles that we started from home with. The building was burnt & all was lost. 'Warren' was a true brave man, he had a kind affectionate disposition, he abhorred any thing like vulgarity. He would blush like a 16 year 'Old Maiden.' He was void of fear, he lived through the horrid struggle and died at his home near Abingdon in 1877.[4]

James King was appointed orderly sergeant by Captain Jones at the 1st organization of the company. He was a native man, was a graduate of West Point, and had seen service on the frontier. He was a noble, kind-hearted, brave, determined soldier, a lover of the Southern Cause. He became offended when Captain Jones was promoted to colonel, and left the company, and joined the 37th Va Infantry. He was killed in the Battle of Kernstown in 1862.

Connely T. [Connally Trigg] Litchfield. Appointed 2nd sergeant in 1861, and was orderly sergeant after James King transferred to the 37th Va Infantry, and served as such until he was elected captain in March 1862, when the company was reorganized. He served in that capacity until the close of the war. He was severely wounded thrice, one wound was in the face just under the cheek bone, by a pistol ball. It remained somewhere in his head for 34 years & caused him excruciating pain at times. To get relief, he used injections of morphine, which made him deathly sick and caused vomiting. On one of these awful wretching spells, the bullet dropped out in the basin at the side of his bed. He was wounded on two other occasions. He was a kind, intelligent officer. When off duty, he was 'Con' or 'Cap,' and engaged in the sport or fun as one of the boys. He won and retained the confidence of his men. A noble, whole souled man, he lived to a good old age; died at his home in Abingdon, Va Aug 6 [5], 1909.

Thos B. Edmonsdon: appointed 3d sergeant in 1861, & became 2nd sergeant by line of promotion. He was elected 3rd lieutenant at the reorganization in 1862. He was a whole souled, rather reckless, brave, and daring soldier, kind and generous to all with whom he came in contact. He was greatly beloved and lamented by his comrades; he was killed by a Yankee sharpshooter at Spotsylvania C.H. in May 1863.[5] He had rushed forward in advance of the company, ordering a charge on the enemy line of sharpshooters, when he was shot and instantly killed.

James M. Byars was appointed 4th sergeant in 1861, and served as such until 1862. He was discharged on the account of ill health and being over 40 years of age. He was a quiet, kind hearted man and a good soldier. He died some years after the close of the war at his home south of Glade Spring. It was my pleasure to visit him and share his genial hospitality on several occasions.

James K. Rambo was appointed 1st corporal in 1861; he was promoted to captain and quartermaster under W. E. Jones; he was finally transferred to Captain Jno. W. Barrs Battery. He died in 1902.

Dr. John A. P. Baker was appointed 2nd corporal in 1861. He did not come up to Captain Jones's idea of a non-commissioned officer, and he removed him. He was finally removed to the surgical department, and was assistant surgeon of our regiment at the close of the war. He died in 1898.

Dr. Gilbert C. Greenway was appointed 3rd corporal in 1861, and served as such until Captain Jones was promoted to colonel. He and James King, who was our 1st orderly sergeant, became offended on the account of the promotion of Lieutenant Blackford to the captaincy. They both left the company; Gilbert went to Beckley's Battalion[6] & afterwards to the 57th Va Infantry, of which he was adjutant. He was a brave, whole souled, generous hearted, man, a fine soldier. He died at the hot springs in Ark.

Jacob L. Fields was appointed corporal in 1861 in lieu of Dr. Baker's removal. He was a good quiet man, always at the post of duty. He died in 1862. [1863]

P. C. Landrum was appointed orderly sergeant in 1862 under Captain Litchfield. 'Paul' was a fine shot with a pistol, and had a hand to hand encounter with a Yankee lieutenant and two privates; he with his pistol, and they with sabers bucking at him. He killed the officer & wounded one of the others; the third one fled. He received a slight saber cut across his right thumb in paring the saber cuts. He was a truley brave, cool, deliberate soldier; he received a severe wound at the Battle of Gettysburg, Pa., in July 1863, from which he did not recover until after the close of the war. He was mayor of the Town of Saltville & also was mayor of the Town of Abingdon. He was a terror to evil doers; he was converted after the war, and joined the M.E. Church South. He was a steady and true soldier of the cross. Under the banner of King Emmanuel, he died in the faith.

M. M. S. Ireson was appointed bugler by Colonel Jones and acted as such until 1862, when he was made 2nd sergeant after Paul Landrum was wounded. He became orderly sergeant and was acting in that capacity to the end of the war. He was in command of the remnant of the company at Appomatox, April the 9th 1865. Mike was as true as steel, a level headed, cool, deliberate soldier; he was placed in more dangerous places than any other man in the company. Through the mercies of God, he was never touched by a bullet. He was a noble Christian man for a number of years before he was called from earth. He died at his home in Tazewell Co., Va., on the 25 [18] of June 1915.

P. C. Miles a native of Jonesville, Lee County, Va., was 3d sergeant at the time of his death, which occured at the Battle of Spotsylvania C.H. May 1864.[7] Pat was a noble, brave, generous hearted man. He and Thos B. Edmondson were congenial spirits. They both sacrificed their lives on the alter of their country in the same day.

Charles H. Dulaney volunteered in the company at its organization in 1861. He was a native of Madison County, Va. He was only 16 years old at the time he was appointed 3d sergeant by Captain Litchfield in 1864, and served as such until the end. He was severely wounded at Spotsylvania C.H. May 1864. Charles was a good, steady soldier. He became a wanderer after the war, and has been an inmate of the Soldiers Home at Richmond for several years.

David A. Fields won the corporal's chevrons in 1864. He was 1st corporal at the death of Pat Miles, and he was advanced to 4th sergeant. David was a fine, jovial, companionable man; seldom down hearted, full of life, fun, and fight. During the raid in Stafford County, on the advanced picket line of Joe Hooker in February 1863, they gave us all the horses each soldier could capture. David and I came back to camp with five head with their equipments. I had to my credit a horse & equipments of a Yankee colonel. A fine bay, I sold him to Lieutenant Edmondson for $400.00. David died in Texas about 1873.

Thos W. Colley was appointed corporal in May 1864. He had just recovered from his second wound; he was shot through the body on the left side—about two inches from the center of his stomach—and left on the field for dead by his comrades. This occurred at the cavalry Battle of Kelly's Ford, 17th March 1863. He served some six months at the post quartermaster's department at Gordonsville, then returned to his company for duty on the 22nd of May 1864, and was on the firing line every day until the 28th day of May, when he was wounded at the Battle of 'Haw's Shop,' and lost his left foot by amputation. By the blessings of God, he still lives to pen these lines in memory of self and comrades; in his 79th year.

C. M. Walden was appointed corporal at some period in 1864. He was a native of Campbell County, Va. He is highly spoken of by Captain Litchfield & the members of the company as a fine soldier. I have never been able to locate him since the close of the war. In 1914, he was alive in Texas.

Samuel J. McChesney was appointed ordnance sergeant for the regiment and served as such until he was wounded in 1863, and lost part of his hand. He was a young doctor, and a clever, whole souled gentleman. He practiced his profession for several years after the war closed, and was deputy treasurer of the county one term. He died some years ago [November 20, 1895]. He was an elder in the Presbyterian Church.

Benjamine Gildersleve [Benjamin Gildersleeve] succeeded McChesney as ordnance sergeant in 1863, and held that position until the end of the war. He was a well-educated man, and a kind, tenderhearted, obliging comrade. He is a strict Presbyterian, is now alive but quite feeble in his years. He was deputy clerk in the U.S. Court at Abingdon for several years.

Privates who volunteered in the original Company in 1861:

Robert F. Beattie: he was a pretty good all-around soldier; he was pretty severely wounded in 1864, he made a lot of fun for the boys by his droll sayings.

Dr. Walter Beattie was a sociable, kind young man; was stricken with camp fever and died in 1861.

Fountain Beattie, he was a kind hearted, jovial young soldier, he was transferred to Mosby's Battalion and was commissioned lieutenant & served with that command until the end.

Thomas W. Bailey, he was a fine soldier always full of life and fun, ready for a fight or frolic. His desire for teasing and fun caused his death. The company came home in the winter of 1863. The day they left for the front, he ran across one Tom Palmer, a member of the home guard, & commenced teasing him and carried his fun to far. He had unhorsed Palmer, when Palmer raised his gun and shot him in the stomach. He died from the effects in a few hours, 1863. [March 15, 1864][8]

Oscar S. Bailey he was quite a young boy when he volunteered in 1861; he was a brave, fearless boy. He was severely wounded in 1863. His home is in Mo.

James A. Bailey Jr[.] he was quite a good all-round soldier.

Joseph H. Baker he made a fine soldier after the first shock. He was killed at Spotsylvania Ch May 7, 1864[.][9] He had endeared himself to his comrades; his death was sadly lamented.

John W. Butt was a fine soldier, a genial, whole souled fellow. He was orderly sergeant; he was killed by a fall from his horse in 1863 [1864] whilst the company was at home.[10]

Randolph Buchanan, he was a fine soldier, rather droll and full of fun & life. He went to Texas after the war and died there.

W. D. Barker: he was a fearless, reckless soldier. One of Stuart's staff rode down to our skirmish line and ordered 'Billy' to press the enemy. Billy tendered his carbine to him & invited him to get down and try it, as he was not a good hand. About that time, a shower of bullets came from the opposite side. The young man [staff officer] put spurs to his horse & left Billy in a rush for the rear. Billy was calling to him to come back and press them. Billy was transferrd to the 63rd Virginia

Regiment & made ordnance sergeant. He was captured in the Georgia Campaign [Atlanta Campaign], and served a term at Camp Douglas in Chicago, Ill. He went to Georgia, and remained there & made his home at Rutledge. His eye sight had failed him. He was in Atlanta & fell down an elevator shaft & killed himself in 1912.

Alexander Buskle [Buskell] was a good quiet man, a fine soldier, always in line.

Richard/Richland Buskle [Buskell] was a fine soldier, he was transferd to Pelham's Horse Artillery. He was killed at the Battle of Fredericksburg in 1862.[11]

David Barr, he was quite a youth in 1861. He was transferred from our company and served in his brother's battery to the end. He is now a minister in the Episcopal Church, Washington, D.C.

A. P. R. Catron, he was a fine young man, modest and quite a good soldier. He attended school at Emory & Henry College and graduated in 1872; he was preparing for the ministry. He fell a victim to that dread disease, consumption, and died in 1872. [1871]

William Riley Clark, a fine young man was shot whilst on picket post. His arm was shattered so badly it required amputation, from the effect of which he died in a hospital at Culpeper C.H., Oct [November] 19 1861.

William F. P. Clark, a noble, generous, brave young man; would have made a fine soldier or citizen. He was accidentally shot by the discharge of a double barreld shot gun, in the hand of a comrade of another company; from the effects of which he died on the 1st [2] day of Nov 1861.

Thomas V. Cole he was one of the rollicking, whole souled fellows, a fine soldier; moved to Missouri. He was wounded and taken prisoner at Gettysburg & held to the close of the war. He died in his adopted state.

David C. Cole, he was quite a young boy, frail and delicate looking, but the out door and rough life of a soldier soon brought new life and vigor to his frail body. He was a splendid soldier. He went to Colorado after the war closed & was killed by a premature explosion of a dynamite blast.

Rufus R. Cassell: he was a young timid boy; he was severly wounded at Union in Loudon County, Nov 1862. After his recovery, he was transferred to the 51st Va Infantry; was captured at Waynesboro & kept a prisoner until June 1865. Died at his Home in Smyth County, Virginia, July 31, 1911. A member of the Missionary Baptist Church. His wife died 12 days later.

Thomas L. Colley. 'Trit' was a good average soldier was quite droll and caused a lot of fun. He moved to Mo and died there in 1875.

Ben C. Crawford, he was a good soldier, a lively, wide awake, companionable man. He went to Texas. He was a Dentist and settled at Georgetown, where he died March 26, 1903. He was a member of the M.E. Church South.

Thos C. Crawford, he was a brave, rollicking, good hearted fellow ready for fight or fun. He was severly wounded in 1863; he stuck to the bitter end. He went to Texas and died there.

J. Frank Cook was quite a boy, in his teens. He was a fine soldier and a good provider. He died in California about 1903.

Andrew M. Crockett, a native of Lee County, Va., he was a noble, zealous defender of Southern rights. He died in Corsicana, Texas, where he located after the war.

John G. R. Davis, he was a fine, steady, true soldier; he loved the Southern cause. He was transferred to Captain Fred Gray's Company, which was in the 21st Va. Cavalry. He was 1st lieut; deceased, January 1905.

Dr. William L. Dunn, he was a noble, true man; he was a true soldier as well as a fine surgeon. He was soon taken from the ranks and placed in Officers' General Hospital No. 5 in City of Richmond. He was later surgeon of Mosby's Battalion, where he served until 1865.

John B. Deyerle: he was a great big, over grown 200-pounder. He was a native of Roanoke Co., Va. Poor fellow, he could not stand the sound of the bullets. He was a fine soldier on parade. I have no knowledge of what became of him.

M. V. Edmondson, 'Van' was a good, genial fellow; he tried to do his part as a soldier, he finally drifted away to 'King's Battery.'

Frank Enk: he was a young French man General Jones brought from France in 1857 to work in his vineyard. He was discharged, being a foreigner and not liable to military duty. I am unable to say where he drifted to or what became of him.

Frank S. Findlay, he was detailed from the company & served on General Stuart's staff until he was wounded in 1862. On his recovery, he raised a company and was commissioned captain, where he served until the close of the war. He died at his home in Abingdon, Va., on the [sentence ends].[12]

Charles B. Fields, he was quite a young man and a fine soldier; he was one of my original messmates, always ready to do his part. He moved to California and settled at Yuba City. He was severely wounded in 1864. I am just informed of his death, which ocured on the 22 February 1916. He was as dear to me as a brother; he was 74 years of age.

Frank R. Fulkerson, he was from Rogersville, Tenn. He was a noble, whole souled, generous hearted, patriotic gentleman—a fearless fighter. He suffered with asthma or bronchitis. I have known his messmate, John Russell, to work with him night after night to keep breath in him. He was advised by the physicians, that he must abandon army life or die. That did not have any weight with him. I am not advised of his whereabouts.

Frederick T. Gray, he was of the mature men who volunteered in 1861. 'Uncle Fred,' as the boys called him, was a kind, affable man, always ready to sympathize with the boys and give them advice. He was one of the trusted men who had the confidence of his superiors. He was discharged in March 1862, being over 40 years of age. He raised a company in 1863 of which he was elected captain. His company was attached to the 22nd cavalry & served to the close of the war. He has been dead several years; a good man & true.[13]

Robert E. Gray: he was a man grown when he volunteered in 1861. 'En' was a shifty soldier, he was captured and taken to Point Lookout. He, in company with two other comrades, made their escape by 'swiming out in the bay.' After many narrow escapes from capture, they made their way back to Confederate lines. He died in 1901 [1902] at his house in the county.

David C. Gray: he was quite young when he entered the service in 1861. He was a tolerable good soldier. He had the knack of getting into some ludicrous scrape. He was placed at a spring to keep the men from riding their horses in to the head of the spring, where we had to get water for drinking & cooking purposes. He was sitting down on post, which was considered a breach of discipline. General Stuart came by & asked him what he was doing there. He replied by stating he was on guard there. The general commanded him, in his short curt language, to get up and walk his beat. David was grossly insulted, and came to the company highly indignant and swore he would resign and go home. That raised a laugh, the idea of a private resigning. [Officers could resign their commissions, enlisted men could not.]

J. A. Gollehon: he had no fancy for war. He was courier for General Stuart for a while. He furnished a substitute and came home in 1862. He lived to a few years ago [December 24, 1907], when he was burned to death in his house in Smyth County, Va.

Melvin Gammon, a native of Tennessee, he accidently shot him self through the hand and obtained a discharge in 1862. The last I heard of him, he was in Rome, Georgia, running a clothing store. I had these facts from Wm. D. Barker.

John Hockett was a truly loyal soldier, always in place. He told me he was detailed as courier to General Stuart and was with him in the Wilderness fight the day after General Jackson was wounded. He said the general was singing a little ditty to 'Old Joe Hooker to come out of the Wilderness.' He married and moved to Texas, where he died in January 1905. He was a Christian.

William Hockett, 'Laughing Bill.' He would see something in the hottest place in battle to cause him to laugh. He was a good all-around soldier. He is alive at this date; he was wounded twice.

Thomas Hubble, he was a Smyth County, Va., man, a quiet fellow. He was stricken with Typhoid Fever in the fall of 1861. He was discharged and drifted away. I had a communication from him a few years ago; he was at Kingston, Tenn. He was urging me to vouch for him so he could obtain a pension. I wrote and asked him to tell me where he was from 1861 to 65. He failed to do so & that ended our correspondence.

Jasper Jones, he was a native man in 1861, a cousin of General Jones, and he had been out on the Texas frontier. He was a fine, deliberate soldier, a true Southerner. He was one of the first men transferred to Colonel Mosby's Rangers & stayed with him until the close of the war. He was twice wounded in hand to hand encounters with the enemy. He was one that made name and fame for Colonel Mosby. He drifted away to South America after the war, where he was drowned in attempting to swim a river with his pack mules.

Henry S. Jones, he was quite a young boy in 1861. He was first cousin to General Jones and Jasper. He was a noble, true hearted boy, always full of fun. He was a fine soldier. He was severely wounded in 1863 but recovered and went back and served to the end. He married Miss Nannie Crow & moved to the west. He died at his home in Grange County, Idaho, July 27, 1900.

John Larimore, he was a great, gaudy, country boy; he was always in a good humor. He was detailed to drive the ordnance wagon. He was always ready for duty, in ranks or on detail. He moved to Missouri after the war; have not heard from him for some 2 years.

David Lynch, he was at the Virginia Military Institute when the war broke out in 1861. He was one of our drill masters; he was a noble, kind hearted young man. He did not live to prove his soldierly qualities. He died of fever early in 1862.[14]

John H. Loggins, he was driven from the company the morning after we camped at Fort Chiswell, Va. He told Miss McGavock a lie to get a bottle of wine. Captain Jones made him leave the company; he went and joined the 37th Regiment.

Stephen D. Meek, Steve was a jovial good-hearted fellow, always full of fun. He was badly ruptured and discharged in 1862. He moved to Texas and died there several years ago. [December 2, 1892]

William F. Montgomery: William was as tough and hard as a pine knot, a splendid soldier, nothing daunted him. He was severely wounded, was true to the end. I visited him a short time before he died. He had been converted a short time before his death. He told me the way was clean.

William W. Morell, a fine specimen of a Confederate soldier. He was my cousin and boon companion. No braver or generous hearted man ever drew breath than he. I have known him on various ocassions to stint himself and give his rations to a more greedy comrade. He was the last man to leave me when I was shot through the body & left on the field at Kelly's Ford, and the 1st to find me when the enemy was driven back. He was killed near Shepherdstown [Kearneysville] Va., July [16] 1863. He was loved and mourned by all.

David H. Morell, he was a mature man in 1861, he was a true man, was wounded at Slatersville below Richmond, by a blow from a saber cut. He was discharged on the account of being over 40 years of age. When the news reached him of the Burbridge raid on Saltville, he shouldered his gun and went to meet them. He was shot and killed in the forefront in Governor Sanders's yard, Oct 1864.[15]

Charles Morell was a truly loyal soldier, a good all-around man. He had Typhoid fever in the fall of 1861, and had a close shave for life. He recovered and came back early in 1862. He was slightly wounded in the arm with a piece of shell, he was made prisoner in the fall of 1862; was exchanged and come back and stuck to the end. He died in 1899. [October 17, 1898].

Leander McNew, he was quite a young, gawky, droll country boy. He was a good average soldier, always in line. He moved to Missouri, where he died in November 1901.

Tobias S. McNew, he was quite a robust looking young man. In 1861 his health failed, and he was discharged in 1862. He was a fairly good soldier and a good sociable fellow. He possessed the elements of a soldier.

James M. McReynolds, he was never any good for a soldier. He drove an ambulance most of the time, and finally deserted and went to the woods.

Wm. McReynolds, he volunteered in the 1st Texas Regiment; he got a transfer to our company in June 1861. He was just the reverse of his brother, he neither found man nor devil, nothing delighted him more than a fight. He got a pass to go to Richmond in 1863 and got in a row some where & was killed, and his body carried out on the Richmond embankment and thrown into Bacon's Quarter Branch in the suburbs of the city. He was kind hearted and liberal with all his recklessness.

William A. Mahaffey was a young man when he volunteered in 1861. He was literally opposed to military restraint and discipline. Captain Jones had a lot of trouble with him; he was a reckless. He raised a row with David Morell in our first camp at Marion, Va., & some two miles east of Marion, he struck Rufus Cassell and Jones had him brought up to the head of the column, & dismounted him and made him walk; which was almost a daily thing with him. He was transferred to Pelham's Battery and served there a while, and finally deserted and hid out until the war closed. William was a dandy; he is now dead.

John S. Mosby, a young lawyer from the City of Bristol, volunteered in our company in 1861. He was a restless, daring man. General Stuart became attached to him and used him as a scout for some time. He finally raised a battalion of rangers & was commissioned major, and finally lieutenant colonel. He done the enemy a great deal of damage, and had a price set on his head. His operations were chiefly against their lines of communications. They would have hung him after the surender if 'General Grant' had not interfered with their aims. He has filled various government positions since the war. He is alive at this time, his home in Washington D.C. He is a vigorous writer.[16]

John Ornduff, he was a great big droll fellow, always in a good humor, it matters not what come or went. I never heard a murmur from him. The captain made him company quartermaster; he drew our corn and hay if we had any. He had a wonderful voice; I imagine I can hear it now, "Boys come and get your corn." He was a good man. He did not survive the close of the struggle very long, but died soon after we returned home. The boys all loved and teased him unmercifully at times. It never ruffled his kind feelings towards them. I hope his honest soul is at rest.

Moses C. Orr, he was a kind, generous young man. He was quite deaf, caused by a severe shock and hurt received in his boyhood. He was discharged on that account in 1862. I do not know what became of him. 1917, he is yet alive in Nebrasky. [Colley entered this Nebraska note at a later date.]

Ruben M. Page, he was quite a young, rosy cheeked boy, he was a good soldier. He was severly wounded in 1864 in the thigh, it gave him trouble and pain all his life. He read law after the war & was County Court Judge for some years. He was one of my original messmates. He died at his house in Abingdon, Va., 1914.

Morgan M. Pendleton, a native of Wythe County, Va., the boys called him 'dad.' He was a fearless man, not reckless. Nothing appeared to excite or disconcert him. He was one of the matchless sharpshooters of Co. D. He did not care anymore for shooting a man than he would to shoot a rabbit. He was appointed corporal & rose to 1st sergeant but could not fill the place being uneducated. He resigned and went back to ranks. Some years ago, he and his son in law—Waymon Suttan—was accused of killing a man in Wythe County, where he lived. Morgan left the county & went west, and I am informed that he was drowned in Snake River.

Dr. Wm. H. Price, he was a fine specimen of perfect manhood in 1861. William was a fine soldier, a genial companion, always ready for wrestle or fight, and always ready & willing to divide rations. He was converted after the war & became a Southern Methodist preacher. Colonel Jones took him to the Valley with him in 1862. He is alive.

John H. Roberts, he was a fine, robust young man when he volunteered in 1861. He was one of the victims of the dread disease Typhoid fever, which raged throughout the various camps in the fall of 1861.[17] He was a true man and had already shown his soldierly qualities. His dust rests in a soldier's grave at Manassas, Va.

Andrew F. Rambo, he was one of the enthusiastic boys, a pale consumptive looking fellow, droll and lively. The captain and his comrades had no idea from his physical condition, that he could bear the hardships of camp life. Captain Jones tried to persuade him to go home and remain with his mother. The trip to Richmond, on horse back in the hot June weather worsened him. Captain Jones had the doctors to examine him in the city. They beat and thumped him, he said, until he was so sore he could scarcely breathe & pronounced him unfit for service. The captain informed him of their decision & proposed to him to stay in the city and go to 'school,' stating he would pay his way. Andy said to him, "Captain them doctors don't know anything about me, I am all right, only a little worried. I volunteered to be a soldier, I am going to be a soldier. I couldn't learn any thing, and you all fighting around here." The captain said, "Damn you, do as you please." Camp life made a robust man of him. This is one example of the material of which Confederate soldiers were made of. And he is alive at this date, quite a dignified old man. He served one term in the state legislature. Droll and full of fun.

James S. Riddle, he came from Bristol, Va., he was quite a young, robust young man, he was one of those poor unfortunate fellows who could not stand the sound of the missiles of death. A good, clever, sociable fellow in camp. He died of brain fever at Fairfax C.H. The doctor said produced by fever in 1861.

Jerry C. Rush, he was a fine, robust young man when he volunteered in 1861. He was a good steady soldier, full of life and vim. One of the boys who took everything as it come in camp and on the firing line, always ready to divide rations and give cheese to the despondent, and sing 'there is a better day coming by and by.' He lived to help build up the waste places before he died.

John Russell, a native of Rodgersville, Tenn., a noble, whole souled, true, loyal soldier. He and Pat Fulkerson were messmates and inseparable companions. He was an ardent lover of the Southern Cause and laid down his life in its defense. He was killed in a skirmish in 1863, and was buried where he fell in Culpeper County, Va.[18]

Frank D. Robertson. Frank was a whole souled Southern man, and has never changed his sentiments. At one time, he was lieutenant of Company L, 48th Va Infantry. He was on 'General Stuart's' staff at the time of the 'General's wounding' and death at Yellow Tavern, May 10, 1864. He says he tried every branch of the service.

J. Alexander Rodefer: he was a fine, strong, vigorous young man when he volunteered in 1861. The cavalry service did not suit his ideas of war, especially the sharpshooting. He was transferred to the 45th Va Infantry in 1863, and finally wound up as clerk in the post quartermasters department. Now dead.

Robert J. Sanders: he was a long, lank, cadaverous looking man when he volunteered in 1861. He was not a coward by any means at Waterloo Bridge Aug 22, 1862. His clothes were pierced by several bullets. He was one of my original messmates. His health failed and the doctors said he would die with consumption. He was discharged in 1863. He lived for several years after the war closed, married, and raised a large family. He died several years ago.

John W. S. Sanders was a fine robust young man in 1861. He was a good, all around soldier, always ready for duty. He was quite severely wounded in 1862, recovered and returned to the company. He went to Colonel Mosby and was with him for a short time but came back to his original company and was wounded the second time on the 8th of May 1864, at Spotsylvania C.H. He was a freight conductor on the Norfolk & Western RR for several years. At last accounts, he was in the State of Georgia.

David P. Sandoe, he was another poor, weakly, beardless looking boy when he volunteered in 1861. He was a good soldier and could handle a carbine equal to the most robust of his companions. The rough, fair, and outdoor life made a man of him. He was a great favorite with officers & men. Captain Litchfield called him 'Bully.' He learned to be a telegraph operator and was in the employ of the Western Union for several years. He died at his home in Abingdon, Va.

Wm. E. Scott was a fine looking young farmer boy in 1861. He was a jovial youngster, a fine soldier. Always ready to fill his place in the firing line. He lived through the war and married a Miss Will of Johnson County, Tenn., soon after the war closed. He is now dead.

William Buck Smyth, he was a man over 40 years of age when he volunteered in 1861, for a 60 days jaunt to Washington City. He soon learned there was something to be done before we got Uncle Abraham's scalp. He had fever & was discharged in 1861. He is now dead.

Thomas Smith: 'Root up Stigens,' the boys dubbed him, he was a great, tall, raw boned specimen of the (Genis Horro) and as droll in speech and actions. He was a fiddler and created a lot of fun and amusement for the company with his droll songs. He was a mimic. The first tight place he got in, he plainly told Captain Jones he could not stand the racket & asked him for an easy place. Jones had organized a pack mule train and put him in charge of it. The boys gave him the title of 'Colonel Stigens.' He was transferred to the 45th Va Infantry, where he remained until the close of the war. He retained the respect of his comrades to the last. He passed to his reward some several years past.

William Smith, he was a brother of Thomas, a young, square built, robust young man; he was a good, average soldier while he remained with us. He had no great love for Southern rights. He was furloughed in 1863 & never returned to the company. He deserted and joined the Federals & is now drawing a pension from the U.S. Government.

William L. Snodgrass, he was quite a young, beardless boy in 1861. William was one of these, steady say nothing kind of fellows, but always ready, day or night, to respond to the bugle call to boots & saddles. He was a man of undaunted courage. He lived through the war and is alive at this time although in quite feeble health.

Thomas Shepherd was not a native of Washington County, he was a man of mature years when he volunteered in 1861. He was a lively, jovial fellow and would have made a fine soldier. He fell a victim to the deadly Typhoid Fever in the fall of 1861. I learned from other comrades he was taken to Richmond Hospital and died there [December 26, 1861].

William W. Vaughn, he was rather a quiet kind of man, rather slow of speech and movements. He was a moderately good soldier, and a clever, sociable man. L. J. Cosby informs me that he was wounded at Chancellorsville in 1863, and he never returned to the company. I have never been able to locate him since the war closed.

William B. White was a man over 40 years of age when he volunteered in 1861. He did not take advantage of his age limit in March 1862, as others did, but decided to share the fate of his comrades, with whom he started out with. He was a good soldier, had the Southern Cause at heart. He was a polite, affable, gentlemanly man with kind word for all with whom he came in contact. He was conductor on the Saltville branch of the NWRR [Norfolk & Western Railroad] for several years. He is now dead.

Rufus C. Williams, he was a fine robust young farmer boy in 1861. He took a delight in a soldier's life, took a delight in driling and maneuvering; when recruits came in he was drilling them. The boys dubed him 'Captain.' He was always addressed by that title. He was a splendid soldier and always in the forefront. Had he lived, he would have made his mark in the world. He was killed at Spotsylvania Courthouse, May 8, 1864. This was a dear spot to 'Old D,' the best men in the company were killed or wounded at this place.[19]

T. D. Wright: I cannot recall him to 'mind.' I had him listed with the recruits but M. S. Ireson says he was one of the original volunteers in 1861. His impression is that he was discharged on the account of some physical disability.

[Colley included the following account at the end of his roster.]

In addition to the names listed in the foregoing pages, I find from a roster published by the *Abingdon Democrat*, a weekly published in the town of Abingdon, of date Friday, April 16, 1861, the day—Miss Lizzie Harden, a teacher at Martha Washington College—presented a silken banner made by her and others of the college girls to our company. The company being formed in double rank in main street, in front of the late residence of John Mitchel Esquire, from the front portico of that building, where she and a host of other ladies of the college & town had assembled for the occasion, and from which she made her presentation address. It was loaded with patriotism gleaned from the pages of history, giving a record of the daring deeds of soldiers of past ages and especially of the Roman soldier, who either turned, bearing his shield in proud triumph of victory won, or borne upon it in the cold embrace of death. She further admonished us never to allow that banner to "trail in the dust."[20] This lovely banner was stored away in the City of Richmond with other luggage that a soldier had no use for in active warfare. The building was burned sometime in the early '6os. Our flag & all was consumed to the regret of all the old company, who through our spokesman, Lieutenant Rees B. Edmondson, had received the flag from the fair dames, and in response, pledged himself and his comrades to defend it and the cause it represented or leave our dead bodies on the field of battle. This and other patriotic demonstrations, which fired the Southern hearts of both males and females at that date, made every soldier who had volunteered at that time resolve in his inmost soul to win or die, and in but few instances, this resolve was faithfuly kept.

The names of the following men were included in that roster, who for various reasons, never went out with the company; whose names are as follows: J. W. P. Dickerson, F. C. Mchaffey, J. T. Grant, J. L. Cato, Daniel Skinner, R. S. Bittle. J. H. Johnson, Elias Dorsey, J. B. Bowser, Stephen Hunt, and Thos W. Clark. The last named one was released by the solicitation of his father on the account of physical infirmities.

Several of the above young men were students at Emory & Henry College & was so anxious to get to the war that they rushed off and boarded the 1st trains loaded with volunteers from states south and west of us, that were at that time passing almost every day and night. We were at the station on most of these occasions, cheering & yelling for Jeff Davis and the Southern Confederacy & they, bidding us to come on immediately or we would be too late to engage in the strife. Some of us, in a rather derisive tone of voice begging them not to kill Old Abe and all the Yankees before we got there.

Both sides were pretty confidant that the strife would end in sixty days. We were assured by some of our windy orators, who I am compelled with reluctance to say, done all their fighting on the stumps and rostrums at home, after they had enthused the boys & got them off to the front, where the actual toil and suffering was to be met and endured, they procured some soft place where shot and shell were not likely to reach them. While there was many honorable exceptions, men who orated and created enthusiasm—and inspired their fellows with patriotism— took their places in the ranks and shared the hardships and toils of a soldier's life and sacrificed their lives in the cause they believed to be right and just, or laid down their arms at Appomatox Courthouse and returned to the desolated homes and took up their various professions, trades, and avocations, and set to work with a heroic determination to build up the waste places made desolate by the savages of four long years of war and four years of reconstruction. Others used carpetbaggers and scalawags, in with the poor deluded negro, as a tool to fill their pockets with filthy income and place them in positions of honor and profit. Through all this, designed by our enemy to humiliate and degrade the old 'veterans' of the Southland, we have been able, by the blessings and mercies of an all wise 'God,' to overcome. And now, at the end of almost half century, we who are left on earth at this distant date—freed from war and its dire calamaties and effects—can look back with a reasonable pride at what has been already accomplished by the indomitable courage and perseverance of the remnant of the officers and privates 'of the Confederacy.' Many of whom have been called to fill places of honor and distinction in the various offices, both national and state, and all who were not too lazy or indolent to toil, have a home and food and [illegible] & the necessities of life. From mines and factories comes the sound of pick & shovel, and the hum of machinery, and from her fields and forests come the various products that find their way to the markets of the world. The desolate land has again been resurrected and placed in the forefront alongside of their sister states in the Great Union of States.

[After recounting various memories of the war, Colley listed the recruits he found in the newspaper account.]

A Roster of Recruits enlisted in Company D., 1st Regiment of Virginia Cavalry from April 1862 to April 9, 1865.

1. James F. Arnett, he was a man of mature age when he came to the company. A married man, he was a fine shot with a rifle, which he soon procured, a long-barreled Sharps rifle, which he used with telling effect. I remember on one occasion where the enemy had 4 pieces of artilery planted in a deep cut in the road and were pouring solid shot into Major Pelham's two pieces. He was trying to get in position to return their fire. The first shot he gave them, he knocked a wheel from under one of their cannon. The next shot blew up a caisson & the Yanks started to run. The officer was waving his sword and trying to rally them, when Arnett said to Captain Litchfield, "Cap, let me try that fellow." The captain told him to go ahead. He got behind a stump, where he could get a rest and fired. The officer threw up his hands and fell backwards from his horse dead. Arnett was taken prisoner in the first Maryland Campaign and served a term at Point Lookout; exchanged & served to the end. Dead: lived some years after the war.

2. Mansfield Asbury was a fine looking mature man when he came to the company in 1862. He was a fine, brave, courteous gentleman and made a fine soldier. He captured the colors of the 5th U.S. Regular Cavalry in a hand to hand fight in the summer of 1863. In a cavalry engagement in 1864, his horse was shot dead and fell on him. His comrades came to his rescue and saved him from capture. He was married after the war: he is now Dead.

3. William Asbury, he first joined the 37 Va Infantry and served there until 1862 when he came to Co. D. His health failed and he returned home; he is now dead.

4. L. D. Asbury, he was quite a young boy, like most of our boy soldiers; took to army life and was a fine soldier. He lived through the war. He became a zealous Christian and died at his home at Chilhowie, Va., in 1913.

5. Abram Allison, he was not a robust man when he joined the company; he was always ready to respond when called up. He did not get to serve long, he died in the latter part 1862 [February 23, 1864].

6. Waller W. Bailey, he was a young man about 23 years of age. He was in Memphis, Tennessee, at the out break of hostilities. He came home in 1862 and joined Co D., where his two brothers were enlisted. He was a brave, generous young man, a fine soldier. He was acting as courier to 'General' Stuart; was killed near Boonesborough, Md., in 1863.

7. William Bailey, a younger brother of the three other members of Co. D. He was a mere boy. He was a noble hearted, patriotic boy, and would have made a fine soldier. He died of Typhoid or camp fever in the fall of 1863 [August 31, 1863].

8. William Bearden, he was not a native of this section of the state. I remember him as being a very quiet, peaceable young man, always filled his place in ranks. I do not know what became of him.

9. Henry C. Butt, he had arrived at the age of manhood, he was a fine soldier and one that carried his religion with him through all the demoralizing effects of a soldier's life. He was a cheerful, companionable man. He entered the ministerial calling, and was for many years a preacher of the Gospel in the Methodist Protestant Church. He was greatly beloved and esteemed by all who knew him. He was elected as the first chaplain of Wm. E. Jones Camp 709 UCV, and served as such until relieved by death; he died in the faith.

10. William Buchanan: he was quite a young man, or I might say a boy. Will was a noble hearted, patriotic young man. He lost his hearing and was quite deaf, which was a great discomfort and annoyance to one, who was like him, of a sociable disposition & fond of company. He was quite a good business man & a good citizen, a splendid soldier, and a member of the M.E. Church South.

11. James H. Bradley, he was a good kind man. I do not know the date of his enlistment. He died since the close of the war.
12. William D. Black, he was no good as a soldier. He played deaf to get a discharge, but failed in that. Then he pretended to lose the use of his left arm and played that to perfection, deceived the doctors, and got a discharge soon after his enlistment. I learn he died near Portland, Oregon.
13. Samuel D. Black, 'Sam' was younger than his brother Bill. He was a pretty fair soldier and was a prisoner at Point Lookout for some time. He came through the war & made some money. He died at his Home in the City of Bristol, Va., 1911.
14. A. H. Byars, 'Old Dad,' the boys called him. He was a fine soldier, a kind, quiet man. He lived through the war; he was quite industrious, a Temperate man, and a strict member of the Presbyterian Church.
15. John W. Bryant, he was a robust, stout farmer boy, and was quite a good soldier. He was severely wounded near Shepherdstown, Va., in 1863. He came home; his father, being a strong Union man, persuaded him to desert, which he did, and was caught and sent to Castle Thunder. I never looked upon this as a disgraceful act. He died at his home about 1901.
16. John Campbell, 'Uncle John' we all called him, was quite an old, gray headed man. He was prompted by a truly patriotic principle, when one of his age came to the firing line. He was greatly loved and lamented by officers and men. He died of Typhoid Fever in 1863 [February 20, 1863].
17. David C. Carmack, he was a transfer from the 4th Tenn. in the spring of 1864. The comrades tell me he was quite a good soldier, he came to the company after I was disabled in May 1864. He served as deputy sheriff, and later as constable in Glade Spring District. He died about 1889.
18. Frank M. Catron, he was a great, gawky, lubberly boy, always getting into some ludicrous scrape or trouble, quite a droll. The company had a deal of innocent fun at his expense. He was a pretty good, average soldier. He cut his foot chopping wood with an ax; I brought him home. He was one of the unfortunate few in our company, whose rations never satisfied the craving of his stomach. He died several years ago with consumption; died 24 Dec 1873.
19. James H. Clark, the boys called him 'Squaty,' on the account of his low chubby stature. He was a fine, lively, cheerful youngster; he soon won the confidance and goodwill of his fellows. A fine, hardy soldier, he was stricken with Typhoid Fever and died at his home a few years ago.
20. William D. Clark, he volunteered and went out with the 37 Va Infantry in 1861—Jacksons foot cavalry. He tired of that and came to Co D., horse cavalry. A great man, he with others in the infantry, thought the 'cavalry' had a soft

job. They soon found out there was no fun in that branch of the service. He was a fair soldier; he is now dead.

21. I. [Isaac] Lewis Clark, he was a man of middle age, he made a good soldier, and was one of the 6 men who went to the fence with me at Haw's Shop, where I was wounded & lost my foot on the 28th May 1864. He was severely wounded in both hands in 1864. He had his carbine raised to fire, the ball passed through his left hand & and through the right hand. He survived this and lived to a good old age. He is now dead.

22. Theo M. Clapp, he was quite a young boy in 1862. He was one of the boys who was on the famous raid around McClellan's [Major General George B. McLellan] army in 1862, and made quite a reputation as a soldier. He was commended in General Orders by General Stuart, he & Sergeant P. C. Landrum were the only two men in the company that was ever so honored. He was severely wounded at Shepherdstown, July 1863.

23. William L. M. Colley, he came to the company in 1862 and was with General Floyd [Brigadier General John B. Floyd] in 1861. He, and our father were both under General Floyd in W.Va., at 'Gauley River.' He was a splendid, fearless, steady soldier. He was wounded at Funkstown, Md., July 1863. The ball passed through his foot; it was quite a painful and severe wound. He recovered and returned to the company, and was again wounded at the Battle of Winchester early in 1864, losing his little finger. He came near losing his arm from inflamation, which was caused by his long ride from Winchester to Charlottesville, where he could get surgical & medical attention. He recovered and was back at the front in time to be at Appomatox, April 9, 1865. In 1879, he was happily converted & joined the M.E. Church South, and still lives in the Faith.

24. Lewis T. Cosby, he was a mere boy when he joined the company in Aug 1862. He was a quiet, kind hearted boy, a good soldier. He received a severe hurt by his horse falling on him in the spring of 1864. He was transferred to General Wharton's [Brigadier General Gabriel Colvin Wharton] Brigade, and was appointed ordnance sergeant of the brigade, and at the close was acting as ordnance officer of the brigade. He survived, and was Clerk of the Circuit Court Clerk for several years, and a member of the M.E. Church South.

25. John D. Cosby, he volunteered in one of the companies attached to the 37th Va Infantry. He had a severe spell of Typhoid Fever, which settled in one of his legs, which unfitted him for infantry service. He was transferred to Co D., 1st Va. Cavalry, sometime in 1863. He was a jovial, rollicking fellow, always full of life and fun. He was at the wagon train when Sheridan captured it near Appomattox Courthouse. He said he started to run in to the pines, when a Yankee hailed him, and said, "Stop your damn feet muscles, you can't run." He

said he stopped and fell down on the ground and commenced laughing. The Yank told him to go back to the rear, & passed on after some one else. Instead of going back, he ran into the pine woods and escaped.

26. William Cubine was transferred from the 4th Tenn Infantry in 1864. Personally, I do not know his record as a soldier. Sergeant Ireson says he was a perfect daredevil as a soldier. If there was any perilous duty to perform, he was the first to volunteer, and led the last charge the 'Old First' ever made at Appomatox C.H., when the remnant of the regiment cut their way through the Federal lines and made their way to Lynchburg and on out to Bedford City, where they disbanded and went to their homes. He went to Texas & made his home there. I met him at Dallas in 1902.

27. John M. Davis was a thorough Southern gentleman. He fought and endured hardships from an inbred principle. He was one of the fearless 6 who went with me to the fence, 28th May 1864. He went to Texas and died there in a short time after he settled in that state.

28. Thomas Davidson: he was a middle-aged man, a fine courteous gentleman, a married man, one who volunteered from principle and love for Southern rights. He soon fell a victim to the deadly Typhoid Fever and died.[21] He was loved and lamented by officers & men; he had the elements in him that make heroes.

29. David DeBusk, he was a good, quiet farmer's boy, one that never bragged of his piousness, but went steadily along in the line of duty. He lived to return to his home; a quiet, industrious citizen, he died at his house in 1913.

30. Samuel DeBusk, another boy soldier, he was a brother of David and equally as good as he in every respect. I have been unable to locate him up to this time.

[Colley skipped numbering with this next entry. To maintain clarity, this editor has inserted the next number in the sequence. Therefore, all subsequent entries appear off by one number from Colley's sequence.]

31. Thomas B. Duff, he was another mere boy soldier, a good and true one; they followed the lead of the older ones. He was killed at Battle of the Wilderness in 1864.

32. J. M. Duff: he was Known as 'Chippy Duff.' He was a good soldier, went to Texas after the war. I met him at Dallas in 1902. He was quite a jovial, broad brimed Texan, and could boast of the good things produced in that fair famed state.

33. John B. Edmondson, he was a man up in his 30s, a married man, and a staunch Presbyterian. He believed it a great sin to press little things in to service—like sheep, hogs, and chickens— and vowed he would not eat a bite of

anything if he knew it had been stolen. The boys put up a job on him and had him steal a lady's pepper, where they had went for dinner. That put a quietus on him about stealing. He was a good steady soldier, a good citizen; he is now dead.

34. Strong Edmondson, he was a mature man when he came to the company. He was a pretty good soldier, he was a railroad engineer. He left this county soon after his return from the seat of war.

35. Thomas K. Findlay, he was in the State of Missouri, & served in Bledsoe's famous battery in General Price's [Major General Sterling Price] army in 1861, but came home & came to Co. D. in 1862. He was a good, kind hearted fellow, he did not like the restraint required by military discipline. He was severely wounded in the shoulder in 1863. He was not a coward by any means. He died suddenly in Lynchburg some few years after the war.

36. Charles H. Fulkerson came to our company from Rose Hill in Lee County, Va. He came of fighting stock; he was a young fellow. Charles was a true soldier, a good companion in camp. His father, Arch Fulkerson, was a bitter Rebel who would not allow a Yankee to come in his house. On my way to Laurel County, Ky., in 1866, I rode up to his gate and said hello. He came down from the front porch, where he and General Peter Johnston were sitting, & took me through a thorough examination as to my whereabouts during the war; as I was a wounded man and carrying crutches. Charles was not at home & I had never met Mr. Fulkerson. As soon as he was convinced I was an old Reb, he bid me to dismount. "If you had been a damn Yankee, you could not have stayed here," he said. General 'Peter' knew me when I went up to the house, and I was kindly entertained. Charles came in that night. He was alive at last report.

37. Samuel Fulcher: he was a very fine, promising young man. He was in Texas when the war broke out, he came home and joined Co. D in the spring of 1862. He was stricken down with Typhoid Fever and died in a few months after his enlistment. He would have made a fine soldier.[22]

38. Jacob Fleenor: Cubine informed me that he was a transfer from the 4th Tenn Infantry. I have no other information. M. S. Ireson did not know much about him; I suppose he was a Tennesseean and drifted away.

39. Charles Foster, he was another transfer from the 4th Tennessee Infantry. Sergeant Dulaney informed me, that Foster was a fine soldier. I have not met or heard from him since the war closed.

40. J. L. M. French, he was a young man who came to the company in 1864 and served to the end. He became a minister of the Gospel and was a preacher in the Holston Conference, M.E. Church South. He died in 1893. He married Miss Mary Stuart & is the father of J. Stuart French of the Holston Conference.

41. W. T. Greenway, he was a captain in the 48th Va Infantry. He got tired of the foot cavalry and resigned his commission and came to Co. D in 1864. He was a man of big heart, he would share the last crumb with a comrade. He died a few years after the war.

42. James Gray, he came to the company sometime in 1862. He was a pretty good soldier. He left the company in 1863, and was elected 2nd lieutenant in Captain Fred Gray's Co., 21st Va. Cavalry, and served to the end.

43. Dr. Robert Grant, he was a native man and a dentist. He was not allowed to remain with us long. He was transferred to the medical department and served to the end. He was an affable, social companion. He is dead.

44. William H. Hall: was a middle-aged man, and one of the solid, fearless heroes of 61–65. A splendid man, he served to the end, and after his return home, which was situated near the foot of Holston Mountain, he was assailed by a lot of robbers or bushwhackers, who came for the purpose of robbing him. They found him at home & ready for the fray. He was shot & wounded but he kept 'up the fight' & wounded one of them. They picked him up, and retreated. He lived several years after the war closed. He was a good citizen; 'now dead.'

45. John D. Hall, a good, clever, sociable man. He was a Northern man, he married a Miss Byars, a Virginia woman. Not being over military age, he was liable to conscription. He came to Co. D and entered the service. I am informed by Sergeant Ireson, that Hall hired a substitute in 1864 and came home.

46. Alex Findlay Harris, he was quite a young boy and was not of a robust constitution, but he served to the end of the war. He was quite proud of his record as a member of Co. D. He graduated at E&H College. After the war, he was a newspaper man and was in that profession up to within a few years of his death, which occurred at his house in 1914.

47. Samuel Hockett, a younger brother of John and William, he was quite a young boy. He made a good soldier boy. He died some years ago.

48. R. M. Hickman: he was a man of mature age. He was captured and was in prison at Point Lookout, Md. 'Bob' was a fine, jovial, fun loving man. He made quite a good soldier, always ready to do his part in camp or on the firing line. He lived several years after the war. He was a druggist and was in that business at Chilhowie, Va., where he died.

49. George Hewlett: he was a native of some county in the Eastern part of the state. He made quite a good soldier. I have never heard anything about him since the war closed.

50. Basil Horne, he was quite a young boy; he would have been a good soldier. What little time he was permitted to live, he was another victim of the deadly Typhoid Fever in a few months after his enlistment.[23]

Monument honoring
Mosby's men, hanged near
Front Royal. Courtesy of
Virginia Division UDC.

51. Robert Jones, a fine, hearty young country boy, he was a number one soldier and a jovial, lively boy in camp or on the march. A crack shot with his carbine. A cousin of General Jones, he was killed at Funkstown, Md., July 10, 1863.

52. David Jones, he was a noble high-spirited boy, a brother of Jasper and Robert. He was transferred to Colonel Mosby's Battalion in 1863, was captured by the Federals and hanged by order of 'General Custer,' in retaliation for some Federal soldiers Mosby had executed for burning Colonel 'Morgan's residence' near Shephardstown. He and six other of Mosby's men were hanged at the same time near Front Royal. There has been a marble shaft erected at the place of their execution, with their names carved on it. A noble, brave boy's life was sacrificed for what? To gratify the hatred of one man?

53. M. G. Keesling, he was another boy soldier. He came to the company in 1862, a native of Wythe County, Va. He took to the soldier's life and made a fine soldier. He came through the war; he was a good, quiet, law abiding citizen. He died at his house in the City of Bristol, Tennessee, in 1910.

54. Robert Keller was quite a small boy. He was as true as steel and stuck to the bitter end. He died soon after he came home. He was greatly beloved by the officers and men; if he was small in stature, he had a big soul in him.

55. H. W. King, another boy recruit from Wythe County, Va., he was a fine soldier as most all the young recruits were, who came in at the age of 16. Rather than join the reserves, they chose the regular service.

56. John Keesling, I am informed by his brother, M. G. Kesling, he was quite young and did not join the company until 1864. He died in Missouri, where he located after the war.

57. Emory Keesling, he was an elderly man. He did not come to the company until late in 1864.

58. M. H. Latham, he was a married man and was up in the 30s. He was as true a soldier and an uncompromising Rebel, and died in that state of mind. He messed with me and I became very much attached to him. Our friendship lasted as long as he lived, and his memory is cherished by me still.

59. L. W. Latham, a brother of M. H. Latham, he was a man advanced in life. He was a very quiet man, he was a good soldier but a more conservative man than his brother. He died since the war.

60. Ben D. Ligeon, he was an elderly man, a noble hearted, jovial fellow. He was never at a loss for something to say that would rally the dispirited. He was a fine horseshoer & was placed at the forge for that purpose, but he did not like it. He always preferred being with the boys in ranks. He was a brave man. He was wounded at Five Forks in April 65—the boys said he done some tall cursing; cussed everthing from Abe Lincoln down to a wagon driver. Ben is dead [June 6, 1896].

61. David Lowry, he was quite a small, young boy. He first went out in 1861 with the 37th Va. Infantry. He left the 37th in 1862. Captain Litchfield procured a transfer for him, swapping 2 men for him; they never reported. He says he was with Colonel Mosby some two weeks. During that short time, he says he helped to capture three of the enemy advanced pickets, 'with their reserves.' M. S. Ireson says Lowry was made color bearer on the 22nd in November 1864, which he carried up to the 9th of April 1865. He then removed them [the colors] from the staff and concealed them on his person and brought them home, and they are still in his possession. He is quite proud of them, and regarded them as the precious relic of by-gone days (This is the Battle Flag). The state flag was saved by Sergeant Page of the Rockbridge Company. David was small of stature, but a more heroic soul never filled the body of mortal man. He is a staunch Presbyterian.

62. D. H. K. Lewark, he was a man of mature age, he did not join the company until late in 1864. I have no knowledge of where he was before that date. He

was a kind-hearted man and a sociable fellow. He moved to Knoxville, Tenn., after the war and died there.

63. John Littleford, he was a transfer from the 4th Tennessee Infantry in 1864; they were good, loyal, true soldiers. I am informed he has been lost sight of since the war.

64. Willis Littleford, he was also a transfer from the 4th Tennessee Infantry, he was a good, true soldier, like all Tenn. 'Rebels.' I have never been able to communicate with him since the war closed.

65. James R. Meek, he was quite a young boy when he came to the company; he was a good soldier.

66. Lilburn Montgomery: he was a man of mature age, a good all-around fellow; he was a horse doctor of some note. I am informed by Sergeant Ireson he was transferred to Co. A of the 1st Regiment, where he served to the end.

67. John L. Morrison, he was another good, jovial boy soldier. He was always cheerful and full of life and vim; a favorite with the company. He married after the war and moved to Lee County, Virginia. I had lost trace of him. Some years ago he visited Captain Litchfield; he had been in South America he stated [to Litchfield]. I have not heard of him since.

68. George McNew, he was another quite young boy, like almost all the boys he took to a soldier's life, with its hardships and dangers; always ready to respond to the bugle call 'Boots and Saddles.'

69. Wallace McChesney, he was a true and loyal soldier, a good young man, he was another victim of the deadly Typhoid Fever; died at Hanover Junction in 1864 [July 10, 1863].

70. Thomas McConnell, he was another boy soldier; he did not come to the company until 1863. He was true as steel and lost his life in the 'Cavalry Battle' at Brandy Station.

71. J. W. Munday, he was a fine, robust young man when he joined the company. He was a member of the company before March 1863. I remember him. He was a good soldier, he was a native of Greeneville County, Tennessee. I learn he is now dead.

72. J. H. Manney: he was a Wythe County, Va., man. He was a good average soldier, I learn from others. I cannot recall him personally. He is lost sight of.

73. Samuel McCall, he was another boy soldier and was always ready for duty. He is alive at this writing.

74. William Mead: this is one of the mysteries of the war. This near barefooted boy, to all appearance about 12 or 13 years old. Captain Jones, with a few men, was on a scout near Georgetown D.C. in the fall of 1861. This boy ran off from his mother and came back to camp. Captain Jones tried to persuade him to return to his mother but he would not do so. He became a part of the

company. The captain used him as a spy. Supplied with eggs or chickens, and barefooted, he would cross Chain Bridge and wander around peddling out his food stuffs and counting cannon and flags and catching from the conversation of Federal soldiers what he wished to learn.[24] He would come back and report. Of course, he was the idol of the company. He took his place in ranks and handled his carbine with as much coolness and deliberation as a veteran. He was to all appearance perfectly void of fear.

On the 28th [22] of August 1862, he was the only one I could get to go with me down in the bend of the river above Waterloo Bridge, to drive away some Yankee sharpshooters who were giving us trouble. We crawled down a gulley until we got to the trees & bushes near the river, where we had a fair view of the boys behind some building on the opposite side of the river. We had a fair shot at some 12 or 15 in line. We did not stay after the first shot, as we had no protection but small bushes. We moved down behind two large Sycamores. There was a fellow, that I knew from shots fired, was up in a tree or house. I was anxious to find him and in exposing my person he spied me and took two fair shots at me. The first cut a piece out of my hat brim, close to my head. The next one struck me on top of my right foot. On the account of the soft sand, it did not penetrate my foot but cut a slight hole in my shoe and sock and bearly scratching the flesh, glanced off and fell into the river. I saw where he was by that time. After my foot got easy, we crawled down until we got square in front of the house. He was at a small window up in the upper story of the house. There was another Yankee at a window down on the first floor. I told him [Meed] to load and fire into the window, and I fired at the upper window & weather boarding until the boys in blue vacated the ranch in a hurry. About that time, they rolled, by hand, a brass howitzer—on the bridge—charged with grape shot. We gave the gunner a salute and crawled out and back to the command. Colonel Jones had become very much attached to this boy and took him to the Valley of Va., and kept him close to his headquarters. He was killed in a skirmish in 1863. I loved him as a brother. Had General Jones and he lived, I have no doubt but what he would have brought him home with him and educated him.

75. James H. Page: he was a mature man, a brother of R. M. Page. He joined the company in 1862 in time to be on the raid around McClellan's vast army. He displayed a great deal of energy and courage on this expedition. He was a good average soldier. The worst trouble—his rations never satisfied the cravings of his stomach. He died several years after the close of the war [1900].

76. John W. Page, they [John and James] were transfers from the 4th Tennessee Infantry. He was a good, steady, orderly man and soldier. I have no trace of him since the war closed.

77. Robert Page, he was also a transfer from the 4th Tennessee Infantry. He was also a good, quiet, steady man and a good soldier. I am informed all these men went back to their homes in Tennessee.

78. Wm. M. Painter, he was a mere boy, hardly 16 years old. He was a brave fearless little fellow; he was a first cousin of mine, son of my mother's sister. The boys put up a job on him to test his courage. McReynolds, an ambulance driver, grossly insulted him, I learned from my cousin Will Morell. This took place after the 17th of March 1863, sometime after I was shot through the body on that date. He was told that the only redress he had was to challenge McReynolds, who was posted on the matter. The pistols were loaded with 'Blank Cartridges.' He met his opponent with out a tremor. At the crack of the pistol, McReynolds was to drop as though he was dead. The boys said he was furiously mad when he found out he had been duped. This made him famous in the company; he was loved and lamented by the officers and men. He fell a victim to Typhoid Fever in the fall of 1863.

79. Hiram G. Pendleton, he was a young boy from Wythe County, Va., a brave and fearless soldier. He was supposed to have been killed in the Wilderness, 7th of May 1864, as he was never heard of after that fight.[25]

80. Joseph Pendleton, another recruit from Wythe County, he was a married man and he was not a reckless soldier but a steady brave man on whom you could depend upon to stay by you to the bitter end. He and Will Morell were with me on the fatal field at Kelly's Ford when I was shot through the body and left for dead. They both ran to me and proposed to put me on my horse but I would not allow them to do so. They were under fire from the Federal sharpshooters & I begged them to leave me, which they did after taking off my belt, saber, carbine, and pistol. Both these brave comrades were killed at Shepherdstown [Kearneysville] July 1863, and buried in the same grave. They were both men who were strangers to fear.

81. Ruben B. Preston, he was another boy soldier and like all the others of his age he made a fine young soldier and lived through the strife and is yet alive and quite a man of thrift; kind and hospitable. It has been my pleasure, on several occasions, to be the recipient of his kind hospitality.

82. Thomas Preston, another quite young boy, a brother of 'RB,' he did not get into the fray until near the close of the war. Of course, he came to do what he could and was always in line.

83. James L. Ritchie, he was another young man; he was a noble, true soldier one who was always cheerful and full of fun. He survived the conflict and made a good and useful citizen. He was the father of 13 children, nearly all of whom grew to man and womanhood. He was a Christian, a member of the Missionary Baptist Church; he died [January 8, 1907].

84. Andrew D. Rosenbalm, he was quite a robust, fine looking young man. He was one of the recruits who came in 1862. He made quite a veteran in a short time. He was quite a good, faithful soldier; he lived some years after the war closed. [Died April 8, 1889]

85. David Ryburn: he was another boy soldier and one of a genial, lovable disposition. He did not get to enjoy a soldier's life but a few months; he was killed in a skirmish at Union, Loudon County [Waterloo Bridge] in 1862.

86. Newton E. Roe, he went out with the 37 Va Infantry in 1861. He was wounded and on that account was unable to march and he obtained a transfer to Co. D. He and I went from home together in May 1864, arrived there on the 22nd; he was killed on the 28th and I lost my left foot, this was at 'Haw's Shop.' He was a kind, sociable man.

87. John B. Richard, he was a great, tall, gawky, consumptive looking boy, subjected to hemorrhages. He was almost always sick and could not of course make much of a record as a soldier. He died in 1912.

88. Stephen D. Sanders, he was a man of mature age, a good all-around fellow and a soldier always ready for duty. He was one of the 6 that went with me to the fence at Haw's Shop on the 28th May 1864. He had a stroke of paralysis and was almost helpless for several years. He died at his home at Meadowview, Virginia 1913. [1914]

89. Jacob J. Schwartz. He was a German recently landed in America. Alex Gallihan found him in the City of Richmond and hired him as a substitute in 1862. He had served his term in the German army. He had a time learning the English language. He was a fine soldier and a kind and obliging comrade. He was wounded at Gettysburg July 1863 and again the 7th of May 1864 at the Wilderness. He came to this county with us and married and lived several years. He was converted a few years before his death. [October 15, 1882]

90. John L. Smith: John was quite a sociable, agreeable fellow, a good soldier. He volunteered in 1862. He survived the war, married, raised a family, and accumulated some property. He is alive now.

91. W. Trigg Strother, he was a fine, hearty, robust young man in 1862. He made a fine soldier; served through the war, went to Louisiana and was there at the time of the great negro and carpet bag riot. He was wounded in the melee and lost an arm. This riot took place in the City of New Orleans.

92. Thos K. Trigg: volunteered in one of the companies raised in Abingdon, Va., in April 1861, and was attached to the 37th Va Infantry. He served with this command until he was taken sick and was confined for a long period on account of the disease settling in one of his legs. He was unable to march

in February or March 1864, and was transferred to Co. D. 1st Va. Cavalry. He was a kind, generous hearted, courteous gentleman and was devoted to the cause for which he fought. He was adjutant of Wm. E. Jones Camp 709 U.C.V. from its organization in 1893; and with the exception of one term, served as commander up to the date of his death. He was a man who was devoted to his family & his comrades. He would, and did, make many sacrifices for their comfort. He and I did not agree on many questions that arose during our long acquaintance and fellowship. We never quarreled, was always in harmony on the one point—the welfare of our more needy comrades. He died at his home Nov 3d [4], 1915, the last survivor of his family.

93. Connely F. Trigg, he did not get in until late, not being old enough to enter the service. He was claimed to be the baby recruit of company D. He was a great favorite with the captain. The company all loved him; he was a boy of a winning nature. I am informed by David Lowry that he was transferred to the naval battalion, where his brother 'Dan' Trigg was serving. He came through the war and read law and made quite a reputation as a lawyer, and was attorney for the William Trigg Shipbuilding Co., and was stationed in Washington D.C. He represented the 9th Dist in Congress for one term.

94. Dr. William White, he organized a company in 1861 and was elected captain and served there until 1863. He resigned and joined Co. D 1st Va Cavalry & served to the end of the war. He was a strong Southern man and devoted to the cause. He was a fine physician and practiced his profession. He was kind to the poor; his office was always crowded with that class of patients, white and black. He was a man devoted to his friends & comrades. He died Oct. 1904.

95. John G. White was quite a young boy when he joined, he was quite an enthusiastic defender of the Southern cause. He was near me when I was wounded at Haw's Shop. When I tried to get up and walk he saw I was about to fall. He and H. C. Butt ran to me and assisted me back to the rear, through a shower of Yankee bullets. They were cutting the bushes off overhead and on the 'right hand & the left.' Through the providence of God, we escaped without being wounded or struck by any of them. He served to the end of the strife & was postmaster for 4 years under the Cleveland administration. He died at his home near Abingdon. [September 6, 1906]

96. A. H. Webb, he was a boy soldier who came to the company in 1862, and was quite a good soldier up to the time he was wounded near Waterloo Bridge in August 1862. He came home, his father was inclined to Union sentiments and advised him to desert the Southern cause, which he did and joined the

Federal Army; and was—when he left this State for Oklahoma–drawing a pension from the U.S. Government.

97. E. W. Wampler, he was a Wythe County, Va., man who came to the company in 1863. I did not know him personally. I am informed by Sergeant Ireson that he was a good soldier. I have had no information of him since the war.

APPENDIX 3

Short Historical Sketch of Officers from the Washington Mounted Rifles Submitted for Publication

Abingdon Va

Aug 1909

Dear Sir:

I wish you to publish a short historical roster of the officers of the Washington Mounted Rifles of Cavalry Company, organized in Washington County, Va., in April 1861, by Captain Wm. E. Jones, who was a graduate of 'West Point' in the class of 1848. His company was attached to the 1st Regiment of Va. Cavalry in June 1861, and was under J. E. B. Stuart, the 1st colonel, and was in the Valley of Va. in front of General Joseph E. Johnston's command. Our camp was near Bunkers Hill until the first Battle of Manassas. In the fall of 1861, the 1st brigade of cavalry was organized and General Stuart was made brigadier general & Jones was promoted to colonel of the 1st, and 1st Lieutenant W. W. Blackford became captain by promotion. Captain Blackford was in command up to April 1862. At the reorganization, Orderly Sergeant Conley T. Litchfield was elected captain by a vote of the company. When Colonel Ashby was killed, Colonel Jones was sent to the Valley of Va., & placed in command of the 7th Va Cavalry; he was afterwards promoted to brigadier general. In the fall of 1863, he was sent out to SouthWest Va., and placed in command of the Department of SouthWest Va & E. Tenn. In June 1864, he was ordered to the Valley of Va., to meet the Hunter 'Expedition,' and fell at his post on the 5th of June 1864.

By the way, his sword was found some years ago and is now in the possession of Dr. W. L. Dunn at Glade Spring, Va. It was very near an accident that it was found. The Federal soldiers had a reunion at Kansas City, Mo. An old 'Rebel' from this Section heard some Yankee vets discussing war times and one remarked that he had Gen. Jones's sword, taken from his body after he was killed at Piedmont, and had kept it up to that time. The old Reb ventured out of his place of business and asked the Yankee if he would give him the sword, if he could find any of General Jones's relatives. He placed a notice in the county papers & got a response from Dr. W. L. Dunn. The scabbard has engraved on it, 'Presented to Gen. Wm E. Jones by the 7th Va Cavalry,' so there can be no doubt about it being the identical sword used by Gen. Wm. E. Jones.

Gen. Jones was a strict disciplinarian and had his men thouroughly drilled. He was as brave and patriotic a man as ever drew a sword, and as plain and unostentatious; there was no display about him. If the men lay out in the woods or in a field, he had his headquarters in a fence cover. It is said that on one occasion, a trooper was looking out for a place to tie his horse. He run on the general lying in a fence corner and said to a comrade, here is a good place. When the general said, "Look out young man you are encroaching on headquarters," and the trooper had to back out. On another occasion, he met a trooper and inquired what command he belonged to, and the trooper cursed him and asked him what was it any of his business what command he belonged to, you dumbed old citizen. He [Jones] said, "Young man you don't know who you are talking to," and the trooper said, "Who are you anyway?" & he said, "I am General Jones," & the trooper was profuse in apologies. The general said, "Get back to your command I may need you pretty soon."

When he first came out to the Department of SouthWest Va & E. Tenn., the soldiers give him the name of 'Old Bawly' because he was quite bald headed. A courier came up one day where the general and his staff and couriers were standing on the depot platform at Carters Station in E. Tenn., & looked around for someone who looked like a general. At length, he said, "Can any of you tell me where Old Bawly is?" & the general said, "I am General Jones." He handed him the envelope, and looked like a culprit whilst the general was reading it. When he was through, the young man said, "General I have an aunt hiding a short distance out here, will you allow me to go out there and get my horse fed and get something to eat?" The general fumbled in his old haversack and produced three ears of corn and said, "Here is three ears of corn, give two of them to your horse & parch the other and eat it. Old Bawly may want you pretty soon." That was all the rebuke he gave him.

On another occasion, a certain colonel complained to him about his rations being so small and meager he could not stand it any longer. The general gave him a cordial invitation to take dinner with him next day. The colonel brushed up his uniform and brightened up his buttons and was on time the next day & sat around looking for a fine dinner to be in preparation. About 2 P.M., seeing no signs of dinner, he got up to depart saying he would got back to his quarters. The general insisted that he remain longer, that dinner would be on hand after while. So the colonel sat down and waited until about 4 P.M. and said he must go, whereupon the general got his haversack and got out a handful of parched corn & handed it to him saying, "This is all I have got to eat." At the same time, he felt in his coat pocket and produced an apple and cut it in halves and handed the colonel one half and ate the other himself, with the remark that a lady had given him the apple. That colonel learned a lesson he never forgot; if he had thought of his men instead of self, he would have reached a sympathetic chord in a heart that was always in sympathy with the men under his command.

I remember a Monday morning after the 1st Battle of Manassas, how he [Jones] came around with a sack with half bushel cracker crumbs, and with a kind word, handed out a handful of the crumbs to each member of his company, saying, "this is all I have got for you this morning." A more kind hearted, sympathetic officer never breathed the breath of life than Wm. E. Jones. One would think to see & hear him at times when something went wrong, that he was a perfect unfailing demon, that no thought of God or anything holy ever entered his heart. On one occasion the writer & he were alone together for some 24 hours visiting the various headquarters of his command. The writer was just recovering from a wound received at Kelly's Ford on the 17th of March 1863, and was thinking seriously of the vow he had made to 'God' on that occasion, that if He would bring him up from death's door, he would seek Him until he found Him. Looking on his general as being something superior to ordinary men, he broached the subject by asking him what he thought of Stonewall Jackson's religion. He said with emphasis and solemninty, "I wish I were as good a Christian as I believe he is."

That same night, when we returned to headquarters, the Inspector General— whose name I have forgotten—was a guest of General Jones, and they had been classmates and associates in the U.S.A. There was at that time some 15 young men at headquarters—staff, couriers & c. After supper we were all around the camp-fire at the general's tent and the subject of religion came up, and the Inspector General claimed to be an infidel and commenced shouting off his infidelity when General Jones brought him to an absolute pause, or stop, by calling him by name and saying to him, "Stop that damned clash. You shall not talk such stuff as that in the hearing of these young men." And he cut it short. That gave me an impression of the man, that time has never effaced from my memory. That he had a profound respect for that which was good and pure and holy & he detested everything that was little and mean.

I will give you an other instance of his utter disregard for personal comfort and ease, related to me by Mrs. Rachel Cook, wife of Colonel Cook.[1] She said her and a number of ladies of the town of Abingdon, when they learned that General Jones had been assigned to command in this department, went to work and prepared a nice room with bed, bureau, wash stand, towels & c., and sent a committee to wait on him and inform him of the preperations made for his comfort & convenience, stating "General your room is ready for you." Mrs. Cook said he thanked them very kindly and politely for their forethought but said he could not occupy it. His men were out in the open and that he never sheltered himself whilst his men had to be exposed to the elements; that he always shared their fate.

I will give you another instance related to me by his Adjutant General W. M. Hopkins in the winter of 63 & 4, when his command was in Lee County, Va. Times were awful hard and the men half starved and thinly clad. A widow lady had several fine hogs & the boys, as usual under such circumstances, helped themselves to porkers. Some days after she had missed her fat porkers, the general and his aides were passing her residence and she hailed them. As Colonel Hopkins was better dressed—he had on a finer uniform—she addressed her remarks to him. Among other things she said was, if she was a general she would see that the men did not commit such depredations. The general listened quietly until she got through with her tirade, and then he said, with an oath of confirmation, "Maybe when you get to be a general you wont do a damned bit better than I do," and rode off and left her to sad reflections of the ways of the world.

I could go on indefinitely and relate instances of his bravery on the field and his noble generous disposition in camp & his impartiality towards his men. Some of the boys were punished pretty severely for their presumptions; including some who were related to him. When we were in camp in the fairgrounds at Richmond in 1861, some of the boys asked if they could not get permits to leave camp, and would go off of their own accord. My old comrade M. V. Edmondson, a cousin of the general, went off on french leave and the general put him under guard on his return, and put him to packing a rail in front of the guard.[2] After he had been at this for some time, the general approached him and said, "Van ain't you getting pretty tired?" Old Van was madder than he was tired & replied in a bad spirit saying, "It don't make a damned bit of difference if I am, I imagine." The general said, "lay down that rail, Van, and come here." He took him to one side and they sat down on a log & the captain said, "Van you 'boys' who are my cousins must come under discipline. I cannot allow you to do as you please and discipline the other men in the company. And the sooner you learn this the better it will be for all concerned." Van said this lecture done him a great deal of good; the captain never had any more trouble with him. He was sent to his mess a wiser, if not a better man.

There was several of the boys who tried to run their own way but they all run against a will that was as firm as the 'Rocks of Gibraltar,' & they all come to obey orders and was said to be the best drilled and disciplined body of men in the regiment.

Captain W. W. Blackford was educated for a civil engineer and did not have much tact for governing or controlling men. He was a brave man and a fine horseman

Reunion of the 1st Virginia. Private Collection.

& an expert with the saber. At the breaking out of the war, he had charge of the mill and plaster bank at 'Buena Vista,' the property of his father-in-law Wyndham Robertson.[3] After his defeat by Captain Litchfield in April 1862, he left the company and served on the staff of General J. E. B. Stuart for some time and was finally placed in the Engineer Corps of the Army of Northern Virginia, and rose to the rank of colonel of engineers before the close of the war. He died at 'Linhaven,' where he resided for several years after the war, and up to the time of his demise, he was a good, kind man and I loved him.[4]

Captain Conley T. Litchfield, who died in Abingdon, Va., on the 6th of August 1909, was a native of Washington County. He was appointed 2nd sergeant by Captain Jones in 1861 & became orderly sergeant under Captain Blackford and acted in that capacity until he was elected captain in April 1862; he served as captain until the end of the strife at Appomattox, April 9, 1865. He was a man who had the confidence and respect of his men and a whole souled, genial, companionable man. When duty demanded obedience to orders he was firm and unflinching. But in camp he was as one of the boys partaking of their jests, their funs and frolicks, and sympathizing with them in their trials, sickness and wounds. The boys all loved him, with few exceptions.

1st Lieutenant Rees B. Edmondson was born in Washington County, he enlisted in the Washington Mounted Rifles in April 1861 and was elected as 2nd lieutenant and served as such untill 1862 when he was chosen 1st lieutenant under

Burial site of Colley at the
Washington Chapel Cemetery.
Courtesy of Charlie Burnette

Captain Litchfield. 'Reese,' as we boys almost invariably addressed him when off duty, was as one of the boys. A brave, noble, generous hearted man, he was almost always selected to command the dismounted men in the skirmish line. He studied law after the war, and was at one time Commonwealth Attorney of Washington County. At one time, he went from this county to Memphis, Tenn.; he finally went to Washington D.C. and died there the 13th of Feby 1901. He was twice wounded, once at Gettysburg in 1863, and at Richmond, Va., on the day before the city was evacuated in April 1865. He married Miss Rebecca Ford who was a native of Memphis, Tenn., who, with their daughters survive him. Peace to his ashes.

2nd Lieutenant George Victor Litchfield, another noble son of Washington County who took his life in his hand and voluntarily went forth with the noble band of heroes who organized in Abingdon, Va., in April 1861, and went forward to the borders of the 'Grand Old Mother State' to drive back the horde of misguided vandals, who under the pretext of saving the Union, rushed forward across the Potomac River with the cry of 'on to Richmond & down with Jeff Davis and the

Rebel horde of traitors.' He was with the number who first met them & gave them a touch of the valor and courage of the yeomanry of the South. Soldiers, who after a severe contest on the field of Manassas, sent the live ones skedaddling towards the Long Bridge at Washington D.C. and left the bloody field strewn with their dead and wounded. He was a brave and true soldier, was twice wounded. He was born January 20, 1837; died October 28, 1903. Comrade Litchfield was married in 1867 to Miss Elizabeth Pierce of Wythe County, 'a woman of marked Christian character.' He was a member of Lodge 48 AF AM of Abingdon, and a member of the M.E. Church South.[5]

3d Lieutenant Thomas Edmondson was chosen 3d lieutenant at the reorganization in 1862 and was killed May 7, 1864 whilst gallantly leading and encouraging his men. [Colley lightly struck through the following with a pencil: He had snatched the colors from the hand of the color bearer and sprang on top of the breast works, when he] was shot down by the enemy's sharpshooters. Of all the genial, whole souled men who followed Wm. E. Jones from the Southwest in 1861, Thomas Edmondson was excelled by none. It is true of the 103 men who composed the company when it first started for the seat of war. These were a number as brave and true as he. To take him all around for kindness of heart and open-handed generosity, he was excelled but by few men. He was the friend of every man in the company and all who came in contact with him. He was the son of 'Col. Buck' Edmondson of Glade Spring, Va. There is none of the old boys who speak of him today but what you can discern a streak of sadness in his voice and probably a tear in his eye. May his soul rest in peace until the great awakening on the resurrection day. And when spirit and body are reunited, may we meet and greet each other on the blissful fields of Eden, there, far from the turmoils and strife of war, the roar of cannon & the bursting of shells & the fire of muskets and carbines & the whiz of minnie balls, the wounds the sickness and all the hardships, and aches and pains incident to a soldier's life, forever to dwell together in sweet fellowship.

    Their Comrade Thos W. Colley

    Late Corporal Co D 1st Regt Virginia Cav A.N.V.

APPENDIX 4

Wartime Letters

[Editor's note: misspellings not corrected in Colley wartime letters, in order to better maintain his feelings expressed on the field.]

Manassas Junction
July 22, 1861

Dear Father

It is with much pleasure that I seat myself this morning to write you a few lines to let you know that I am well. I know that you will all be uneasy after hearing of the battle that was fought hear yesterday. There was a great many men killed on both sides. Our loss is supposed to be abought 1,000. That of the Federals about three times as many. Our troops entirely routed them. We will persue them on to Alexandria, and on to Washington City. We have about 1,500 prisoners besides what was killed. I was in the thickest of the fight where the bombs were a flying as thick as hail. We did not lose a single man out of our company. Rufe [Rufus Cassell] was right smartly frightened, right when the bombs were a falling about us. I have not time to tell you any more about the fight now. It lasted about five hours. I would like to see you all right well. Tell mother not to be uneasy about me. I have not had much to eat for six days, till this morning, and never had the saddles off our horses. The enemy ran us from camp near Winchester. I will write to you as soon as I can. James King sends his love and respects to you. I do not know where to tell you to direct your letters. You may direct them to Winchester. Nothing more at present but remain your affectionate son.[1]

Ths. W. Colley

It is raining so I can't write any more.

———

Fairfax Court House
Fairfax County, Va.
July 26th, 1861

Dear Sister

It is with great pleasure that I seat myself to write you a few lines to let you know that I am well & hope these few lines may find you enjoying the same blessing. We were in a terrible battle on Sunday the 21st inst, we had a pretty hard time of it for 11 or 12 days. We had to be close to the enemy and watch their movement for night and day. We had to keep our horses saddled all the time, we have had a little rest since Tuesday. We came down and back that day from Manasas Junction; we are at this time within 7 miles of the enemy, they are at Alexandria, about place they could stay there. I will now endeavor to give you an account of the battle as near as I can. It commenced abought 2 oclock Sunday morning with cannon; about 9 oclock the small arms commenced, it was nothing but a continual roaring of course. Musketry until 3 oclock in the evening when the Federalists gave away in the greatest disorder with confusion, which continued so till a message arrived. We pursued them a good five miles with cavalry, and had a battery of artillery. Tore up everything they had. We captured every cannon, amounting to 11 pieces of the best cannon in the North. We heaved some 15 missiles on the road the enemy took from the battlefield, and the road is lined with everything that a man could call for: wagons, harnesses, provisions, field packs, and blankets and clothes. Almost every house on the road is full of clothes that they [the Federals] had to dress up in anything. Once they got to Richmond, it [the clothes] was to be forwarded to them at Richmond.

They anticipated a fine time at Richmond, but I guess they haven't got there yet, at least not all of them, and they got there in a way they did not expect—they went as prisoners, about 12 or fifteen hundred. It is not ascertained what their losses were. They commenced to haul there dead and wounded off, along 1 oclock, and continued to do so til they had to retreat. All that was left on the field, could assure you that there is as many a one left. They may come back to bury their dead. Soldiers were at work Tuesday a burying them and taking care of their wounded. There was a great many of their troops that were wounded that had to lay on the field for 24 hours. Most all of our company were on the field on noon Monday after the fight. I did not go myself and was glad after the company came back and told me what they saw. I will not horror your feelings with a description of their story. I saw enough to see, til five oclock Sunday evening, when we pursued them. The road along which we went, I saw several dead bodies and wounded men of the Yankees. All of our dead and wounded were well cared for. I have no exact account of the loses, the Yankees admit of 6,000 on their side. Our loss was in killed and wounded between 1,500 and 2,000. I am informed that they had a fight in Alexandria, and many of their soldiers, they had to raise the draws of the bridge to stop their men from running close off, and before they would stop they had to have a fight. I do not think there were any in among us worse whipped and confused. They had one of our generals a prisoner, and he escaped from them. He says he never saw an army worse confused than they were, a great many of them threw away there arms and everything they had.

General Beauregard estimates their loss at 2,000,000 of dollars; that will help us ought right smart. It looks to me like there is enough of things left to supply the whole South. I was in the battle but did not get to fire a shot; we were held in reserve, our company and another company of our regiment. The rest of the regiment made a charge on their battery with great success. They took every piece of cannon they had except one. We were exposed all the time, a heavy fire of bomb shells and grape shot but we were fortunate enough not to get a single man killed or wounded in our company. Our captain was very much pleased with the way we acted in the field. None of our men were very much frightened; I was not at all frightened myself. I must draw my letter to a close. Lewis has volunteered; I expect I have written several letters to him but have not received but one answer yet, and that was the one that you put that piece in. Tell mother that I am well and have had my health first rate since I left Ashland.

I am in fine spirits now, have plenty of clothes and a tolerable plenty to eat: Yankee beefs and crackers. You must write to me soon I am very anxious to hear from home. I have not heard from father since he left me at Richmond; I wrote to him on Monday just to let him know that I was still alive. I want to know whether you have got the picture I sent him. Tell Mr. Cassell's folks that Rufus is well; he acted very well in the field. And also give my love to them all and to Jesse Greenway and his family and Mr. Aston and all my friends in general. I have got a Yankee's Testament with 'Samuel McDaniels' name in it, he was from Vermont. I want to bring it home with me when I come.[2] Tell Laura and Sue howdy for me. I do not know where to tell you to write to, you may direct it to Winchester as before, and one to this place. I will tell you all when I come home, from your affectionate brother Thos. W. Colley.[3]

P.S. I stated that I did not know where we would go. I heard we will drive on to Washington, that is the talk now. There is a great force collecting at this point, or in a few hours march of this place. Please write soon, T. W. Colley

Fairfax C.H. Fairfax County, Va.
August 1861

Dear Mothers & Sisters

It is with great pleasure that I seat myself to write you a few lines to let you know that I am well and hope these few lines may find you all enjoying the same blessing. I have not heard anything from you all for some time. We have been here ever since the day after the battle and will have to stay some time yet. I do not think we will ever be attacked here any more. The Yankees got enough of us up this way. We gave them their portion in the battle of the 21st. I have written to you twice since then but have not received any answer from you yet. I want you to write to me as soon as you receive this. I wrote a letter to Mr. Browning a few days ago. I have not time to write any more at present. I send you enclosed the Lord's Prayer, which I captured from a Yankee. Put it in a frame and keep it nice and clean. I have several things I would like to send home. I have a set of gold bosun studs I captured. I will send them in my next. Tell Uncle Adam, Rufe is well and has not received but one letter from him since we left home. The rest of the company is well. We have had but little sickness in our company. Nothing more but remain your affectionate brother.

T. W. Colley

P.S. Please write and tell me whether you hear from father and Lewis. I have not heard any thing only that Floyd's Brigade was at Staunton.

Address   Fairfax C.H. Fairfax County, Va.
Care of Cpt. Wm. Jones
1st Regt. Va. Cavalry

I want to know whether you got my picture I sent home.

August 28, 1861

Dear Mothers & Sister

It is with great pleasure that I seat myself to write you a few lines to let you know that I am well and hope those few lines may find you all enjoying the same blessing. I have no news of importance to write. It has been very quiet since Sunday, and Friday the 23, we were all ordered out to Falls Church. It was reported that the enemy were advancing on that place from Georgetown, but it proved to be a mistake and on Sunday the 25th it was reported they were advancing on Annandale, 6 miles east of our camp. Our regiment was ordered out but it also proved to be a false alarm. Our infantry are a throwing up breastworks at both the above named places. They had a skirmish with the Yankees yesterday near Falls Church in which there was 5 Yankees killed and some 15 taken prisoners.[4] We lost one man. I believe the cavalry was not in the engagement. We drove the Yankees from a hill that we have been wanting to get possession of for some time. We can now see Alexandria on a clear day. Our regiment expects to move down to Annandale in a few days. We expect a movement of the whole army in a week or two. Our army extends from 10 miles above Mannassas to this place, making in all about 25 miles. The tents are as thick as they can be for health and comfort. It will not be long till they will be drove back across the Potomac, where they ought to be made to stay forever. The health of the company is generally good. Charles Morell has been sick for a week but is better. He had a light attack of the bilious fever. I have not been able to ride for three or four days on the account of the boils. They have got near about well. I never enjoyed health better in my life with the exception of a few boils. I want you to get Mrs. Hagy to make me enough good blue jeans for two pair of pants and a hunting shirt. You had better speak to her in time, before someone else gets in before me. There will be a great demand for jeans this fall. Those things I spoke of in my last letter, I would like to have as soon as possible. We have not been paid off yet. I do not know what the reason is. I would not care how soon myself. I have written to you every week since the battle and will continue to do so as long as I have time. Give my love to Mrs. Hogue and all my old friends. So nothing more at present. I hope to be able to see you all soon. Tell Laura and Sue howdy for me. Your affectionate son and brother.

    T. W. Colley

Write soon

Adress Fairfax C.H. Fairfax County, Va. care of Capt. W.E. Jones 1st Regt. Va. Cavalry

---

        Camp Rex
        Fairfax County, Va.
        Sept 8th, 1861

Dear Mother & Sister

It is with great pleasure that I seat myself this evening to drop you a few lines to let you know that I am well and hope these few lines may find you enjoying the same blessing. The mails were not stopped as was reported. I have no news to write. Things are generally quiet here. No fighting, only a few skirmishes between ours and the enemy's pickets. We have not lost any of our men since I wrote to you last. Charley [Charles Morrell] has been very sick since I wrote to you last. He is a great deal better at this time. They think he will be able to come back to camp in a few days. I have not seen him since he was removed to the hospital. We are kept very close in camp. We could not get a permit to go to see our fathers, if they were dying in two hundreds of us. They did make out to let David [Morrell] go and wait on Charles. All the sick that were sick are on the mend. Mr. Mosby [John Singleton Mosby] that was thrown from his horse is able to come back to camp. You recall that I mentioned in my last that the doctors thought it very doubtful whether he would recover or not. It proved that he was not injured inwardley as was first thought to be the case. I am in hopes that they will all be well in a short time. We have not received our pay yet. The paymaster has been here this week and paid all the companies but ours and another. The reason we could not get our pay was that there was something wrong with our payroll, so I expect we will have to do without till next pay day comes around, which will not be very long if it comes when it is due. It will be the 15th of this month. I want you to get some blue jeans and get James Hagy to cut me a pair of pants and you send them as soon as you can. I want broad black stripes down the legs if you can get some black cloth. That is what the rest of them has. If you have not sent the other things I wrote for you had better keep them till you get all ready. I have not heard from you all for some time. I want you to write as soon as you can and let me know how you all are. I have nothing more to write at present but remain your dutiful son and brother until death.

Thos. W. Colley

Give my love to all my friends. Tell Mr. Browning that I have not received any answer to my letter yet. You must send me some thing to eat in the box if there is any room for it.

P.S. Give this to Mr. Cassell. I want him to get George Mantz to make me a pair of cavalry boots and send them to me by express with Rufus's. I want you to have them made for me and settle for them. We have been foiled out of our pay this time. The paymaster was here this week, but owing to the payroll being sent to Richmond, we will have to wait till the next pay day comes around which will not be long, the 14th of this month. We will then have 4 months pay due, as all the regiment was paid, but our company and another. I want you to be sure to have the legs of our boots made long enoug. You will oblige your friend very much by doing this favor for me. Give my love to Jane and Samuel and receive a portion to yourself, from your friend

T. W. Colley

Send our box to Fairfax Station

Address Fairfax C.H.

Fairfax County, Va.

Care of Capt Wm. E. Jones

1st Reg. Va. Cavalry

Our camp is 7 miles from Washington Citty. Munson Hill is 5 miles from the city.

———————

Mr. Cassell

Dear Sir. I am under many obligations to you for your kind offers. I want you to get Mantz or Dickerson, whichever will make them the cheapest.[5] $10 is as cheap as I can get them anywhere. Some of the boys have had boots made in Richmond. They have to pay $12 for them. If you can get them made, the 15th of October and later will do if you can't do any better. Whenever I get the money I will send it to you. We have four months pay due us now; about $1.50 due us for our clothing and wages. Give my best to James T. Alinades. From your sincere and true friend.
Thos. W. Colley.

———————

Camp Cooper
Fairfax County, Va.
November 4, 1861

Dear Father and Mothers, Sisters and brothers,

It is with a sad heart that I seat myself to write you a few lines to let you know that I am well with the exception of a bad cold. I hope these few lines may find you all in good health. Sister, I received your letter a few days ago but have been kept from answering it by a fatal accident which happened to one of the best friends and messmates, Mr. Wm. T. F. Clark. He was accidentialy shot by one of Captain Yancey's about 8 o'clock on the 1st inst., while we were turning out to roll call. Captain Yancey's company is next to ours, only 60 feet apart. Will Clark had just come out of our tent and advanced some 5 paces from it when Mr. Anderson started out of his tent right opposite where Will was, when the hammer of his gun caught against the side of the tent door and instantly discharged his piece, which was a double-barreled shot gun charged with 8 buck shot; all of them entering Mr. Clark from the left side. Two lodged in his Testament, which was in the side pocket of his jacket immediately over his heart, which saved him from immediate death. One entered his abdomen just below the naval, passing through, one just above the hip bone passing through the lower part of his stomach and coming out the opposite side causing severe vomiting, which lasted until within a half hour of his death. Three struck him in the left arm, one in the elbow, one between the elbow and hand just grazing the bone and passing on through a tent in the next company of Captain Smithers, doing no other damage unless making a hole in the tent. Fortunately, they were all out at roll call. One passed through his little finger on the left hand breaking the bone and very near taking the next one to it off. One passed through Gilbert Greenway's pants and entered Mr. Clark in the thigh and the hip joint. It did not come out. All the rest passed through except the one that struck in the elbow. I was with him all the time after he was shot till he died, which was about half past 3 o'clock on the 2nd inst., living only abought 8 hours. He was sensible to the last. He thought he would die all the time. He suffered a great deal of pain from the wound in the stomah and thigh. He would ask, when I would have to raise him up, "Tom raise me this time, you will not have to raise me many more times." Billy Morell raised him up the last time and he smiled and he said, "I am gone Billy, I am gone," is the last words he said. I had to wash him the morning he died. I did get two of the company to help me dress him. It rained all night he was shot and all the next day. I had to be in it all through the day, a fixing to send him home. Billy Morell had to go to the junction to get a coffin, which he fortunately found already made. We put him in an ambulance and carried him to the junction, and there put him in his coffin. I was sorry that I could do no more for him. We got a very nice walnut coffin and case which cost $25.00. Mr. Catron took the corpse in charge at the junction. If not delayed, will arive at Abingdon this evening. I feel very sorry for his parents. They will take it so hard—I and Billey Morell wrote a letter to his people stating all the particulars about his death and offering our sincerest regrets for the loss of a sincere and true friend. Our mess also wrote another [letter] offering deep regret for the loss, both to them and ourselves, and begging them to submit calmly to the will of God for depriving them of a son and brother, and us of a kind and confident friend. I feel that I have done all that I can do for him while he lived and after he died, that is all I could do. I believe that is all the particulars of his untimely death. The man that shot him takes it very hard.

You wrote to me that Mr. Dickerson had made me a pair of boots. There must be some mistake about them somehow or other. I have a pair of boots that came today by Mr. Samuel Hultcher. He says that Mr. Mantz sent them to me. Mr. Cassell has not written to me or Rufus since I wrote to him last about the boots. I do not know who he got to make them. If Dickerson made a pair you need not send them.

Camp Cooper
Fairfax County, Va.
Nov. 13, 1861

Dear Grandmother and Uncle

I have been neglecting to write to you for a long time but I have at length come to the conclusion to write you a few lines to let you know that I am still in the land of the living. I have had my health as well as I ever had in my life, with the exception of the tooth which I have had for several days. It has swollen my face up considerably. I think it will get better in a few days. I have no news worth writing you at this time. Everything has been very quiet since the little bushing we gave them at Leesburg. I do not think we will be plagued with them any more this fall. Some people think they will advance again this fall and some think they will not. If they do we will try and send them back a little faster than they come up. I think it very probable that we will not have any fighting for several weeks at any rate. General Jackson's Brigade has been sent to Winchester and it is reported in camp that they were fighting there yesterday but I cannot vouch for the truth of it. There is so many false reports originated in camp that it is impossible to tell when the truth is told. I must draw my few lines to a close. Billy Morell wishes to add a post script and I thought that I would leave him plenty of room. Give my respects to sister and Uncle John's family. Nothing more at present but remain your affectionate grandson and nephew

     Thos. W. Colley

                       Camp Cooper
                       Fairfax County Virginia
                       Nov. 15, 1861

Dear Sister

I received your very kind letter of the 1st inst. with much pleasure. It found me well with the exception of the toothache which has swollen my face right smartly. It is some better at this time. My box came to hand safely. My pants and boots fit splendid. The roundabout is almost too short and too tight around the body.[6] I can make out to wear it; I have nothing but it to wear. It is not quite heavy enough for the cold weather. I was very much pleased with the box and contents. You wished to know what I needed. I have written several things since your letter started. I will try and give you a list of all I want. Two pair of wollen slips, two wollen under shirts, 1 pair of pants, 1 pair of socks, 1 heavy blanket. If you can make me another heavy roundabout, have it cut about 3 or 4 inches longer than this one, and about 3 inches larger around the boddy. The sleeves is just right. I want it well wadded all through. I think those articles is all I will need this winter. Send them as soon as you can. I wrote to Mr. Browning about some caps, 5 if he had them. I want 1 for myself and the other 4 for my messmates. We need them very badly. I wrote to him 4 weeks ago but have not received any answer from him. I want to hear from him as soon as possible so I can send to Richmond and buy me a cap. I have some metal buttons at Mr. Stewart's in Abingdon that Mr. Rambo sent there from Richmond. There is a dozen of them. Put 6 of them on my roundabout. There is no news worth writing you. Everything is quiet here. We hear this morning that the enemy are advancing on our county. I am in hopes that it is not true. If it is true

I am in hopes that they will send us back there to help to defend you all. Tell Mr. Cassell that Rufus has been sick some three or four days but has got well again. Give my respects to Mrs. Casell and Alinande, Uncle Adam, Mr. Browning and lady, Mr. Stewart and family. Tell Lewis I will write to him in a few days. Nothing more from your

> Dear brother
> Thos. W. Colley
Address Tudor Hall

> Camp Cooper
> Fairfax Co., Va.
> Nov. 18, 1861.

Dear Brother

I received your kind letter some time ago. I was very glad to hear that you and father had got home and that you was almost well. I am in hopes that you and him will conclude to stay there. I know mother would be a great deal better satisfied if you would stay at home. I know she must suffer a great deal of uneasiness when we are all gone from home. I wrote to sister a few days ago. I mentioned in it all the articles I need, with the exception of a pair of suspenders and my reading comforter I wore last winter. I have no news worth writing with the exception of some little skirmishes. On the 14th Major Martin took 60 of his men and went down in the enemy's picket line and captured 31 prisoners, 5 four horse wagons loaded with corn. There was some 50 Yankees with the wagons when he came upon them. The rest made good their escape. He brought the wagons and prisoners safe to camp. Today a portion of our regiment went out on a scout down towards Falls Church. There was a portion of our company out when they got within Falls Church they came on abought 50 of the enemy. They all ran but 15 who gave fight. We killed six of them, wounded two and took 8 prisoners. Colonel Lee lost his horse.[7] He was shot from under him. When his horse fell, he drew his pistol and commenced firing on them. We lost 1 man killed and three wounded, 1 dangerously, the other too only flesh wounds. The man that was killed belonged to Captain Drake's company, and one of the wounded men also. The other two belonged to Captain Yancey's company. Billy Morell and Sam Halcher and Fountain Beattie and John Mosby pursued two of them that ran some distance through the woods. One of them wheeled and fired at Fountain Beattie but missed him. Mosby immediateley dismounted and shot one of them through the head. Billy Morell fired two shots at the other one but missed him. A South Carolinian came up about that time with a double-barreled shot gun and fired at him and killed him. Billy had a carbine and my pistol. He did not fire but one barrel of the pistol.

I do not recollect whether I said anything abought the day that I went out in sister's letter or not. Myself and Docks Dunn and Baker came on five of them some three week ago. There is where I got the pistol I mentioned above. I had to drop my letter abought the time I wrote 6 lines, to go out and aid Colonel Lee. Two men came in with an awful tale, said he was fighting abought 60. Colonel Jones had the rest of the regiment ordered out. I said I had just lit a candle, and commenced writing this letter. I was sent on in advance to see what he needed. I did not get more than 3 miles before I met Colonel Lee coming in with the prisoners. We all came back to camp well satisfied. I concluded I would finish my letter to close. Cousin Will sends his respect to you all. Give my love to all, father, mother and sister and friend.

      Your Dear Brother

      T. W. Colley

I have not heard from you all since I received my box

Tell Jesse Browning if he don't write to me soon I will pull his hair when I get back and also send them caps I wrote to him for.

      Camp Suward

      Fairfax County, Va.

      Dec. 7, 1861.

Dear Brother

I am happy to say to you that your letter found me well. I hope these few lines may find you all enjoying the same blessing. I was glad to hear that father had got better. Tell him that Dumsey McReynolds is at the junction and Gilbert Greenway is well and sends his respects to him. I heard from Dempsey and Rufus Cassell. He is also sick and has been for some time. They are both better. Rufus is able to come back to the regiment. He will be here in a few days. The rest of the boys is well except Thomas Bailey. He has been sick with a headache for a day or two. I had a severe spell of head ache the day after I received your letter but have got entirely well of it. Tom is also better. It is nothing but cold. I think we are exposed to wet and everything that comes along. I wrote to sister a few days ago an answer to her letter that she mentioned in your letter, for fear she did not get it. I will mention what she wished to know abought my box. Everything came to hand safe, except the vial of ink. It was broken. It was a small loss. We have plenty of ink here. About the shirts, I do not care about any fancy overshirts. If I can get some good flannel under shirts and a couple of good strong colored cotton shirts and two pair of wollen slips, 1 pair of socks, the comforter I wore last winter, and the blanket you say is ready. Get some of the ladies to knit me a pair of yarn suspenders. I do not know whether to have the things sent yet or not. You can get them all ready. If you have not started them wait till you hear from me again. Colonel Jones is trying to get this company back home this winter. I do not know whether he will succeed or not. General Johnston promised him an answer in a few days. If we have to go down on sand, I do not care whether he gets us out or not. There is no news worth writing you.

We are still expecting the enemy to advance. There was a small party of them come up to the Court House picket on the 27th inst. and exchanged a few shots with our boys. Billy Morell and Gilbert Greenway were on post where the enemy came to. They fired on them. As soon as the firing was here at the reserve, they was joined by some 10 more of our boys. They exchanged some 40 shots with the enemy. There was abought 60 of the enemy. They could not stand our fire. They took to their heels and left us. We did not hit any of them. We wounded one of their horses. They did not hit anything on our side. We sent out a scout the next day but could not see anything of the enemy. You said I did not mention my horse. He is in about as good fix as he was when I left Richmond. He has had the distemper twice since I left Richmond. He has got over it now and has improved very much in the last three weeks. We have had pretty plenty of food for our horses this fall. It has been getting tolerable in the last few days. They are on half rations today and tomorrow. If this kind stile lasts long, we will be all on foot [on our way] back.

I wrote to Jesse Browning some time ago. If he is going to answer my letter I want him to let me know and if he don't I will pull his wool when I get home; that is if the Yankees do not get me and those caps. I do not want him to forget them and also not to forget the price, $2.50, that is all I can give. Give my respects to Mr. Cassell and lady and Uncle Adam, Jesse and Mrs. Browning and Miss Ann and all my old friends. Tell old friend Hague that I hope the militia may be ordered out so they can get him. Tell him if he will come and take my place awhile he can get shed of going in the militia. Tell Mr. Steward that I and Will White would be glad to see his face down this way with a jug of whiskey. Write soon and tell me all about the girls. Tell mother that I have became quite devout. I read a chapter in my testament every night. I and Will Morell both read a chapter every night. Will sends his respects to you all. Tell Sue and Laura howdy for me. Nothing more at present but remain your affectionate brother

Thos. W. Colley

Camp Copper, Va
December 14th, 1861

Dear Sister

I received your kind letter of the 9th inst. with much pleasure this evening. I thought I would without delay answer it. I was very glad to hear that my things be on the road, if I can only get them, which I hope that I shall. There is some talk of us getting to come home in a short time. I do not know whether there is anything of it or not. I can come home by enlisting for two years more, which I shall have too befor my _____ [illegible] 12 months is out. I can get a furlough for 60 days by enlisting for two years. Colonel Jones thinks he can get us all off to come home this winter. I was just fixing to write to you not to send any things till about the first of January, but as you have started them they will get here before we can get ready to start. It will take about two weeks to get ready to start home, if we get off, which is in doubt about us coming home till our time is out.

Damn such office as I have got. I get that of picket duty and get to sleep in misery every night and have to work like thunder sometimes. Sometimes it is two weeks before I have anything to do. My office is pioneering, making roads and such other things as they want done. I had a tolerable easy time of it. Tell Ms. Stewart's people that Will says he wishes that they would write to him occasionally and let him know how they are doing. Tell them he is well and has been looking for some things for some time but has not received them yet. Tell Mr. Cassell that Rufus has come back to the company, he appears to be well enough at this time, he looks very pale, but not bad. I have no news to write you at this time, everything is quiet here at this time. There is no prospect for a fight here this winter. They may have one down at Evansport, some 30 miles from here. There is no sign of an advance of the enemy here. The morning papers came in whilst I am writing. It prides an account of the destruction of Charleston, S.C., by fires.[8] I have not time to give you any of the particulars, you will have an opportunity of seeing it by the time this comes to hand in the papers. You wished to know if I needed anything more than what I had written for; I do not think that I shall. When my blanket comes we will have 4 blankets apiece, myself and Samuel Fulcher and Will Morell tents together. What I have written for will be all I need at this time. I must bring my letter to close, the mail will start in a few minutes. I give my respects to all my friends and to mother and father and Louis & Laura and Sue and receive my best love to yourself, your afectionate brother

> T. W. Colley
> Company L   Tudor Hall
> 1st Regt Va Cavalry   Prince William County Va

I will try and send you some envelopes as soon as I can

Camp Cooper
Fairfax County, Va.
Dec. 18th, 1861

Dear Sister

I received your letter of the 10th with much pleasure. I was glad to hear that you was all well at that time and happy to say that your letter found me enjoying fine health. I think it is all up, about us getting to come home, till our twelve months is out. We all thought some time ago that we would get home for Christmas. General Johnston told Colonel Jones that he would not spare any of the cavalry, so we may give up to stay all winter. You wrote to me in your letter of the 9th that you had heard that Cousin Frity was dead. There is nothing of it. He is as hearty and as well as a man could be. We have but three men out at the hospital at this time. Thomas Leopard, Thomas Huble, Fountain Batie, the latter who is at home on furlough. You said that Miss Molie Moor wished to know whare Mr. Sheopard was. You can tell her that he is at Richmond in the hospital. The last I heard of him, he was on the mend. My box is lost, I expect. I was at the junction yesterday and found it registered on their books but could not find the box. I will go again tomorrow and try again to find it. I want father to send the express receipt. He ought to have sent it to me when he started the box. I want him to see the express agent and see what he says about paying for it, if it can't be found. It must of come safe to the junction or they would not have registered it. The express office is so crowded there, that is impossible for anyone to get anything that is there. They say they are not bound for anything that is lost. If they are not I do not see the use of an express office. I would hate to lose the box, for I need everything that was in it. Tell Mr. Browning I will pay him for the caps, the first one that comes down here that I can send the money by. You said that mother wished to know if I wished her to pay Mrs. Hagy for the jeans. Certainly I do. That is what I sent the money home for. You said that Cousin Mrs. McDaniel said that she had written to me. I have been looking for an answer for some time. I have not time to write any more at present. You must write soon. Give my love to all my friends. From your affectionate brother

> Thos. W. Colley
> Company L Tudor Hall
> 1st Regt Va. Cavalry

You said something abought sending me some brandy. A little would be very acceptable about Christmas—You need not send less than two gallons.

Camp Jackson
Pr. William County, Va.
Jan. 1st, 1862

Dear Brother

I seat myself to answer your kind letter of the 29th of Dec. which came to hand a few days ago. I was glad to hear that you was all well and happy to be able to say that your letter found me well. I never enjoyed better health in my life than I have for the last two months. I have no news worth writing you at this time. I suppose you have heard all about the fighting the general [Stuart] had at Drainesville.[9] It was tolerable hard on our side. Our loss was 160 killed, wounded and missing. We do not know what the enemy's loss was. The citizens of Drainesville say their loss was 300. The Yankee papers give their loss at 10 killed and 15 wounded. They outnumbered us 5 to one. We got all our dead and wounded the next morning. There was some few of the enemy on the field next morning when we went back for our dead. We carried all our wounded of the evening of the battle except 15 which the enemy captured. We got them next morning. Our regiment was not in the fight. The first Kentucky Regiment suffered the most and the artillery. We had 20 artillery horses killed. We did not lose any of our artillery. One piece had to be hauled off by hand, all the horses being killed. The enemy did not molest a thing that was left on the field by our men. We had two caissons blown up, full of bomb-shells, which killed several men and horses. General Stuart did not make anything by that fight, only saved his wagons which he had 215. He started on a foraging expedition and it appears that the enemy had started on the same errand. I believe that is all I can tell you of the fight. We have moved back to within five miles of the junction. The whole cavalry brigade is close here. It consists of 6 regiments. We are all cussing, and building winter quarters. We left the battlefield on the 21 July. There is some few graves in our encampment. We have got our huts pretty well built. We have given out all hopes of geting home till wintertime is out. Bailey is in the tent at this time writing a letter. He said to tell you to come down and answer as a substitute for him, till he goes home a while, and for you to write to him. Tell Bill Cassel that I am very sorry that he tells my girl to get married. I do not know what I shall do for a wife now. I had calculated to take her next spring. I want to know whether she was a Union girl or not. If she was I do not care. I want him to write to me and Rufus. All the boys are well. I am sorry to say I have lost my box—I have almost given it out. I am going again tomorrow to look for it again. I have been waiting for the receipt. Father ought of started the receipt when he started the box. I can buy me some pants and wollen shirts here if I cannot get the box. I can buy everything I need that was in the box except the blanket. Tell mother she need not make me anymore wollen underclothes. I will buy them here.

I think she said she only sent one flannel shirt in the box. If she did not, she may send the other with my other things and the wollen gloves you spoke of, and also a comforter if you can get one. You will have a good chance to send my things if you get them ready in a week or ten days. Alexander Gollehon is coming home in a few days. He will bring all packages to our company. I would like to have a blanket if you can get one. We will be paid off again in a few days and will send the money to pay Mr. Browning for the caps. You said there was five of them I think. Give my love to father and mother and sisters and my respects to all my friends. From your affectionate brother

        Thos. W. Colley

Address as heretofore

If you can get it, you may send me a couple of slips. Tell Miss Molie Moor that Mr. Sheopard is in Richmond yet and that I have not heard from him for some time. He was very low the last account.

Camp Jackson, Jan 17, 1862

    Dear Sisters

I take the present opportunity of answering your kind letter of the 9th. Most, I was glad to hear that you and all were well. I have not been very well for some six or eight days. I have had the toothache and face swollen very badly. It is not a great deal better. I hope it will get well in a few days. We are very comfortable fixed in our winter quarters where all things bids fair for us to stay for the next 4 months. There is no prospect of the enemy advancing this winter. The roads are so bad that it will be improable for them to transport their army this winter. The late Northern intelligence is that they are in readiness to advance. They have not gone into winter quarters yet. As we can learn, they must calculate on advancing by not going into winter quarters. I have no news worth writing you at this time. I am sorry to say to you that my box is lost for good. You need not try to get me any shirts or slips. I have bought myself two pair of slips, two woolen shirts, and two linen shirts and I also happened to get those two shirts that you sent me in the summer to Richmond. How I came to get them, when Earnest was down here, as he went back through Richmond he looked in the express office. He found my package and fowarded it to the junction and it hid there till three or four days ago when Mr. Litchfield, our agent happened to find it. There has been a new arrangement since my box was lost. There is only two men from a regiment that can get anything from the express office. There will not be so many things lost as heretofore has been. You may send me another blanket, 1 pr. pants Brenda bought,

1 of my vests I left, and at home 1 pair of woolen gloves and something to eat. Some butter. Mrs. Slagy has sent apple butter. I want some pickle cucumbers. You can pickle them and put them in a jar or crock. Salie Skagy wrote to me that she had some fine apples to send and I would like to have some brandy if it can be got and a couple of gallons will do. I have not got any money to send home this time. I had to pay a considerable price for what clothes I get. I will be home when my time is out, if I live and they don't tie me to some smart general who has been putting a bill before the legislature to draft all the 12 months men as soon as their time is out, and not give them a chance to re-enlist again. I do not think it will pass the House of Representatives. If you cannot get my things ready to send by Mr. Gollehon, Charles Morrell will be a coming down before long and if not send it by express. I believe that I had mentioned all that I want at this time. Tell Miss Mollie Moor that I have not heard anything from Mr. Shafer since I wrote to you before. He is still alive yet or the surgeon that he is under would have reported him to the captain. Tell Mr. Cassell that Rufus has got his box. Give my respect to James Loyd and tell him that I am much obliged to him for the name and that I will dress him out and out when he gets large enough to know his manners. It is a mistake abought my boots being worn out. They are as good a pair of boots as I ever had. Tell Miss Mollie that I will be sure to call on her next spring, to wait on me. Give my respect to Mr. Browning and family and all my friends. Give my love to mother, father, brother, and sisters. Tell Lewis that I will answer his letter in a short time. Nothing more from your brother
Thos. W. Colley

P.S. Will Morell sends his respects to you all . . . Give my love to Cousin Miles if you see her and tell her I will write to her soon.

———————

King William County, Va.
Jan 21, 1862

Dear Sister

I got here yesterday morning after a hard ride of 16 days. I had very good luck with the horses. My horse and Mr. Edmundson's was sick two or three days on the road. They did not eat anything for several days. I could not see anything the matter with them. There is no news stirring in camp. Some of the boys have tents and some have cabins. There is no sign of winter quarters. Our brigade is here for the purpose of getting forage. It is impossible for us to get any fodder or hay. Corn is all we can get for our horses. Lewis is here yet and some 15 others with out horses. General Lee says he will not let but one go at a time. It is uncertain when Lewis will get off. Mr. Edmondson got my satchel down safe with my clothes. You can say to Father that Mr. Sneed wants to buy that horse of mine and I think we had best let him go. He charged Catron, had to pay $20.00 for a month instead of $12.00. Our contract said I will have to pay for 2 months and probably three before I can get him away. Charley Grey has gone back home. I expected to get him to take my horse home when he went. I did not see Mr. Sneed myself. He said to Catron that he would give $150.00 for him. I think he will give more. It will cost me abought $75.00 to pay the expense on him home. I want him to let me know if I shall see him or not. Charles Grey started with Lewis's horse and got him first in a lodge and got his leg hurt so he could not travel and had to leave him. He was offered $125.00 for him. Tell Father to get him a horse and he will get to come after him in a short time. Him and Cousin Charles will get home as soon as all the other boys gets back. Lewis only got his boots a day or two ago. He got a pair of boots from Corby. That done him very well. I will close for this time. Your brother

　　　　T. W. Colley

Address Hanover C.H.

Please send the letter back that Lewis sent home in a letter.

———————

　　　　　　　　　　　　　　　Camp Stone Wall Jackson
　　　　　　　　　　　　　　　Pr. William County, Va.
　　　　　　　　　　　　　　　Jan 31st, 1862

Dear Sister

Not having received a letter from you for some time I came to the conclusion that I would write you a few lines to let you know that I am well and doing very well. There is nothing stirring here at this time only plenty of rainy weather and mud. The mud is about 18 inches deep here in camp. I have good news to write about. My box. Mr. Litchfield found it on the 29 inst. One of Colonel Radford's men had taken it out of the express office through a mistake and had never returned it till a few days ago. Everything was safe in it. He had not disturbed a thing in it. I have more under cloths than I needed at this time. I would like to send some of them home if I could get a chance. I have been looking for father down here for several days. Rufus got a letter from home a few days ago. It stated that father and Uncle Adam was to start in a few days. I would be glad to see them here. I begin to need a pair of pants pretty bad about this time. If you have not started my things yet you need not send me any blanket or undershirt. Send all the rest of the things I wrote for. He is a list of what I want: one roundabout, one pair of pants, a pair of woolen gloves and something to eat and something to drink. I believe that is all I want at this time. Tell Jesse Browning that my caps came safe after so long a time and I will send him the money as soon as some person comes down that I can send it by. I believe I have nothing more to write at this time. Give my respects to all my friends and my love to all at home. Tell Lewis to write to me soon. I reckon I will get to come home when my time expires. I expect to volunteer in Kentucky next year. So nothing more at present but remain your affectionate brother

    Thos. W. Colley

         Culpeper Va.
         Feb. 20, 1862

Dear Sister

It has been some time since I have had an opportunity of writing to you. We have got settled down in camp once more and I embrace the present opportunity of writing you a few lines to let you know that I am at present doing very well at this time. We went on picket on the 15th and came in on the 18th. We had a pretty severe time of it. Commenced snowing on the 17th and continued until the morning of the 18th when it changed to rain and rained all day on us. The signal post is about 20 miles from camp. Our relief got there about 3 oclock in the evening and we had to travel all the way to camp in the rain and dark. There is no news here at this time. Everything is quiet heare. It is expected that the Yankees are falling back towards Washington City. We did not see any whilst on signal. The roads are in an awful condition at this time. The snow was several inches deep when it commenced raining. It has about disappeared. I get plenty to eat since we came up to this camp. Pork and flower. We get nothing but corn for our horses. Tell father I do not see any chance of getting my horse sent home at this time. He has been there three months the 23rd of this month. That will cost me $10 and Mr Guy came by there for his horse and says he does not think my horse will stand the trip from there home. He says he has not improved any since he has been there. I wrote to Mr. Sneed to know what he would be willing to give me for him. I have not received an answer to it yet. I hardly know what to do with him. The old man Sneed told Mr. Grey that he would sell him to pay the expense if I did not take him away in a short time. I have nothing more to write at this time. My love to mother, father, Laura and Sue and may God's blessing rest upon you all is the wish of your brother

    T. W. Colley

[The following written in the same letter.]

 Dear Brother

Being as I have more paper to spare, I will write you a few lines to let you know how we are geting along. The regiment started the same morning you left for home and I left for Miss Saddie's sweet abode. I arrived there abought 10 o'clock in the morning and stayed until Saturday, 10 o'clock the next morning, when I left with a sad heart. I over took the regiment that night about 11 o'clock at Walers Tavern, Louisa Co. We made the trip to Culpeper in 2 days. After I caught up with them, we camped near the C.H. two nights and then moved out to our present camp 3 miles east of the C.H. where we will stay for some time. We have to signal down on the Rappahannock about 20 miles from our camp. We have to stay out 4 days at a time. We had a glorious time whilst we were on picket. It snowed abought 10 or 12 inches then turned in to raining. You ought to be here now. Our theater opens tonight at Culpeper C.H. It will be a great thing. I expect Lewis. I want you to see Thompson Twill and see if he can get me 3 bushels of salt and what it will cost me and let me know soon. I want it for a friend. I wish you a happy time at home. I will close for the want of space and something to say. Bring me a pair of pants when you return. Your affectionate brother

      T. W. C.

If you have not started them before this comes to hand. If you have I will try to sell them to some person in the company. I want you to send me one pair of pants by Mr. Ramba if you had not started them, two pair of woolen slips, two pair of socks, the jeans roundabout I wrote for, one good blanket, a colored blanket would be preferable for five if he had them. Those furred caps are the ones. I spent $2.50 too. I will send some money home by Cal Earneer. Him and Mr. James Buchanan is here at this time. They will stay with us a few days till they get tired of camp life. I was glad to learn from Colonel Earnest that father and Lewis had got home and that they were as well as they were when they arrived at home. I want them both to write to me as soon as they can. I do not want you to forget my butter and cheese and return my thanks to Mrs. Poley Clark for her kindness towards me. I have not space to write anymore at present. My love be with you all and God bless you from your son and brother

      Thos W. Colley

  Address Manassas Junction
  Care of Capt. Wm W. Blackford
  1st Regt. Va. Cavalry

———————

Richmond, Va.
June 5th, 1862

Dear Mother and Sister

I now write to the 4th time since I arrived at Richmond without receiving an answer. I had almost come to the conclusion you had forgotten me or had not received my letters. Father arrived here on 29th last month. He would not get to the company until yesterday. He has been out at the baggage wagons. I have not had an opportunity of seeing him but twice since he came here. He left here yesterday evening to go back to the baggage wagons for the purpose of starting home. This morning he has some 10 or 12 horses to take back with him. Mr. Cassel is going to help him with his horses until he can hire some person to help him. Alexander is very anxious to get home. You may expect father about the 20th of this month. It will take him some 18 days to get there. He has had his health very well since he left home. I was very sick yesterday evening when father was here. I had something like the sick headache. I am a great deal better this morning. I feel very sour in the breast on the account of straining so much vomit. I will be well enough in a day or so. I started to [illegible] my last. I think about Lewis having the mumps. He has not been with the company for 3 weeks. Him and Rufus Casell were both in the hospital when father came to Richmond. He took them out to the baggage or just happened to get there as they were starting ought themselves. Lewis is well but is quite weak yet but gaining strength as fast as he can. Charles has got well and is with the company. David has not quite recovered yet. The wound in his shoulder does not appear to heal so fast, it being in the joint. I fear it will always be stiff. I suppose you had saw an account of the Battle of Saturday 31st and Sunday 1st.[10] It will be useless for me to try to give you any account of it only that we drove the enemy from their entrenchments and captured all the artillery they had on this side of the river, amounting in all to 16 pieces. Everything has been quiet since with the exception of occasional shot with artillery. The artillery has commenced pretty rapidly this morning. It grows more rapid every hour. It may bring on another fight today. We are stationed about 2 miles east of Richmond near the York River Railroad and about 2 miles in the rear of our advanced forces. It is so marshy that cavalry can't do anything here so we have to lie still near the battlefield. I must bring my letter to a close. Give my respects to Uncle Adam and Mrs. Browning and family and Mr. Kid's family and to Mr. Stewart's. Tell them Will is well. My love to mother and Laura and Sue and receive the best wishes of your affectionate brother

Thomas W. Colley

P.S. I omitted to mention to you that some person has been kind enough to steal my satchel and everything I had except what I had on, and had them on 4 weeks, when I came to look for my satchel. I had to buy a shirt and pair of slips in Richmond. They are not match account altho I had to pay a big price for them. I sent by father for what I need. Please give the package that I send by father to Cousin Kate Williams.

        I remain your affectionately
        T. W. C.

        Camp near Brook Church
        Henrico County, Va.
        June 18, 1862

Dear Sister

I received your kind favors on the 1st inst. I was glad to hear from you all and to hear that you was all well. I am happy to be able to say that I am well and have been since I came back to the regiment, with the exception of a bad cold and sore throat. I had the sick headache the evening father started home. Lewis returned to his company a few days after father started home. He is well also, ever since he recovered from the mumps. He was exposed so much at first that I feared they would go a great deal harder with him than they did, it being at a time when I could not give much attention to him. The colonel required every man to turn out that was excused by the surgeon.

Everything has been quiet since the 1st with the exception of an occasional artillery duel and an occasional cavalry scout, one of which the 1st participated in. We left our camp near this place on the 12th inst. and proceeded north west on the Charlottesville Turnpike. Not a man knew where we was going. Everyone thought from the direction we had taken that we was bound for the Valley to join General Jackson. I will clip the account from the *Dispatch* and enclose it in this letter. It does not give the 1st all the praise due them. The account is somewhat exaggerated by the *Dispatch*. General Stuart estimates the enemy's loss at 150,000. We burnt 3 transports in the Pamunkey and some 60 to 75 wagons and captured 250 horses and mules of which we lost 50 on Friday night, and owing to the brushy country we had to pass through and the number of prisoners, is all so exaggerated. We got through with 198 privates 6 officers and 16 contraband Negroes. We was three days and nights that we was not out of the saddle— We all stood the trip first rate and there was only two men wounded in our company— Gilbert C. Greenway, he was wounded by one of our own men. He does not know whether it was one of our own company or one of the Maryland Company. They belong to our squadron. He was wounded in the charge at Old Church in which our company led the charge on the enemy's camp. They all fled at our approach, with the exception of two officers surrendered. One was their commissary and the other was a lieutenant. We pursued the enemy on beyond their camp some distance. We found a little of everything in the camp. We had not time to get anything but a few overcoats that were hanging on the bushes and fence around the camp. I got a good coat for Lewis. He was afraid to take hold of anything for fear it would not be right. We had pretty hard times of it but I would not have missed the trip for $500 as poor a man as I am. Lewis stood the trip first rate. I have not time to write much more at present. We had to move camp this evening down on the James River at the Charles City Road. To mention here the other members of our company that was wounded. He is Mr. Clapp from the lower end of the county. He was shot by a Federal Dragoon. He demanded the Federal to surrender and he paused to do so when Mr. Clapp raised his carbine and shot him through the heart. The Federal had his pistol cocked in his hand at the time and in his deathgrasp pulled the trigger whilst the ball penetrated Mr. Clapp's right leg just below the knee inflicting a very painful wound but not dangerous. Mr. Greenway was wounded on the instep. The ball struck on the spur buckle driving it through his boot and some distance in the flesh inflicting a very ugly wound. He starts home this morning. I must close. They are fixing to move. I will write whenever I can. Lewis said he did not feel like writing today. Give my respects to Mr. Stewart and family, and Mr. Browning's family and my love to mother and Laura and Sue and believe me ever your affectionate brother.[11]

    T. W. Colley

Address Richmond, Va.

———

Charles City County Va.

July 5, 1862

Dear Sister

    I received your kind letter some 10 days ago and have been so busily engaged that I have not had time to answer it and have but very little time today. Myself and Lewis are both well and have been since Lewis recovered from the mumps. We have been moving ever since the 25 of June. We left our camp near Richmond on Wednesday night 25th to join Jackson at Ashland. We arrived there about 3 o'clock the next morning and rested until sunup. Whilst we were resting the 37th Va. Regt. came along and I saw several of my old friends and acquaintances. Among the number was Cousin Will Hagy and Pleasant Clark. They were both well and in fine spirits. We started again after they passed and traveled about 12 miles when we came up with the enemy at Cole Harbour about 3 o'clock Thursday 26th, when the fight commenced and has lasted 5 days with very little cessation throughought the whole five days.[12] We have been in the saddle ever since until yesterday, we got a little rest. The enemy are under cover of their gunboats on the James River. They are getting on their gunboats and transports as fast as they can. There is a great many of them on shore yet. Jackson, Longstreet and Ewell's Divisions came down yesterday to attack them but have not done so yet. They were drawn up in line of battle all day yesterday and last night and are still in the same position yet. This morning they cannot draw the enemy from under their gunboats and I do not think there will be any more fighting at this place. The enemy would have been completely routed if it had not been for their gunboats. We had them entirely cut off from their gunboats on the Pamunkey River and they had to make their way to James River, a distance of 25 or 30 miles through swamps and thickets. We captured very near every piece of artillery they had. If we can succeed in routing them in this place it will end the struggle for Richmond. I do not think they are staying here for a fight. It is only to guard their wagon train. They have about 600 wagons at Westover, about 30 miles below Richmond at which place we are advancing on at this time. Our boys are about 3 miles from the above named place and it lies immediately on the bank of James River and Heren Creek which forms an Island. It is a very strong position with their gunboats to back them. I have not heard any of the results of the battle yet. We was kept in rear of the enemy all the time. That is, the enemy was between us and Richmond. It is reported we captured 25,000 prisoners with 80 pieces of artillery, 60,000 stands of small arms and a large amount of wagons and ambulances. Tell Will Hagy that I saw Will yesterday morning and he was well and hearty. I did not have a chance to talk with him any time. This is twice I have saw him since the battle commenced. They have lost their colonel [Samuel Vance Fulkerson]. I suppose you have all heard that he was taken to Abingdon to be buried. I also saw Pleasant Clark. He was well. I fear I have not time to write any more at this time. Our company all got through safe with one exception. Pendleton was wounded in the foot slightly. There was only one man killed in the regiment. The cannon have began to roar. We will have to move directly so I will have to close. Give my love to father and mother, Laura, and Sue and receive a portion to your self. From your brother

     T. W. Colley

I would like to write a great deal more if I had time
Direct your letter as before. Lewis sends his love to you all and says he has not time to write.

———

Hanover C. H.

July 23rd, 1862

Dear Sister

I received your kind favor of the 14th a few days ago and also received one that was written 30th of June at the same time. There was so much stir and excitement about Richmond at that time on the account of the battle that was in progress at that time that they did not attend to the mail or anything else. It is all over now, and our capitol rests in peace and security once more. I hope it may rest so as long as God permits it to stand. We moved up to this place yesterday from Atlees Station where we was encamped when I wrote my last letter. The whole brigade is here at this time. We have come here for the purpose of getting forage for our horses and to drill. All the recruits need drilling. None of them know anything about drilling. It would not do for them to go in to a fight without knowing any thing abought drilling. I expect we will stay here some time if the enemy does not run us out. I heard yesterday that Jackson was at Warrenton on the 21st. I do not know where he is by this time. He is a very hard man to keep up with. One day he is at Gordonsville and the next day at Manassas and the next day you cannot hear anything about him. I did not get to see Cousin Will Hagy but a very little while he was at Richmond. I would of liked to have stayed with him some time but I could not get the clearance. I had to steal off from camp what little time I got to stay with him. You wished to know if I received your letter that contained the one from Cousin Suize. I received it. It was a tremendous Union letter. I do not know whether to answer it or not.

Myself and Lewis have both been well all the time. David and Charles are both well. Will Morell has been very sick at this time. We have got him at a private house. It is very nice place. He is at the Widow Carter's, about 5 miles from our camp. Charles was to see him yesterday. He was a great deal better yesterday. I have not heard from him this morning. The doctor said he had the bilious fever. There is not much the matter with him now only he is so weak and has awful diarrhea. He has never been confined to bed, yet he keeps his bed very near all day. He can get up and walk about the house. I am in hopes he will be well in a few days. We have to lament the loss of one of our best friends, Samuel Fulcher. I suppose you have heard of his death. He died of Typhoid Fever at a private house in Richmond. During the battle, none of us had a chance to go see him before he died. Will Morell stayed with him all the time he was sick. His father got to him before he was taken away. That will be a great satisfaction to them to know he was well cared for. I sincerely sympathize with his family in their bereavement. In him we lost a kind and obliging companion and a good soldier. Everyone in the company thought a great deal of him. I do not think he had an enemy in the whole company. It is very distressing for one to part with their best friends but alas they must, to whenever it is God's will to take them from us. I sent some Yankee books home by David Sandoe. When you get them, you will see the names of the ones they are intended for. I must close and give Lewis a chance to write some. Give my respects to Mr. Stewart's family and Mr. Browning's family and Mr. Cassell and James Loyd if he is at home, and Shorlot. Tell Mrs. White that Will is well. He is out on a scout at this time. I started out with them and came back with a dispatch to General Stuart. They will be in this evening. They sent in 6 prisoners yesterday evening. They are scouting in the neighborhood of Fredericksburg. The enemy have a small force at that place yet. Give my love to mother and Laura and Sue and believe me your true brother

T. W. Colley

P.S. I was compelled to buy some clothes in Richmond. They cost me very dear, $18.00 for pants, $4.00 for a shirt, $2.00 for slips, $5.00 for shoes. It took very nearly all the money I had to get them and I was compelled to have some clothes [rest of sentence cut off].

Your affectionate
Brother T. W. C.

Lewis says he will not write today. He sends his love to you all.

———————

Rappahannock County, Va.
Aug. 31st, 1862

Dear Sister

I received your kind letter several days ago but have not had time to answer it. We have been on the march for some three weeks. We have been fighting most of the time. The regiment was at Sudley Mills yesterday and Jackson was at Manassas. They had a pretty severe fight near Manassas on the 29th inst. in whitch Generals Ewell [and] Taliaferro was dangerously wounded. We suceeded in driving the enemy back with heavy loss.[13] Our loss was between 700 and 800 men killed and wounded. There is another fight expected to day. I have not been with the regiment since Monday. I was slightly wounded in the foot at Waterloo Bridge on the Rappahannock River. It is not a very severe wound; just grazed the top of my foot. It caused my foot to swell very much. I think it will be well in a few days. I was at a private house for several days. They treated me very well while I stayed with them. We are near Flint Hill in Rappahannock County with the baggage wagons. We will leave here in the morning for Gainesville near where we was last winter. Lewis has been with the wagons all the time since we left Hanover. C.H. His horse has not been fit for duty for some time. Tell Cousin Mitia that I heard from Cousin Will yesterday. He was well and doing well. I have not time to write any more at this time. I wish you would send me a pair of pants and a shirt with Cousin Will Morell when he comes down if you can get them. Tell all the folks I will write to them whenever I get time. Give my love to mother and sisters—So may God bless you is the wish of your

> Brother
> T. W. Colley

———————

Camp Near Bunker Hill, Va.
Oct 12, 1862

Dear Sister

I seat myself to let you know that myself and Lewis are both well and have had our health well ever since we left Richmond altho we had some pretty hard times through the Maryland Campaign. I have not done any service since we came out of Maryland. My horse has not been fit for service for some 3 or four weeks. I have had him in pasture some 15 miles from where I am at this time. The captain made a detail of two men to take all the horses that were unfit for duty when we came from Maryland. James McReynolds took mine and some 6 or 8 others up to Rockingham County. I heard that he had got first rate pasture. My horse was graveled.[14] The gravel worked out above the hoof. It made him very lame for several days. His back was very sore. I hurt it riding sideways while my foot was sore. I didn't stop but a few days when my foot was hurt. It was sore and swollen up for some 4 weeks. It is quite well now. I went in the great fight at Sharpsburg with the 2nd South Carolina Regt. I experienced some pretty hard fighting in that battle. I have a notion to swap places with John Alison in the 37th Va. Regt., Captain Graham's company. I am getting tired of cavalry. It wears out too many horses. I cannot afford to buy another horse and I do not think mine will stand service much longer. It is thought by a great many that peace will be made before long but I doubt it very much. There is nothing stirring since the battle of Sharpsburg. We have some skirmishing with the Yankee cavalry but it does not amount to much. Stuart is on scout at this time into Md. and Pennsylvania after horses.[15] He has been gone two days. We have not heard from him yet. The men took five days rations so we need not look for them for several days yet. There is some 30 of our company dismounted. Some of them have no horses at all. They have been speaking about letting the men that would buy horses go home and get them, but I think they will talk about it until they wore it out like they did last fall about taking our company out home to winter. Lewis is with the regiment at this time. I have not seen him for several days. He was up here at the wagons some six or eight days ago. His horse were in tolerable good fix. His back had been very sore but was getting better. I heard from him this morning. He did not go on the scout. There was only a detail from every company, 20 men from ours. There is no sickness in our company at this time. David Morell started to go home some six weeks ago but I heard of him up in the Valley of Virginia some two weeks ago. He was still there yet. Sister I wrote to you some four weeks ago but not receiving an answer I came to the conclusion that you did not get it. I wrote to you to send my boots and a pair of pants and a couple of shirts by the first opportunity. I have the last shirt on I have, and the last pair of socks and those white and black specked pants that I brought with me from home last spring. I have wore them for the last 4 months steady. If you can send me some good heavy shirts and the pair of socks and a pair of pants and my boots I think I can do for a while. I cannot get anything here without you send it by some person that is coming to the regiment. I saw Joseph Anderson since he came back. He informed me that you was all well when he left home. It was the first I had heard from you all in a long time. Dr. Hutton told me also that you were all well. We have been encamped close to the 37th and 48th Va. Regts. for some time. I have saw a great many of my old friends and acquaintances. Nothing else to do at this time. There is a great many places vacant since I saw them in Abingdon before we left there. Cousin Will Hagy is a great loss to us all. I cannot think there is any chance for him to be alive. Very near all the prisoners that was taken in the Sharpsburg fight have bein paroled but we can hear nothing of him. I deeply sympathize with Uncle Joseph and the rest of the family for the great loss they have sustained in a dutiful son and a kind and affectionate brother. We must all submit to God's will, let be hard or easy. Give best respects to Cousin James Hagy's family and Mr. Stewart's family and Mr. and Mrs. Kenady and Mr. Cassell and Mr. Aston. My love to mother and father, to Laura and Sue and may God bless and protect you all from all harm is the wish of your affectionate brother

       T. W. Colley

Address Winchester, Va.

Co. D

1st Va. Cavalry

———————

Gordonsville, Va.
Nov. 11th, 1863

Dear Sister

I arrived here yesterday. I was a signed to duty today. I will start to Lynchburg in the morning with horses; broken down horses that have been turned over to the Q M at this place. I suppose that will be my business this winter, driving horses back and forth from here to Lynchburg and bringing fresh horses from there down here. I think I can do very well as long as the weather keeps dry. I do not know what arrangements there will be made after awhile. I will try one trip to Lynchburg and if I can't stand it I will tell Major Richard that it is too hard for my constitution. I will write to General Jones in a few days. I think I can get a transfer to him yet if the thing is managed right. I will write and get him to advise me what to do. Major Richards is perfectly willing that I should have a transfer but it is not in his power to give it. A Adj. Gen. can give me a transfer. I will try it soon. I got here very well, had good luck all the way. I have no news to write you at this time so I will close. Tell Aunt I can buy over shirts down here. She need not make any flannel for me. Get some yarn from here to knit it for me, as soon as you send her the yarn. My love to father, mother, Lewis and Laura. I will write to Lewis in a few days when I get to Lynchburg if I have time. Give my best wishes to Mollie. Tell Aunt Kidd I did not see James as I passed Dublin. He was about a mile from the railroad. Believe me as ever your kind and affectionate Brother

T. W. Colley

Charlottesville, Va.
Nov. 19th, 1863

Dear Brother

I seat myself to write you a few lines this morning to let you know that I am well and doing well at this time. I returned from Lynchburg yesterday morning to this place. We start again in the morning with another lot of horses to Lynchburg. I do not know what I will do when we get through moving this lot of horses. They are all that is to go for some time. I will try for a transfer again as soon as I get back to Gordonsville. Major Richards said he had no objections to me getting a transfer if I could. I shall write to General Jones in a few days for him to advise how to proceed with the arrangement. If I fail in that I will go back to the company and report for duty. I can do a great deal lighter duty in the company than I can get to do here. If this is what they call light duty, I don't want to see the hard part. It will suit a man very well that is afraid of bullets. That is all the difference I see in this and doing duty in the company. So if I cannot get a transfer I will tell Major

Richard to send me back to my command. I wish you would see about getting that leather from Mr. Litchfield and get my boots made in four or five weeks. Tell James Loyll that I did not have the money to spend to get them knives for him when I was in Lynchburg but I will get them this time and send them to him if I can find any person in Lynchburg that is going out home. I wrote to Jane a few days ago. I told her to get some yarn and get Kattie Williams to knit me a comforter. I will get buttons and trimmings for my coat and send it home as soon as I can. Give my respects to Mollie and Emma. My love to father, mother, Janet, and Coural. Write soon to me at Gordonsville care Major Steward's and believe me as ever your loving brother

    T. W. Colley

Gordonsville, Va.

Dec. 11th, 1863

Dear Brother

I received your kind letter yesterday evening and I take the first opportunity of replying to it. I am happy to say to you that it found me well and doing very well. I hadn't had very much to do since I wrote to you last. I was truly glad to hear that you were all well. You can say to mother that she need not go to any more trouble about geting me that flannel shirt. I expect to go to Lynchburg again next week and I can get one there. You need not be in any hurry about sending my comforter. I do not want any thing sent until you get my boots ready then I want my trunk sent and all my things sent together. I want my boots as soon as you can get them ready, a comforter and a pair of pants and a fine shirt. I will send you the key of my trunk when you get all my things ready. I do not expect to get to come home until next spring. I should like a dark grey jeans pants if you can get any. I want them for Sunday go to meeting pants. I will get some buttons for my coat next week. I have not been able to get any yet. I do not want my suit Aunt Mary wove for me this winter. I want it made up and kept at home until I send for it. Let me know what trimmings you can get there. If there is nothing suitable in the stores at home, I will try and get something here. A merchant here promised to get me a set of buttons next week. I will send them home as soon as I find an opportunity. You did not state whether Janice Spoyd wanted them shop knives or not. I do not know whether to buy them or not when I get to Lynchburg. You gave me no satisfaction about anything I wrote to you about. I want you and her both to write a letter and put them both in one enveolope and if both of you can't write two pages you can call on some of the neighbors to help you. If you are all afraid to write, I will quit entirely. I want something to eat sent in my trunk for Christmas. I do not get anything here but mutton and bread, very good living for a lousy soldier. I will let you know what all I want when I hear from you again. I was truly glad to hear that there was such a great revival going on at Antioch. I hope all of the familys professed religion in the neighborhood and will stick to it. I sincerely wish I was a good Christian and then I would not fear death in any shape or form. So I will close hoping to hear from you soon. My love to father, mother, Jane and Laure. My best wishes to Aunt Kid, Mollie, Emma, Sam Byors and Miss Mollie. Believe me as ever your true brother

   T. W. Colley

Gordonsville, Va.

Jan 24, 1864

Dear Brother and Sisters

I received your kind favors a few days ago. I was truly glad to hear from you all and to hear that you were well. I was sorry to hear that mother's health was not good. I have no news to communicate to you at this time. There is nothing stirring at this time down this way. I was glad to hear that you had such a fine meeting. I sincerely hope that all who joined will hold out faithful to the end, but alas I fear there will be a great many that will not hold out. I am very sorry to hear that my boots are not done yet. My boots that I have on are getting quite thin. They are not fit to wear in such weather as this. I will have to do with these until I can do better. I am sorry that Cousin James has lost my measure. I would like for you to be working on my coat some. I want my suit as soon as I get home. I want to get married some time in the next month if I can make all arrangements. We have the day all ready set, but I have not decided whether I will come up to it yet or not, but I think I will if all things work right. I do not know when I will get to come home. I have put in a furlough but have not heard from it yet. I am looking for it every day. I hope it will come in this week. I think it has had time to have been approved and returned to me. If I get it by the first of February I will be satisfied. That is as soon as I want to come home. I will get some needles and pins before I come out. Laura, I am sorry to hear that my dearest Emma is gone away to S. Carolina. I fear I will never see her loving face again nor hear that winning voice of hers. I am also sorry that I cannot be at those weddings you spoke of, but never mind, I will have one of my own some of these days before long. Please give my love to Molley and Mrs. Kidd Lewis, I am truly glad to hear that you are still at home and hope you will stay there until you get well, don't think of going to the company until you get entirely well whether you get a detail or not. No person is going to arrest you while you are not fit for duty. If they do shoot them down. You had as well die one way as another but you need have no fear of being arrested while you are unfit for duty.

I am in hopes you will have a fine time at the weddings you spoke of. I would like very much to be there myself.

Mother, I am in hopes that this may find you better. I can never expect to see you well while this war lasts for I know you cause yourself a great deal of unnecessary trouble about myself and Lewis. If you can command your feelings so as to think as little as possible about us, it will be a great deal better for you. We are both bound to serve while the war lasts or until we are killed. My love to all my old friends and believe me as ever your dutiful son and affectionate brother

   T. W. Colley

[Written in margin of letter.] Tell James Loyd that I will bring him some awls and the knives if I can get the knives in Lynchburg and tell him to call his daughter Kattie if he wants me to have the name.

           Gordonsville, Va.

            Jan. 29th, 1864

Dear Brother

I write to you a few lines to let you know that I am well and hope these few lines may find you a enjoying the same blessing. I do not know when I will get a way from here. I shall try next Monday. I have to go before the Medical Board at the hospital. I will try and get away if I can. Cousin Charles wrote to me that he had drew my money. I wrote to him to send it to me. I do not know whether he received the letter or not. I saw General Fitz-Lee the other day. He stated to me that my company was gone home. I wish you to get my money from Charles and send it to me by mail. He ows me $30.00 for taking his horse out home. You will also send that I want sixty dollars, if I can get it before I start home. Start it by the first of Febuary and oblige your brother

   T. W. Colley

           Gordonsville, Va.

           Febuary 7th, 1864

Dear Brother

I received your kind letter a few days ago. I was truly glad to hear that you were all well. This leaves me well. I have had my health first rate for the last five weeks but I feel almost as stout as I ever did. My wound has almost ceased hurting me, I think in the course of two or three weeks. I do not know when I shall get to come home. I must get home by the 17th of this month. I must get there by that time if there is any chance in the world. You must get some of the girls to help me out.

There is no chance for me to get back to my company for another month. I went before the Medical Board on the first of the month. The physicians would not let me return to my company yet. I will not get before the Board again until the 1st of March. I have told them all here that I am to be married on the 17th inst. I think I will get a furlough on that account. If they require me to get a certificate from my sweethart, if they require that of me, you must get Mollie to send me a promise of marriage. I think Major Richards will give me a 10 or 15 days furlough to get married. If they do let me go, I will tell them she is sick and we could not get married until she gets well. If I can work this scheme out, I will be at home by the 14th and if not I do not know when I will get home. I should like very much to be at home with the boys. I hope they will have a fine time whilst they are at home. Well times are tolerable exciting here. Today heavy firing on the Rapidan this morning. Some pretty heavy artillery firing this morning, some musketry firing. The Yankees crossed at Mortons Ford yesterday evening.[16] It was driven back by our forces across the river. It is thought they will try to cross again. They have been shelling all along the line today. I do not think there will be much fighting yet a while. I will close for this time. Write soon and let me hear from you all. I wrote to you to send my money that Charles drew for me, and what he owes me besides for bringing his hoss ought home. Give my love to mother, father and sisters. My love to Mollie, Mrs. Kidd and Jones, James Loyd and Lendy Tremain. As ever your true and affectionate brother

    T. W. Colley

Have my boots home soon

Gordonsville, Va.

Feb 9th, 1864

Dear Brother

I wrote to you several days ago to send me the money Charles drew for me and what he owes me besides. I should like to have some $50 or sixty dollars. If you have not sent it I wish you would. Send it as quick as you can. I also wrote to you a Sunday. You will be apt to get that letter today. Major Richard told me this morning that my papers had been sent to General Lee. As there is nothing to do but for him to sign them and send them back, I expect to get them by Friday, so you may look for me to come home some time next week. That is if you send the money in time for it to get up Sunday or Monday. I think there will be no difficulty in my getting off if it is left to General Lee. I do not know what sort of a certificate the doctors sent to Major Richards. I think from what he said to me this morning that he thought I would get off. He said to me this morning that he thought I would get to return to my regiment. That it was left with General Lee to say whether I should return or not, so I think there is no danger of me staying here any longer. Send that money as soon as you receive this. Send it by mail as I directed before. Give my love to all the girls and believe me as ever your affectionate brother

> T. W. Colley

My love to mother, father, June and Laura.

Gordonsville Va.

Feburary 14th, 1864

Dear Brother

I received your kind letter a few days ago. It found me well and doing tolerable well. I have been building some chimneys for the last two or three weeks. I am very near through with them at this time. I have one to finish up yet and then I have no idea what they will put me at.

I have been looking for my papers to come back from General Lee's Hd. Qrs. every day since they were sent there but they have not returned yet. It will be a week Tuesday the 16th since they were sent there. I am greatly in hopes they will come in a few days—for I get more and more fed up with this place every day I stay here

I have no news to communicate to you at this time. Everything is quiet along the Rapidan at this time. I should like very much to get home before those weddings comes off that you spoke of. I heard of another one that interests me more than any that I have heard of heretofore. It is Cousin Kate. You will say to her that she must put it off until I get there. I want to have something to say in her marrying. I think I will be in time for Molie B. and also the other Mollie's.

I am glad to hear that the boys are having such a gay time at home. I wish I could be there but as it is I will be satisfied to remain where I am until I can do better. Give my love to father, mother and sisters and my best wishes to Mrs. Kidd, Mollie Jones and Uncle Adam, Mr. Stewarts and Mr. Kestner, Hamilleys and believe me as ever your affectionate brother

> T. W. Colley

P.S. I hear Thomas Edmondson had the smallpox. I was truly sorry to hear of such distress and malady getting a hold in our county and more so to hear of one of my best friends having it. I also heard that James Onnigan had the same disease as James Rybussrs.

> Your Brother T. W. C.

Gordonsville, Va.

March 25th, 1864

Dear Sister

I wrote to you several days ago. I have not received an answer to it so I come to the conclusion that you did not intend to write to me any more. I haven't received but three letters in the last two months back. I received a letter from brother some 10 days ago. He stated that the company would leave home in a few days after the date of his letter, which was the 13th of the present month. By that I suppose they are on their way to the army. I shall look for Lewis to come and see me as he goes on to the army. He stated to me in his letter that Captain Litchfield was down this way some where. I expect he would call to see me but I have not seen or heard anything of hime since I left home. I don't suppose he cares anything about me any more. I have wrote to General Jones for a transfer to the 8th Va. Cav. I expect the answer to my letter is at home by this time. I expected to be at home by this time so I wrote to him to direct the answer to Emory. If it has come to hand, you will oblige me by enclosing it to me as soon as possible, or any other letter that may be at home for me. I need some boots and clothing very much but I am afraid to have them sent down here for it is uncertain how long I will stay here. Tell Cousin Millia he owes me a letter and to send it on as soon as possible. I have been kept in suspense so long that I do not know what to get at sometimes. I have been expecting to get away from here for two months and still on uncertainties yet. I have not received a letter from any person for 3 months with the exception of four letters from home. I have written to Cousin Kate some 3 or 4 times and have received no answer from her. I suppose she has gotten entirely too good to correspond with a sinner like myself. I will close for the present, hoping those lines may find you all as well as this leaves me. I am fleshier now than I have been since I went in the army. I get plenty of corn bread and bacon to eat and do nothing but ride a little every day. Give my love to Mrs. Kidd, Mrs. Moore, Mollie and Janice and my respects to all my friends. My love to father, mother and sister and believe me as ever your affectionate brother

Thos W. Colley

Gordonsville, Va.

March 28, 1864

Dear Sister

I received your kind letter of the 27th inst. last night. I was truly glad to hear that you were all well. I have no news worth writing to you. Lewis and Cousin Charles spent the night with me last night. I can assure you it did me a great deal of good to see them and to hear what a gay time they had at home. Charles was telling me of some marvelous things he had done whilst at home. It was quite laughable to hear him talk. The company did not come by here. They passed in six miles of this place. Lewis and Charles flanked out and came to see me. They went on to Orange C.H. this morning to join the regiment, which is encamped some ten miles from that place. They were both well and their horses were both looking well. Charles swapped his horse off this morning. I think he got a great deal better horse for cavalry than the one he brought from home. I had heard of the sad fate of my friend T. W. Bailey before I received your letter. I was truly sorry to hear of such a sad affair. Tom was a noble hearted boy. He will be missed more by the whole company than any other member that could have been lost. He was the very life of the company. He was my next best friend to Cousin Will Morell. I will be entirely lost when I return to the command. I studied a great deal about Tom and dreamt abought him several days and nights before I heard of his untimely death. From what I can learn, the young man was perfectly justifiable in shooting him. He was a stranger to Tom and did not know what Tom's intentions were towards him, and consequently I think he was justifiable in shooting when he did. I know positively that Tom Bailey would not of hurt a hair on a farmer's head. I understand that Tom had not been drinking any that day. All he did was through fun. I do not know when I will get off at this time. As soon as Captain Litchfeld gets here, I will try to get off. I need a pair of boots very much. I am almost entirely barefooted. Tell father to try and get me some leather and have my boots made as soon as possible. You may send me a pair of pants by Captain Litchfield if he has not started by the time this comes to hand. If he is gone, I will make out with out them until I get home. I had no idea that Mr. Litchfield would treat me as he has done. He promised me faithfully that he would let me have leather by Christmas, but alas I see that all promises are made to be broken. There was times I thought he would accommodate a soldier sooner than any person else, but alas I see it is not so. I haven't much to write to you this time. I wrote to you a few days ago. Has Mr. Milmors ever heard any thing of Jack Fleas? Let me know. I did not think to ask Lewis. I will close for the present. Give my respects to all my friends, Aunt Kidd and Mollie especially, my love to father, mother and sister. My love to Dave and James Hagys when you see them. Laura, tell Miss Mollie Stewart that Lewis has gave her to me. I do not know by what authority. Believe me as ever your kind and loving brother

    T. W. Colley

I have gotten you one paper of needles. They are not new as you specified. You wished to know what I was doing, I am courier for Major Richards. I stay at the camp all the time.

Camp 1st Va. Cavalry
Mount Pelia
April 2, 1864

Dear Sister

I write you a few lines to let you know that I am well and have returned to the
company. I expect I will get a furlough in a few days to come home for a horse.
From what I have heard it will be quite a difficult matter for me to get a horse at
this time. I understand that General Longstreet is pressing all the horses in the
country.[17] I hope father will get me a horse soon. It will not be longer than two
weeks before I will get home. I have been trying to come for a great while. I reckon
I will have a good furlough when it comes. There is no news to write to you at this
time. Everything is quiet at this time and I hope it will remain so for some time to
come. General Grant is in command of the Federal forces at this time. He will be
for making a move pretty soon if the weather will admit of it. I will close for this
time hoping these lines may find you all well. Give my respects to all my friends
and my love to father, mother and sisters. Believe me as ever your true brother

T. W. Colley

Lewis is well and sends love to you and all.

Jackson Hospital
June 3rd, 1864

Dear Brother

I thought I would write you a few lines today. I have felt quite well since you
were here to see me. Yesterday I wrote a letter home. Today I thought I would
write a few lines to you. My foot pains me severely every night. It is quite easy all
day. I have no fever today. The doc says I am doing well. Come and see me soon.
Tell Charles to come as soon as he can

Yours Truly
Brother
T. W. Colley

Jackson Hospital
June 3rd, 1864

Dear Sister

I thought I would write you a few lines to let you know how I am getting along.
Lewis has written to you of my wound and the extent of it. I will say it is a pretty
severe wound but not a dangerous one. I was shot in the ankle joint. I thought

I would have it amputated before I would risk suffering what I am. I am doing quite well. My physician says he never saw a wound doing better in all his experience. He says if I have good luck I will be able to go home in six weeks. I hope I shall. Lewis was to see me day before yesterday. He is waiting for a horse detail. He thinks he will get it by the time I am ready to go. I am in hopes he will. I will hardly be able to come by myself in less than 2 months. I think with good luck and plenty of it I will be able to be moved in a month. I am very well attended to. Very seldom we get any wheat bread. Corn bread all together. It is very well baked. I can't say that I want for anything to eat or in any other way. You must excuse hand writing. I have to lie on my left side all together, consequently, I do not do much towards writing. Tell mother to suffer no uneasiness on any account. I am in no great danger. My love to father, mother, Laura and Bettie and believe me as ever your affectionate brother

       T. W. Colley

Jackson Hospital
1st Division
Ward H.
Richmond, Va.

Jackson Hospital
June 5th, 1864

Dear Sister

I wrote you a few lines the other day. I feel so much beter today. I thought I would write to you again. I know that you are all anxious to hear every day if it was so you could. I am doing very well, a great deal better than I expected at first. My foot, or stump rather, will not be as nice as I expected. The doctor that performed the operation left the sole of the foot as a flap. When he got all the bones out, he turned that up over the ankle and fastened it with strips of adhesive plaster. He cut all the arteries off and there being no blood to support that flap, it is nothing more than a dead piece of flesh consequently, it will all have to rot off. In fact, it is very near all off at this time. That won't hurt it materially, it will only hurt the boots a little. Tell Mrs. Kidd to let me know where I can write to Jim. I should like very much for him to come and see me. I wrote to the Richmond P.O. to him but I reckon he did not get it. His letters are all directed to the care of some person. How did Billy Moor come ought in the fight? His division was very near all captured. Father was talking of coming down to Richmond when I left home. If he has got his arrangements fixed so he can come at this time, it would be a great deal of comfort to me, but if he has not I do not want him to put himself to unnecessary expense to come down. If he comes, I would like for him to bring me some apple butter, some jam, or jelly. My love to father, mother, Laura and Kattie

      T. W. C.

Please write soon. I haven't heard a word since I left home from anyone out that way.

Jackson Hospital

June 7, 1864

Dear Brother

I have written to you several times and have not received an answer from you yet. I would be glad to hear from you and more so to see you. I am very anxious to know what you have done with my mare. I am so much afraid that the captain will put some person on her. I cannot rest easy. If she was sold and I had the money here under my head I would feel better satisfied. You must sell her for as near $2,500 dollars as you can get. I am doing very well. My foot has not pained me a great deal for several days. It is watering and running pretty smart yet. I have nothing more to write to you at this time. You will come and see me as soon as you can so nothing more. I remain as ever your

      Affectionate Brother T. W. Colley

      1st Div. Ward F.

Jackson Hospital

June 10, 1864

Dear Brother

I have written to you some 5 or six times without being able to hear a word from you since the day you came to see me. I have been puzzled to know what can keep you away from me so long. The idea struck me that they had put you on my mare and sent you to the company. It has caused me a great deal of uneasiness. If I knew she was sold 4 all things right, I could rest a great deal better. Father was to see me last week. He wished to see you very much. He told me to say to you to sell your horse for what ever he would bring. If you haven't sold my mare I want you to sell her as soon as you possibly can and come to see me soon. I will be able to go home in 3 weeks if I have good luck. My foot is doing as well as it could possibly could do. It is healing very rapidly. In 3 weeks at the furthest, it will be entirely healed over.

I will close for the present hoping these lines may find you well. My love to Charles and all the boys and believe me as ever your

        Affectionate Brother

        T. W. Colley

                                   Jackson Hospital

                                   June 26, 1864

Dear Sister

I take the present opportunity of writing to you. There is a gentleman going to Lynchburg, I will send this by him. I wrote to you some days ago. I do not know whether you will ever get it or not. I will send you a letter every time I get a chance. I am doing quite well and my foot is healing as fast as it probably can. In 3 weeks I will be able to come home if I have good luck. I received a letter from Lewis, written the 22nd. He was down below Richmond near Charles City C. H. He said he was well and Cousin Charles was well. He has sold my mare for 2,700, twenty-seven hundred dollars, he stated in his first letter to me. In the next letter, he said he had sold her for 2,650.00. She was very well sold I think. I want you to send me something to eat. Some bread, butter and a cheese if you can get one. I can eat everything I can get and more too. Rations comes quite slim here sometimes. Sometimes we get a plenty. There is nothing that we can buy but what we have to pay forty prices for, and not much at that price. None of the boys that are here have started back yet. The railroad is tore up for some distance beyond Lynchburg. Hunter [Major General David Hunter] tore up things generally wherever he went. He makes a great bust of the way he ruined private property. He said he would have turned the lunatics out of the asylum at Staunton if he had not been over persuaded by Crook and Averil [Brigadier Generals George Crook and William W. Averell]. He said if he ever got the chance again he would surely turn them out. He is the grandest villian I ever have heard of since the war commenced. I will close for the present hoping this may find you all well. I am in fine health myself. I have never enjoyed better health in my life. The weather is exceedingly hot here. I stay here and sweat all day. I can sit upon the bed. Give my love to father, mother, and Laura. My respects to Mrs. Kidd and Mollie and believe me as ever your

        Afectionate Brother

        T. W. Colley

Jackson Hospital
July 2nd, 1864

Dear Brother

I take the present opportunity of writing you a few lines to let you know how I am getting along. I am doing quite well. My foot is healing very rapidly. In two weeks I think, with good luck, I will be able to go home by the 15th or 20th of this month. I have not heard from home since father was here. I wrote to you about father being here to see me in three letters before this. You did not say anything in your last whether you had received a letter from me since father was here or not. Father told me to say to you to sell your horse for what you could get. Get the new issue if you can for both of our horses. I wish you to ask Doctor Owens to give me a piece of sponge. There is so mutch Erysipelas and Gangrene here that I would like to have a piece of my own. I want you to come and see me as soon as you can. I have looked for you almost every day since you was here but I have not seen you since. I went to the captain a few days ago about not letting you come to see me. I will close for the present. Hoping these few lines may find you well and also that you will soon get to come and see me. Give my love to Charles. His father was not better when father left home. So I remain as ever

Your brother
T. W. Colley

———————

Jackson Hospital
July 7th, 1864

Dear Father

I thought I would write you a few lines today. I do not know whether I will ever reach you or not. I am doing quite well My wound is almost healed. Mabey in two more weeks it will be well enough for me to come home. My health has been very good since you left me. I never enjoyed better health in my life than I have done since I have been here. I received a letter from Lewis yesterday. He said he was well. He has sold his horse for $800. He had give out. He could not keep up with the command. He told me he met with a fellow that was going home and sold to him. The Yankees have damaged the road so bad beyond Lynchburg that it will be a long time before it can be repaired. It will be a month before it will be repaired and father, that will be a great obstacle to my getting home. I will get home sometime before the war closes if I have good luck. Lewis said he thinks he would have gotten out by the 15th of this month. I fear I will not be able to go with him. I have written to Jane several times since you left here. I do not know that any of them ever went through, the road being torn beyond Lynchburg. I do not know whether the mail passes over the road or not. Lewis stated that none of the boys had returned yet so I came to the conclusion that the road was not in running order. Yet, the doctor said he thought that I would be able to come home with Lewis. I am in hopes I will. Nothing more at present. My love to mother and sisters. I remain as ever your dutiful son

        T. W. Colley

                                   Oakland, Va.
                                   Sept 7th, 1864

Dear Brother

Yours of the 26th last month came to hand last night. It found us all well. I am getting along pretty well considering the weather. My foot is healing up quite fast. I think it will be healed over in another week or two at least. The galls pester me so I can't get along as fast as I would if there was none about. There is no news of any consequence. General Morgan was buried in Abingdon today.[18] He was surprised at Greenville Sunday night. That is all I have heard of the affair. We haven't heard the particulars of the affair yet. It is reported that Atlanta has fallen into the hands of the enemy. We have no official report of it yet. Nothing said of our loss. Great excitement through the country about peace but I do not credit anything I hear about it. Democratic nominee for president is not very favorable to us. I don't think if Abram don't get mad and make peace before McClellan is put in the president's chair, our chance is a bad one. I don't think he will offer any terms that we can accept at this time or at anytime. Here after our only alternative is to clean out the Yankee armies that is in the field at this time, and by that time we will have no army, and so we will be obliged to make peace on some terms. Our only hope is that the peace men will resist the draft at the North. It is reported that they are determined to do so. If they do and Abe fails to fill up his ranks this fall he will be obliged to offer an armistice. I was sorry to hear that the captain was hurt. I hope his hurts are not serious. I was glad to hear that Will Montgomery wasn't to badly hurt. All the girls are well. Old Marney Stewart was down to see me yesterday evening. She made me laugh till I like to busted right before her. Give my love to Charles and tell him to write to me soon. I will have to close for this time. It is getting so dark I can't see the paper, let alone seeing a line. Write soon to your

        Affectionate Brother
        Thos. W. Colley

APPENDIX 5

An 1887 Account of His Wounding at Kelly's Ford

An event in the life of a Confederate soldier, today, the 17th day of March 1887, bring vividly to my mind the 17 day of March 1863, the day of all other days to me at that date. Fitzhugh Lee's Brigade of cavalry was in camp about one mile East of Culpeper C.H. They were picketing and guarding the upper fords on the Rappahannock River about sunrise on the morning above alluded to. The news came that the enemy were driving in our pickets at Wheatley's and Kelly's Fords. In a few short minutes, everything and everybody that was about to move was saddling and mounting their horses and moving out to the front. They were hardly under good headway before another order came directing the tents to be struck and the wagons packed and moved back west of Culpeper, C.H. At that time, there was a sick soldier laying on one of the tents who had not tasted food of any kind for 36 hours. When the officer in charge of the camp directed him to prepare to move his reply was, if I must move I must move towards the front. And suiting the act to the words, he proceeded to saddle his horse and buckle on his arms and accoutrements and move out towards the front.

About a mile from camp he met up with the general in command and he accosted him in this summer hello. "C what in the world are you doing out here? I thought you were sick," said he. "I am general, but I had to move and when I move I always went toward the front." The general said, "I have a little flask of whiskey in my haversack. You had better take a little" of that panacea for all ills, so he drew forth his flask and the soldier took it and drank a small quantity and thanked him for his kindness. He rode on with him to Brandy Station, where the general said, "Here C, take this dispatch to captain Litchfield, who is in command of the front picket on skirmish line. This soldier obeyed the order with alacrity and soon sped away on his fleet charger to find Captain L., who by the way was his own captain. The captain was greatly surprised to see him and said, "What on earth are you doing out here, you are too sick to be up out of bed." "Captain I had to move and it was easier to move to the front than the rear." Another drink of brandy from the captain's canteen put new life and new strength in the feeble body and about this time the noble General JEB Stuart arrived on the field and took command and ordered a change on the extended lines, drawn up in rear of a long stone fence that ran up from the river near one mile. So our charge availed us but little. We lost several men and about three hundred horses.

This soldier stopped at the stone fence and discharged all the cartridges he had in the top compartment of his catchbox, and then looked around to find himself alone and confronted by 1,500 or 2,000 Federals, and tried to turn about and seek saftey in a stint of fires. Some 1/2 mile off, across a level bottom field, was the work of but a few moments but there was many missiles of death hurled after him, but none took effect. When he arrived at the skirt of fires, he came on two of his company, one a kinsmen and messmate. We had scarcely each argued a few commonplace remarks when to our surprise, a squad of the enemy's sharpshooters slipped up within 75 or 80 yards of our position and sent a shower of balls around our heads. One of which struck the writer of this sketch about 2 inches from the pit of the stomach, on the left side and passing through his body, coming out at the small of the back near the spine. He thought at this moment his earthly career was about ended. His two companions, who were unhurt, had started to move off but one of them turned and saw him fall and came to him and raised him from the ground, but being so near dead they both fell to the ground together. By that time, the other comrade came up and said, "Let us put him on his horse and carry him off." I said, "No don't attempt that, but leave me to my fate and try and save yourselves. I cannot live." So they stripped off my arms and accoutrements and bid, as they thought, a sad and last farewell. That is the last I remember for some two hours.

I swooned and laid there on the cold frozen ground, insensible for the space of time above named. By that time, the enemy had advanced and were fighting some 1/2 mile beyond where I lay. Then the thought flashed across my mind, I am a helpless prisoner, and with what little remaining strength I had left I tried to crawl off on my hands and knees and get under a stack of rails piled on a stump nearby. But the effort was more than the weak frame could stand and I fell over in another swoon. When I came to again, a young Federal soldier stood near me on horseback, and I spoke to him and asked him to please get me some water. I had not had a drop of water all this time and when I was conscious I suffered terribly from a burning thirst. He replied he had no water and began to question me about my pistol and horse. I assured him I had no warlike _____ [illegible]. I was not at that time in anyways belligerent. Just at that time, whilst I was begging him for water, a squadron of cavalry came along near where I lay and the officer in command accosted the young man in a very abrupt and angry tone, to know what he was doing there being out of the fight. The young man replied by informing him that there was a wounded Rebel over there. The officer asked him if he was put there to guard him. He replied he was, which I knew to be a lie. When they passed up by me I was in a deadly swoon and did not need any guard. The officer stopped his command and rode out to where I was and spoke kindly to me and asked me the matter and extent of my wound, and I told him as best I could and requested him, if he pleased, to get me some water. He replied certainly I will, and immediately sent a sergeant to send a man with water in his canteen. I heard one say, "Sergeant I will go," and he ordered him to go. He came to me on his horse and let the canteen down by the strap but I was so benumbed with cold and so weak, I could not hold the canteen to my lips. He saw the condition I was in and immediately dismounted and placed his canteen to my lips and I drank pretty freely and was somewhat revived. He sat down by me and talked very pleasantly.

One of the Federal generals rode up to where I was and put a number of questions to me about the number of men we had engaged that day and who was in command, and I answered him satisfactorily, and he then asked about my wounds and said he would send his own surgeon to me at once, which he did. The surgeon came, he was quite a pleasant and kindly disposed man. He examined the wound and said very kindly, "My friend, you have not long to live. If you have any message to send to loved ones or any request to make, you have not long to do it in." I replied, "I have lived longer now than I expected to when I fell here." He gave me some whiskey, said that was all he had in his power to do for me. He left me a quart bottle full of good rye whiskey and bade me goodbye. It was a sad moment to me. I was and had been all my life a wild, reckless, drunken, hairbrained scamp and today God had brought me face to face with the grim monster—death. I had been taught in my youthful days to pray and had read a number of good little books from the Sunday school library at old Washington Chapel and I had read my Bible pretty closely and prayed all my life, at times when I was sick or in trouble. But at this time and under these circumstances I prayed with all the fervency of a truly awakened heart, and I did not cease until that still small voice whispered to me, you shall live. Hope sprang up in my heart and now the fear came that the enemy would carry me off across the Rappahannock and send me to prison.

I was alone after the surgeon left me. The soldier who brought me water had gone to hunt up an ambulance to take me up off the field. Whilst he was gone, an Irishman rode up near me and halted. I said to him, "Will you be kind enough to get me some water?" He said, "No be Jesus, I haven't got a drop of water in me canteen, but I got some of the best whiskey ye ever tasted." I thanked him; I had plenty of that by me. By this time my soldier friend returned and brought

The Bible Colley
carried during the
war with his name
on the outside.
Private Collection

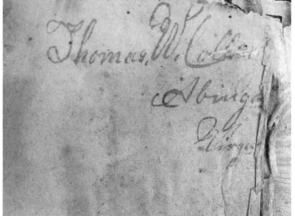

Colley wrote his
name and city of
residence inside.

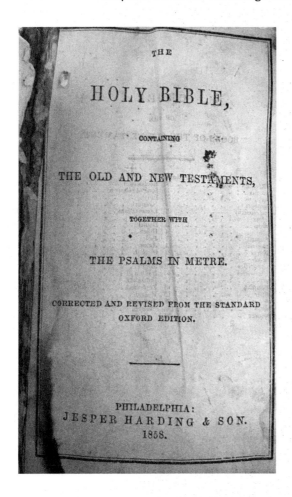

Title page of
Colley's Bible.

the ambulance and two or three rough looking scamps who grabbed me up like I was a log of wood, and they caused me great pain, and I cried out to them not to hurt me and the soldier who stood by drew his saber and threatened them with vengeance if they did not handle me lightly, which they did. After that, they put me in the ambulance and ordered the driver to move on. He was a kind-hearted Irishman, and the place was a new piece of ground just being cleared off and was quite rough and stumpy. Ever few feet the wheels would strike a stump or root. He would stop and say to me "Be Jesus, does it be often hurting you now?" I replied, "No, drive on." The enemy was falling back across the river and I feared our men would come on them and cause a stampede, and I did not have any desire to be in an ambulance with a frightened driver, so I urged him to drive on. Presently, they stopped and put in another wounded soldier of the 4th Va. Cavalry, and by that

CHAPTER XXII.

...es had slain Saul in Gilboa:
...he brought up from thence
...s of Saul and the bones of Jona-
...s son; and they gathered the
...them that were hanged.
...the bones of Saul and Jona-
...son buried they in the country
...amin in Zelah, in the sepulchre
...his father, and they performed
...the king commanded: and after
...d was intreated for the land.
...oreover, the Philistines had yet
...in with Israel; and David went
...nd his servants with him, and
...gainst the Philistines: and Da-
...xed faint.
...d Ishbi-benob, which *was* of
...as of the giant, (the weight of
...spear *weighed* three hundred
...of brass in weight,) he, being
...with a new *sword*, thought to
...lain David:
...t Abishai the son of Zeruiah suc-
...him, and smote the Philistine,
...illed him. Then the men of Da-
...are unto him, saying, Thou shalt
...more out with us to battle, that
...quench not the light of Israel.
...nd it came to pass after this, that
...was again a battle with the Phi-
...es at Gob: then Sibbechai the Hu-
...ite slew Saph, which *was* of the
...of the giant.
...And there was again a battle in
...with the Philistines, where Elha-
...the son of Jaare-oregim, a Beth-
...mite, slew *the brother of* Goliath
...Gittite, the staff of whose spear *was*
...a weaver's beam.
...And there was yet a battle in Gath,
...re was a man of *great* stature, that
...on every hand six fingers, and on
...y foot six toes, four and twenty in

of my salvation, my high tower, and my refuge, my saviour; thou savest me from violence.

4 I will call on the LORD, *who is* worthy to be praised: so shall I be saved from mine enemies.

5 When the waves of death compassed me, the floods of ungodly men made me afraid;

6 The sorrows of hell compassed me about; the snares of death prevented me;

7 In my distress I called upon the LORD, and cried to my God; and he did hear my voice out of his temple, and my cry *did enter* into his ears.

8 Then the earth shook and trembled; the foundations of heaven moved and shook, because he was wroth.

9 There went up a smoke out of his nostrils, and fire out of his mouth devoured: coals were kindled by it.

10 He bowed the heaven also, and came down; and darkness *was* under his feet.

11 And he rode upon a cherub, and did fly: and he was seen upon the wings of the wind.

12 And he made darkness pavilions round about him, dark waters, *and* thick clouds of the skies.

13 Through the brightness before him were coals of fire kindled.

14 The LORD thundered from heaven, and the most High uttered his voice.

15 And he sent out arrows, and scattered them; lightning, and discomfited them.

16 And the channels of the sea appeared, the foundations of the world were discovered, at the rebuking of the LORD, at the blast of the breath of

Throughout the Bible, Colley marked favorite scriptures as identified.

This Bible was Presented to me by Mary Hicks. When I volunteerd in April 1861. It was Kept and read by me during the War &c. &c.

Colley made a notation in the Bible so he would remember the lady who presented the scriptures to him.

Colley's Bible

time, they were in the field and near the tenant house of Mr. Wheatley, where we were both taken out and placed in a vacant room. There was no one at the house but ladies and they were very much frightened.

My soldier friend still stood by me. He could not get anything to lay me on and he went out and took his blankets from his saddle and brought them in and laid them down on the floor and placed me on them. In moving me so much, it caused me to swoon again. When I came to, they were rubbing me with whiskey and had a great fire built, and I began to get warm and to suffer pain in my chest, as I had not bled any outwardly whilst laying out on cold earth and the bitter cold air. I began to roll and tumble to get ease. At last. I turned on my face and the blood gushed out at the place where the ball entered, and I began to feel quite easy. The blood ran freely for some time. I heard the sharp reports of the Confederate carbines not far off, and I said to my kind soldier, "Friend you had better leave me or you will be taken prisoner and sent to Richmond." I could not think of him being a prisoner after all his kindness to me and I urged him to leave me. He requested me to give him my spurs. I told him to take them off my boots as I never expected to need them anymore. My great fear was then of bleeding to death in a short time. He bade me farewell with tears in his eyes. I have never seen or heard of him from that day to the present, but of all men, I would rather see him than any mortal on earth.

He had scarcely reached the river some 3/4 of a mile away when one of my own regiment rushed into the room where I was lying. He was overjoyed to see me alive and said my cousin had you to the lace, where he left me in the fore noon. He went out and found my cousin and brought him to me and he was delighted to see me still alive. He said I must have a surgeon and he went out and found our regimental surgeon and brought him in. He examined my wounds and said it was impossible for me to live. All that could be done was to apply wet cloths to the wound and let me rest quietly. The blood soon ceased to flow and I became perfectly easy and calm and lay that way for 8 days and nights. I could hear and knew all that was going on around me. My hands were folded across my breast. My eyelids were closed and never opened them unless some one spoke to me, then they would close again mechanically. All this time I lived on rice water and cream. Today, my father came to me, the 3d day after I was wounded and remained with me until I was able to start home.

My company and regimental officers supplied all my wants, and the citizens visited me and brought me what delicacies they could command at that time. About 10 or 12 days after I was wounded, I commenced craving something substantial to eat, and the doctor put me off from day to day, until I firmly told him I would not be trifled with any longer. I only wanted a half glass of milk and a small piece of corn bread and one boiled egg. About the thirteenth day he agreed I might have that, and so I got it about 2 oclock p.m. In about 2 hours, I was doubled-over with cramp colic, and for 12 hours I suffered the most excruciating pain. It was all the doctor, father, and my cousin could do to keep me in head by force and entirety. The doctor was very much alarmed by my constant exertion, for fear the wound would burst out to bleeding a fresh and cautioned me time and again about it. I was in so much pain I did not care much what happened. At one time, he took hold of me and forced me back on the bed and said. "My dear sir you must keep quiet or you will bust the wound out to bleeding." I said, "burst thunder, how do you expect a man to be quiet when he is torn and sucked with pains?" After a long

_____ [illegible] they succeeded. I can assure you I did not dictate to the doctor what I would eat or drink any more.

On the 16 day after I was wounded, father and all attendants went out to dinner and left me alone in the room, snugly tucked up in bed. I had heard about the appearance of the battlefield, which was just outside the yard enclosing the house. I had been forbidden to get up or try to walk, but I had a great desire to see outdoors and especially see the battlefield, so I slipped up from bed and went quietly out of the house, and held to it to support me; but when I got to the corner of the house, I could not see anything beyond the yard fence. It was only a few paces from where I stood to the fence. I felt like I could make that distance easily, so I let go of my hold on the house and made two steps, when a guest of wind came and blew me down. I crawled back to the house and clambered to my feet and made my way back to bed, and covered up snugly before any one came in. I never told any of them about it until after I got well.

As I have stated, the house I was in was not more than 3/4 of a mile from the ford of the river that was our outposts. I began to feel uneasy for fear a scouting party of the enemy would cross the river and find me and take me a prisoner, and carry me off and send me to prison. I always had the greatest abhorrence of being a prisoner. I would rather have died any time, so I commenced begging the doctor to have me moved, and let me go home until I got well. He said I could not be moved, and I finally told him, if he did not send some conveyance to move me, I would move myself; his previous experience with me satisfied him that I would make an effort to move if it killed me. So, on the 18 day he sent an ambulance to move me. I was taken to the residence of Douglas Wallach. He and his wife, and one daughter, were very much attached to the Union. He was not at home. He was at that time editor of the *Washington Star*. Mrs. Wallach had been on a trip to Washington City a short time before I went there, and she had returned with a good supply of coffee, tea, sugar, & things that were not found in many Virginia homes at that time. They had one daughter who was heart and soul for the South. They were all extremely kind to me, and then later on in the war they were forcibly taken from their beautiful home on the hill east of Culpepper CH, and sent through the lines to join the husband and father in his voluntary exile. My heart went out in sympathy for them. If it had been in my power, I would have prevented their removal, but those in authority thought it best for them to be beyond our lines. I do not know that they ever conveyed any intelligence to the enemy, but they were suspicious, and that was enough in those dark and stormy days. One thing I know, that no mother could have been kinder to a son than Mrs. Wallach was to me, and no sisters could have been kinder to a brother than the two young ladies were to myself and my father. I enjoyed their hospitality for some three weeks before the doctor would decide for me to start home.

At last the furlough and the news came that I could go home to see the dear ones who had for several days mourned for me as dead. A telegram was sent to my father, on the night after I was wounded, that I was dead; they knew nothing to the contrary for several days afterwards. So, one bright morning we took our leave of our kind friends. My father insisted on paying Mrs. Wallach, but she would not accept one cent. We promised to send her a few sacks of salt but could not at that time get transportation for them, and so I am still indebted to her for her kindness. All I can do now is to ask God to bless her and loved ones, and hope for an opportunity to repay her, or some of the family, in some way for their kindness to me. It was almost as hard for me to part with them as it was with home folks. So, we bade them an affectionate farewell and started for home, in the cloud-capped mountains of SW Virginia. The home of the brave, the land of the free, as we were wont to sing. We came on with out any mishap and found our house with mother and sisters. They were glad to welcome the lost boy home again. I gained strength quite slow, but in these perilous times, I got but little rest or quiet.

In May, the Battle of the Wilderness [Chancellorsville] took place. A poor widow had a son in the war and a pretty daughter at home; the son was severely wounded [in the Wilderness fighting], and mother and daughter wanted someone to go and see about him and to bring him home. I went to Richmond and found him but he was not able to move. I done what I could for his comfort and left him. I went on to Fredericksburg where my regiment was in camp, and brought my horse home, and five others home. It was a heavy task to me in my weak state. I never flinched from anything that I thought it was my duty to do. I came upon by Waynesboro and near Staunton, in Augusta County, to get two horses that were there, belonging to two of my company who had been killed in battle. I got my horses together and came on, the 1st night to within three or four miles west of Lexington, and got a good place to stay and feed. The next night I came on to 6 miles north east of Salem and got a good place and plenty of feed. The next night, I could neither get feed nor any place to stay. Beyond Christiansburg, about a mile, I called at a very comfortable looking house and asked politely if I could get to stay, and the answer was no; at the same instant, the door was slammed in my face. In an instant, my hand was on my pistol and it was drawn and the hammer pulled back and ready to fire on the ranch. The first thought was to riddle the door with bullets, and then my better nature prevailed and I moved on.

I came into the town of Christiansburg and rode up to the tavern and called the landlord out and asked him if he had any thing to feed my horses on. He said he had not a thing but a few shucks. He said, "I will tell you what to do. You go about a mile out of town until you come to a large brick house. There is a man lives there, Mr. Hall. He has plent of corn and hay." I could not think of tying-up those poor starved horses without something to eat, so I thought I would try Mr. Hall, altho I had but little faith in him. We stayed all night with him. When My company went to Richmond the first year of the war, he owned some 50 or 60 negroes then, and he would not allow the milk woman to give us a drop of buttermilk. At that time, he came out and laid down on a rustic seat under a large tree near the spring, and some of the boys, through fun and frolic, when they found out he had ordered the women not to give us any buttermilk, surrounded him and got to singing a song. *'You shant have any of our good whisky when your old whisky is gone and you shant have any of our good buttermilk when your old buttermilk is gone.'* They sang to him until the women had gotten through putting things to rights in the spring house, and locked the door and brought the key to him, and then he slipped out of the crowd that had gathered around him.

I jagged along with my tired self and horses until I came to Mr. Halls. I rode up to the stall and hollered hello. There was a light in the house and it was put out in a twinkling. It was near 12 o'clock at night and I was not going to be bluffed quite so easy, so I continued to holler hello, and finally an old colored man came out from somewhere and came up to the fence. I told him I wanted some hay and corn for my horses. He said, "Old mans gone to bed and don't like to be 'sturbed." I whipped out an oath, and pistol too, and said, "'stirbed thunderation, a man out at this hour of the night who has been fighting to protect him and his property, and now he cannot so much as give him a few ears of corn and a little hay. If you don't go and tell him what I want, I will put a pistol ball through you in an instant." He started off in a run and that is the last sight I got of him.

I waited for some time for him to return but I guess it was hard to tell which the poor old darky was under the most fear of. I tied my horses up to the fence. I took my pistol in hand and walked down to the front door and knocked on the door with the stock of the pistol, and then went to the blinds and knocked on them, but got no response from within. I then walked around to the rear of the house and around to the negro quarters. The doors were all closed and no sign of life or light in any of them. The cribs and stables were all on the opposite side of the road from the house, so I thought I would go over and see what I could find. Everything was locked up tight and I could not get an ear of corn or a bunch of hay. I tried to burst the lock on the crib, but I was so weak and so near exhausted by my long day of travel, I could not do anything with what I had to work with, so I had to give up and went back to _____ [illegible]. I thought I can do nothing for you. I managed down from my saddle, and laid down on the still, thinking I would remain there until morning, and when they came out to feed their stock,

I would get something for my horses to eat. I could not sleep for thinking of the poor hungry horses. I rested there about an hour and got up, and with my horses, started on towards home.

I had come about a mile, I think, when I came to a log house. There was a light shining through and I hailed hello. Presently, a man came out and asked what I wanted. I told him the distance I had traveled that day, and asked him if he had anything to feed on. He said he had nothing near the house. He had some oats about a mile a way, but said you can turn your horses down in the clover lot until morning. So, I told him I would do that and he helped me unhalter them and turn them in. He was a soldier, just returned home about 30 minutes before I got there. His kind wife insisted on getting supper for me, and I would not allow her to do so. It was near 2 o'clock in the morning. Then I told them to go to bed and I laid down on a blanket before the fire and was soon sound asleep. I awoke at sunrise and the good man and wife were soon up and striving around getting breakfast, and he was off to his stock after oats. He soon returned and we distributed them to my horses, who had been doing quite well on the fine grass they were in by this time. The good little housewoman had our meal ready, and I, after my long fast, done a justice to it. After getting Mr. Hall's biography, I got up my horses and started on another long march.

About 2 miles east of Wytheville, I commenced trying to get to stay all night; some there were sick and some had nothing to feed upon, and so I came on to old Mt. Ara about 2 oclock at night. Called on Captain Peat Snavely, and called him out. I said, "How are you captain? Can I get feed for my horses and stay with you until morning?" He said he reckoned not, as feed was very scarce and hard to get. Then I commenced telling him about the big table and big dinner he had set in his yard the 1st year of the war as we went on to Richmond. He said, "Was you there?" I was said I was. "Well I guess you can stay," he said. I said, "I think not. If one soldier is not welcome, another will not be, so if you will direct me how to get to Dr. Shaw's I will go there."

So, I soon found my way to the doctor, a hospitable man in whom, I am told, a hungry soldier was never turned away at anytime either day or night. I rode up to the gate and hailed and the doctor came out in person, and to my inquiry about horse food and so on, he said, "I can feed you and your horses but I fear we can not give you any place to sleep." I said, "If that is all my dear friend, I will find a place to sleep." I carried my bed with me, so a colored man was soon called and horses fed and I was well fed myself. There were only 15 soldiers lodging with him that night, so I found a place to sleep and a good meal. Next morning, and after a tender of some of the new issue, which was refused by my friend, I thanked him kindly and pulled out for home.

When I left there, I thought I would reach home that night. As I came down to Colonel Beatie's, this side of Seven Mile Ford, the old gentleman was down at the road and hailed me and told me to get down and he would have my horses taken and cared for, that I was not going any farther that night. It did not take much urging to get me down and we went up to the house and there I met an old school-marm and another lady, who since that time and up to her death was more than friend. To a great extent, she was the instrument in the hands of God, in leading me to Christ, and was for several years afterwards a great stay and help to me in my Christian infancy and childhood. I thank God that she was spared to us so long She was my sister and my friend—Miss Susanah T. A more devout Christian woman never lived. I think I will tell you more about her further on. I did not now anything about Christianity at that time. Colonel Beatie was a kind, genial, whole souled man and his wife was a kind, motherly woman. They had two sons who were out in the same company with me the 1st year of the war. Dr. Walter Beatie then Fountain Beatie Dr. Beatie died in the early part of the war and Fountain went to Mosby's command and figured in all his daring raids and narrow escapes from the enemy. So, I was as near home as a solider could get.

About this time, the enemy were moving up from Cumberland Gap and threatening Bristol and Abingdon. The colonel tried to persuade me not to go on home but to remain there a few days and see what the result would be. I told him no, I will go on until the road is blocked so I can get no further, and then I will stop. I had my horses brought out and started. I had not gotten far before I began to meet refugees from Abingdon, and they all insisted I must turn back. I said no I will go as far as I can, and I pressed on towards home. At Cedarsville, 7 miles east of Abingdon, at Captain Strawther's, I left one horse and pressed on with the others to deliver them all that day and night. The last one I delivered in Abindon about 8 oclock that night. It belonged to David Lynch, who had died in the army, and I brought his horse home, and then turned toward home.[1]

NOTES

Introduction

1. Brian Craig Miller, *Empty Sleeves: Amputation in the Civil War South* (Athens: Univ. of Georgia Press, 2015), 70.
2. Megan Kate Nelson, *Ruin Nation: Destruction and the American Civil War* (Athens: Univ. of Georgia Press, 2012), 172.
3. Eric T. Dean, *Shook Over Hell: Post-Traumatic Stress, Vietnam, and the Civil War* (Cambridge, MA: Harvard Univ. Press, 1997), 5, 26, 70.
4. Ibid., 111.
5. Ibid., 199.
6. R. Gregory Lande, *Psychological Consequences of the American Civil War* (Jefferson, NC: McFarland Publishing, 2017), 193.
7. Jeffrey W. McClurken, *Take Care of the Living: Reconstructing Confederate Veteran Families in Virginia* (Charlottesville: Univ. of Virginia Press, 2009), 5.
8. Nelson, *Ruin Nation*, 176.
9. Miller, *Empty Sleeves*, 172.
10. Nelson, *Ruin Nation*, 188.
11. William A. Hill, "Thomas W. Colley" letter, Boone, NC, 1897, Courtesy W. L. Eury Appalachian Collection, Appalachian State Univ., Boone, NC.
12. Miller, *Empty Sleeves*, 12.
13. "Charlene Roche Family Tree," Ancestry.com, 1997, accessed February 7, 2017, http://trees.ancestry.com/tree/40850494/family?usePUBJs=true.
14. T. W. Colley. "T. W. Colley as a Soldier 1861 to 1865," *Confederate Veteran* 7 (Jan. 1899): 12.
15. Thomas W. Colley Collection, Ms2003-017, Special Collections, Virginia Tech, Blacksburg, Va.
16. Miller, *Empty Sleeves*, 137–38.
17. Dean, *Shook Over Hell*, 8, 90, 233
18. Miller, *Empty Sleeves*, 131.
19. Lande, *Psychological Consequences*, 143.
20. Nelson, *Ruin Nation*, 178.
21. McClurken, *Take Care of the Living*, 69.

22. Ibid., 55.
23. Nelson, *Ruin Nation*, 219.
24. L. T. Cosby. "Thomas W. Colley," *Confederate Veteran* 29 (July 1921): 309.

1. A Signal without a Word of Command

1. William Edmondson Jones, a native of Washington County, Virginia, graduated from Emory & Henry College and West Point, and then saw service on the frontier, where he served in the U.S.A. Mounted Rifles. John H. Eicher and David J. Eicher, *Civil War High Commands* (Stanford, CA: Stanford Univ. Press, 2001), 325.
2. The Maryland Regiment consisted of approximately 300 troopers in Company K, originally the Howard Dragoons. Robert J. Driver, *1st Virginia Cavalry* (Lynchburg, VA: H. E. Howard, 1991), 124.
3. Brigadier General Irvin McDowell, not Banks, commanded the Federal forces at Manassas.
4. William Willis Blackford, also a native of Washington County, Virginia, took a leading role in raising the Washington Mounted Rifles. He later served as Major General J. E. B. Stuart's aide-de-camp before joining the Confederate Corps of Engineers, rising to the rank of lieutenant colonel. Michael Shaffer, *Washington County, Virginia, in the Civil War* (Charleston, SC: History Press, 2012), 53.
5. Thanks to the screening action of Stuart's cavalry, Johnston moved his force to Manassas, using the railroad for the first time in the annals of military history. His forces arrived at Manassas in time to bolster General P. G. T Beauregard's troops and defeat the Federals of Brigadier General Irvin McDowell.
6. Georgia native Francis Stebbins Bartow held the rank of colonel during the Battle of Manassas/Bull Run where a shot ended his life. Barnard Elliott Bee Jr., a South Carolinian, served as a brigadier general and gained lasting fame as the officer who reportedly gave Thomas J. Jackson the famous moniker "Stonewall," as Bee attempted to rally his troops behind the Virginians. Soon after, Bee fell dead on the field from a wound. Eicher and Eicher, *Civil War High Commands*, 125, 589.
7. No record of a Colonel Thomas G. Preston exists.
8. Colley references Colonel, later Lieutenant General Wade Hampton III, a wealthy South Carolina native who raised and funded the famed Hampton's Legion. The Legion consisted of infantry, cavalry, and artillery.
9. Regarding the Brooklyn Zouaves, historian John Hennessy describes the 14th Brooklyn as " . . . nattily comparisoned in red pants, trimmed jackets,

and nifty red kepis." John Hennessy, *The First Battle of Manassas: An End to Innocence July 18–21, 1861* (Lynchburg, VA: H. E. Howard, 1989), 97.

10. Cub Run: a creek, which spanned the Warrenton Turnpike. The Confederates shelled the bridge across Cub Run, impeding the Federal retreat. Ibid., 120.

11. During the Battle of First Manassas/Bull Run, the Confederates turned a near defeat into victory, after Johnston moved reinforcements from the Shenandoah Valley via rail, marking the first use of the railroad in moving troops during time of war. The arrival of fresh troops, coupled with Jackson's stand on Henry House Hill, reversed the tide of battle and produced a Confederate triumph.

12. Colonel J. E. B. Stuart established his headquarters atop Munson's Hill, located just outside Washington, D.C., where he could see the "spires" of the city. Major Henry B. McClellan, *I Rode with Jeb Stuart: The Life and Campaigns of Major General J. E. B. Stuart* (New York: Da Capo Press, 1994), 41.

13. Debate continues regarding the decision of the Confederates to refrain from pursuing the Federal forces into Washington City. President Davis, who arrived on the field at Manassas near the end of the fighting, met with Johnston and Beauregard to discuss next steps. Often in war, the victor stands as vanquished as the defeated, and the same held true at First Manassas. After a day of brutal fighting, the Southern troops, low on ammunition, hungry, and short of other matériel, did not possess the battle readiness to march on Washington, a well-defended city.

2. I Suppose the Yankees are Human and Will Not Murder Me

1. Eli Whitney Jr. designed and built several different versions of a six-shooter. Jeff Kinard, *Pistols: An Illustrated History of Their Impact* (Weapons and Warfare) (Santa Barbara, CA: ABC-CLIO, 2004), 92.

2. Clark passed on November 2, 1861, because of his wounds. Driver, *1st Virginia Cavalry*, 161.

3. Bilious fever was an umbrella term applied to various diseases, including malaria and typhoid fever. The Ohio State Univ., "Common Civil War Medical Terms," accessed November 28, 2016, https://ehistory.osu.edu/exhibitions/cwsurgeon/cwsurgeon/commonterms.

4. McClellan initially planned to land his troops at Urbanna and advance on Richmond, but lingering concerns over the threat posed by the CSS *Virginia* prompted a change. Instead, McClellan landed his force at Fort Monroe. Stephen W. Sears, *To the Gates of Richmond: The Peninsula Campaign* (Boston: Houghton Mifflin, 2002), 18–19.

5. Johnston sent a dispatch to General Samuel Cooper dated March 12, 1862, informing officials in Richmond of the Confederates leaving Manassas. United States War Department, *The War of the Rebellion: A Compilation of the Official Records of the Union and Confederate Armies*, ser. I, vol. 5 (Washington: Government Printing Office, 1880–1902), 526–27. Cited hereafter as *OR*. Unless specified otherwise, all citations are to Series I.

6. Christian M. Colley, born in 1813, was Thomas's father. "Charlene Roche Family Tree," Ancestry.com, 1997, accessed January 3, 2017, http://trees.ancestry.com/tree/40850494/family?usePUBJs=true.

7. Macadamized roads were made by placing crushed stone over dirt roads to improve transportation, especially during wet weather conditions.

8. Per the 1860 Census, Jacob Merchants, age 65 in 1860, lived in Smyth County, Virginia. "1860 United States Federal Census," Ancestry.com, 1997, accessed November 28, 2016,

9. On April 2, 1862, Major General George McClellan landed almost 60,000 troops at Fort Monroe, with the intention of advancing up the Peninsula to capture Richmond. The resulting engagements, known as the Peninsula Campaign, failed to deliver the Confederate capital. Sears, *To the Gates of Richmond*.

3. The Wonderful Feat Accomplished by a Few Cavalrymen

1. The 1863 Richmond City Directory described the Columbian Hotel as "a large and commodious building, located in the business portion of the city . . . comfortably furnished, and its tables supplied with the best the market affords." "1863 Richmond Directory," accessed November 29, 2016, http://www.mdgorman.com/Written_Accounts/1863%20Richmond%20Directory.htm.

2. No W. D. Barber found in the regimental records, but a William D. Barker was present at the time. Driver, *First Virginia Cavalry*, 149.

3. On March 1, 1862, President Jefferson Davis suspended the Writ of Habeas Corpus in the City of Richmond. *OR*, vol. 51, 482.

4. Colley probably references "Boudinot," as in Elias Boudinot, a member of the Cherokee Nation. Angela F. Pulley, "Elias Boudinot ca. 1804–1839," March 9, 2002, accessed November 29, 2016, http://www.georgiaencyclopedia.org/articles/history-archaeology/elias-boudinot-ca-1804-1839. The term "Digger Indian" represented a derogatory name given to Native Americans working during California's gold rush. PBS. "THE WEST—Diggers," 2001, accessed November 29, 2016, http://www.pbs.org/weta/thewest/program/episodes/three/diggers.htm.

5. The Battle of Williamsburg, fought May 5, 1862, took place as McClellan moved his force up the peninsula.

6. Colley described the sounds of the Confederates scuttling the CSS *Virginia* on May 11, 1862. The draft of the *Virginia* prevented her from navigating up the waters of the James River; after the fall of Yorktown, rather than let the ironclad fall into Federal hands, the Southern troops sank the ship. John V. Quarstein, *The* CSS Virginia*: Sink Before Surrender* (Charleston, SC: History Press, 2012).

7. A Biblical reference found in Judges 7:3.

8. During Stuart's first ride around McClellan, Captain William Latané fell mortally wounded near Linney's Corner, Virginia. Emory M. Thomas, *The Bold Dragoon: The Life of J. E. B. Stuart* (Norman: Univ. of Oklahoma Press, 1999), 116.

9. In December 1864, Major General George Stoneman led Federal troops into southwest Virginia, targeting the saltworks in Saltville and the lead mines in Austinville.

10. The White House on the Pamunkey River served as a Federal supply depot. Previously, the house was home to William Henry Fitzhugh "Rooney" Lee. Paul C. Nagel, *The Lees of Virginia: Seven Generations of an American Family* (New York: Oxford Univ. Press, 1992), 292.

11. Colley misidentified the trooper captured at White House; John Jacob Schwartz, originally from Switzerland, served as a private in Company D. Driver, *First Virginia Cavalry*, 224.

12. The initial Confederate prisoners arrived at Fort Delaware in early April 1862 after the First Battle of Kernstown. The prewar fort, converted to a Federal prison, later became, as historian Lonnie Speer noted, "the proverbial Union hellhole." Lonnie R. Speer, *Portals to Hell: Military Prisons of the Civil War* (Mechanicsburg, PA: Stackpole Books, 1997), 193.

13. Lieutenant James Breathed commanded two guns from Major John Pelham's Battery during Stuart's First Ride around McClellan. Thomas, *Bold Dragoon*, 113.

14. Colley used—perhaps as a metaphor—the term "P Coats," more commonly referred to as "watch coats," and usually associated with Naval personnel. He most likely used this reference to indicate troopers on guard-duty at the time.

15. Operating under orders from General Robert E. Lee, Stuart assembled 1,200 of his horsemen to determine the exposure of the Federal's right flank. Riding behind enemy lines, Stuart feared returning from whence he had come, so he proceeded to encircle McClellan's force. In a daring raid, one, which elevated morale in the South, the Confederate cavalry captured 165

prisoners, several hundred horses and wagons, and destroyed $250,000 in Federal supplies. Robert W. Black, *Cavalry Raids of the Civil War* (Mechanicsburg, PA: Stackpole Books, 2004), 13–20.

16. Major Johann Heinrich August Heros Von Borcke, a native of Prussia, served as adjutant general on Stuart's staff. Eicher and Eicher, *Civil War High Commands*, 590.

17. Von Borcke described his wounding: "I suddenly felt a severe dull blow, as though somebody had struck me with his fist on my neck . . . my left arm hung stiff and lifeless, and the blood was spouting from a large wound on the side of my neck, and streaming from my mouth at every breath." Heros von Borcke, *Memoirs of the Confederate War for Independence*, Primary Source Edition Containing Volumes 1–3 (U.S.A: ICG Testing, 2016), 420. Von Borcke's wound prevented him from serving on Stuart's staff until his death, as Colley described.

4. The Air Was Literly Poluted with the Stink of the Dead

1. After two days of indecisive fighting—May 31–June 1, 1862—at Seven Pines or Fair Oaks, which resulted in the wounding of General Joseph E. Johnston, President Davis elevated General Robert E. Lee to command the Confederate's main army in Virginia.

2. Jackson's soldiers made rapid marches during the Valley Campaign of 1862, thus gaining the moniker "Foot Cavalry."

3. Two Virginia infantry regiments containing sizeable numbers of soldiers from Washington County, Virginia. Shaffer, *Washington County.*

4. Battle of Mechanicsville, or Beaver Dam Creek, fought June 26, 1862, marked the second of the Seven Days' Battles.

5. Samuel Vance Fulkerson, a native of Washington County, Virginia, fell mortally wounded during the June 27, 1862, Battle of Gaines Mill. Shaffer, *Washington County*, 55.

6. Elements of Stuart's cavalry engaged with the USS *Marblehead* on June 29, 1862. Pelham brought up a couple of his guns and began shelling the boat. Recalling her skirmishers, the *Marblehead* navigated away from the scene. Burke Davis, *Jeb Stuart, The Last Cavalier* (New York: Bonanza Books, 1957), 140.

7. The 2nd Regiment Virginia Infantry mustered into service in Wheeling, Virginia, on May 9, 1861. Frederick H. Dyer, *A Compendium of the War of the Rebellion*, vol. 3 (New York: Thomas Yoseloff, 1959), 1661.

8. The Seven Days' Battles culminated with the Confederates attacking at Malvern Hill on July 1, 1862. The battle produced over 5,000 Confederate

casualties but ended the Federal threat on Richmond. National Park Service, "Battle Summary: Malvern Hill, VA," accessed November 30, 2016, https://www.nps.gov/abpp/battles/va021.htm.

9. Colley described a constant nuisance to soldiers: lice.

10. The Second Battle of Manassas, fought August 28–30, 1862, produced a Confederate victory and resulted in Pope's reassignment to fight Native Americans in the Department of the Northwest. Eicher and Eicher, *Civil War High Commands*, 434.

11. On a raid to hit Major General John Pope's supply lines, the troopers of the 1st Virginia clashed with the Federals near Waterloo Bridge on August 22, 1862. The various engagements during this period often are listed in accounts as Rappahannock Station. Von Borcke, *Memoirs of the Confederate War for Independence*, 82–83.

12. Thomas Lafayette Rosser, a native Virginian, eventually rose to the rank of major general. Ezra J. Warner, *Generals in Gray: Lives of the Confederate Commanders* (Baton Rouge: Louisiana State Univ. Press, 1997), 264–65.

13. On September 4, 1862, General Robert E. Lee issued Special Orders No. 102, which included guidelines for the soldiers in the Army of Northern Virginia to follow upon entering Maryland. The specific clause Colley mentioned is contained in the following passage from Lee's order. "This army is about to engage in most important operations, where any excesses committed will exasperate the people, lead to disastrous results, and enlist the populace on the side of the Federal forces in hostility to our own. Quartermasters and commissaries will make all arrangements for purchase of supplies needed by our army . . . thereby removing all excuse for depredations." *OR*, vol. 19, pt. 2, 592.

14. Warren Montgomery Hopkins, a prewar teacher at Abingdon's Male Academy. Eventually rose to the rank of colonel with the 25th Virginia Cavalry. At the time of the Confederate move into Maryland, Hopkins served as aide-de-camp to Brigadier General William E. Jones. Bruce S. Allardice, *Confederate Colonels: A Biographical Register* (Columbia: Univ. of Missouri Press, 2008), 202.

15. On September 14, 1862, the 1st Virginia crossed the Catoctin Mountains, entered Boonsboro, and fought a rearguard action to cover the soldiers of the Army of Northern Virginia as they fell back from engagements at Fox's and Turner's Gaps. Driver, *1st Virginia Cavalry*, 46.

16. The 37th Virginia Infantry had fought in the West Woods, while the 2nd South Carolina Infantry engaged near the Dunker Church. "The Battle of Antietam on the Web," Antietam on the Web, December 23, 2016, accessed January 3, 2017, http://antietam.aotw.org.

17. On September 17, 1862, the bloodiest day in American history with over 23,000 casualties. General Robert E. Lee, fresh off a string of victories in Virginia, took his army onto Northern soil seeking a victory, one that might prompt Great Britain and France to support the Confederacy. The defeat of Lee's Army of Northern Virginia gave President Abraham Lincoln the victory he sought, and he issued the preliminary Emancipation Proclamation five days after the battle.

18. After the Battle of Antietam, the Army of Northern Virginia forded the Potomac on their way back to their namesake state. On September 19, Federal forces crossed at Boteler's Ford and attacked the rear guard of the ANV under Brigadier General William Nelson Pendleton outside Shepherdstown. Thomas A. McGrath, *Shepherdstown: Last Clash of the Antietam Campaign, September 19-20, 1862*, 5th ed. (Lynchburg, VA: Schroeder Publications, 2016).

19. John Opie also used the term "Buttermilk Rangers" in his postwar account of cavalry operations in Virginia. "It was the custom of the infantry to taunt and jeer the cavalry whenever the opportunity arose. They called them 'Buttermilk Rangers.'" John Newton Opie, *A Rebel Cavalryman: With Lee, Stuart and Jackson* (Breinigsville, PA: Kessinger Publishing, 2010), 54.

20. Mr. Cyrus Rhodes, age 52 on the 1860 Census, resided outside Harrisonburg with his wife and 12 children. The daughters Colley referenced ranged in age from 12 to 25. "1860 United States Federal Census," 1997, accessed November 30, 2016, www.ancestry.com.

21. Colley refers to Major Generals David Hunter and Phil Sheridan; both left their marks on the Valley region in 1864.

22. Members of the German Baptist Brethren were commonly known as the Dunkers because of their baptismal method. Patricia L. Faust, ed., *Historical Times Illustrated Encyclopedia of the Civil War* (New York: HarperCollins Publishers, 1991), 229–30.

23. The Chambersburg Raid—October 9–12, 1862—also known as Stuart's Second Ride Around McClellan, consisted of some 600 troopers and four artillery pieces. Stuart, operating with General R. E. Lee's permission, sought to gather intelligence on the various positions of the Army of the Potomac. Thomas, *Bold Dragoon*, 173.

24. Major John Pelham led the Stuart Horse Artillery Battalion until receiving a mortal wound during the March 17, 1863, Battle of Kelly's Ford. Stewart Sifakis, *Compendium of the Confederate Armies: Virginia* (Bowie, MD: Willow Bend Books, 2003), 92.

25. The engagement at Union, in Loudon County, Virginia, took place November 2, 1862. Robert O'Neill, note to editor, March 28, 2017.

26. Ryburn was killed on November 10, 1862 at Waterloo Bridge. *OR*, vol. 19, pt. 2, 802.

27. During the period from Colley's missing journal, Stuart reorganized the cavalry into four brigades. The cavalry saw little action at Fredericksburg as Major General Ambrose Burnside repeatedly threw his troops against the well-fortified Confederates in mid-December. Stuart conducted his Christmas Raid, seeking to destroy the Federal supply base at Dumfries, while Brigadier General Fitz Lee and his troopers attempted to destroy the bridge (they failed) across Accotink Creek. Ibid., 51–52.

5. I Am Always in the Ring

1. Colley describes the action at Hartwood Church on February 25, 1863, when the 1st Virginia, along with Fitz Lee's other regiments, engaged the Federals. Driver, *1st Virginia Cavalry*, 55.

2. Colley evidently made a mistake in identifying the regiment. No 16th Virginia Cavalry exited for the Union; a 16th West Virginia Infantry Regiment was stationed in the area Colley describes in 1863. Sifakis, *Compendium: Virginia*, 236. Perhaps he meant to indicate the 16th Pennsylvania Cavalry. Colley also indicates the captured officer held the rank of colonel and also served as paymaster; it is unlikely the same individual held both positions. Thanks to historian Robert O'Neill for suggesting clarification on the 16th PA and the colonel.

3. George B. McClellan, part of a military group sent to observe the Crimean War, wrote a military manual and designed a saddle based on his observations abroad. The US Army adopted both. Stephen W. Sears, *George B. McClellan: The Young Napoleon* (New York: Ticknor & Fields, 1988), 47–48.

4. Captain James Breckinridge with the 2nd Virginia Cavalry was the officer who put up resistance at Kelly's Ford. *OR*, vol. 25, pt. 2, 61.

5. Hessian: a term sometimes applied to German soldiers.

6. No location known as Shepherds, Virginia, exists. One possible supplier, which provided saddles, harnesses, and other equipment to the Confederacy is Steward & Spragins in Petersburg. Thomas M. Spratt, *Confederate Property and Material Suppliers in Virginia, 1861–1865* (Athens, GA: New Papyrus Publishing, 2003), 36.

7. The Battle of Kelly's Ford, fought March 17, 1863, pitted a force of 3,000 Federal cavalry troopers under the command of Brigadier General William Woods Averell against Confederate Brigadier General Fitzhugh Lee's 1,000 horsemen. Colonel James H. Drake commanded the 1st Virginia during this battle, and the trooper Colley references in the 16th Pennsylvania Cavalry

fought under Colonel J. Irvin Gregg. Gregg's regiment belonged to Colonel
John B. McIntosh's Brigade, part of Averell's Division. In addition to Colley
receiving a severe wound during the fighting, the South lost a promising
young artilleryman, Major John Pelham. Eric J. Wittenburg, "St. Patrick's
Day Melee: The Battle of Kelly's Ford," *North & South* 11 (December 2009):
35–49; Wiley Sword, "Cavalry on Trial at Kelly's Ford," *Civil War Times
Illustrated* 13 (April 1974): 32–40.

8. Averell reported taking 3,000 troopers to Kelly's Ford. *OR*, Vol. 25, pt.1, 47.
9. After the late February 1863 engagement at Hartwood Church, Fitz left a
    note for his old friend Averell: "put up your sword, leave my state and go
    home . . . if you won't go home, return my visit and bring me a sack of cof-
    fee." Edward G. Longacre, *Fitz Lee: A Military Biography of Major General
    Fitzhugh Lee, C.S.A.* (Cambridge: Da Capo Press, 2004), 97.

6. I Came to the Conclusion "God" Could Not Smile
upon This Kind of Thing

1. Probably Daniel P. Brown, listed on the 1860 Census as a neighbor to
    the Wheatleys. "1860 United States Federal Census," Ancestry.com, 1997,
    accessed January 3, 2016, www.ancestry.com.
2. Colic: patient suffers from stomach pains and cramping. The Ohio State
    Univ., "Common Civil War Medical Terms," accessed December 2, 2016,
    https://ehistory.osu.edu/exhibitions/cwsurgeon/cwsurgeon/commonterms.
3. William Douglas Wallach served as editor of the *Washington Evening Star*;
    his wife, Margaret, tended to Colley's wounds. District of Columbia, Register
    of Wills and Conditions, "Probate Records [District of Columbia], 1801–
    1930," 2015, accessed December 2, 2016, http://search.ancestry.com
    //cgi-bin/sse.dll?ti=0&indiv=try&db=usprobatedc&h=89109.
4. The saltworks in Saltville, Virginia.
5. Otis, Dunlop & Company owned two slave trading houses in Richmond.
    Elizabeth Kambourian, "Richmond Slave Trade," accessed December 2,
    2016, https://www.google.com/maps/d/viewer?mid=11AeMB-8ElBEyVEY
    xHiFYTAeFtS8&hl=en&11 =37.55456919380494%2C-77.5180499741821
    3&z=12. Colley talked with his friend about the Battle of Chancellorsville,
    fought April 30–May 6, 1863.
6. Richmond's Winder Hospital, one of the largest in the Confederacy, even-
    tually grew to 98 buildings capable of treating over 4,000 patients. Mike
    Gorman, "Winder Hospital," July 17, 2008, accessed December 2, 2016,
    http://mdgorman.com/Hospitals/winder_hospital.htm.

7. William Hill Bailey succumbed to fever in camp on August 31, 1863, and David Campbell Lynch died from disease on April 3, 1863. Driver, *1st Virginia Cavalry*, 148, 201.

8. According to the 1860 Census, several Halls resided in Montgomery County, Virginia, and listed farming as their occupation. "1860 United States Federal Census," Ancestry.com, 1997, accessed December 2, 2016, www.ancestry.com.

9. The 1860 Census indicates an Isaac Sawyers, age 78, lived in Smyth County, Virginia. This location matches with Colley's estimate of about 40 miles to his home in Washington County. Ibid.

10. Leonidas Baugh, a prominent resident of Washington County, held several positions during his life: newspaper editor, postmaster, county surveyor, and many more. John G. Kreger is credited with removing valuable records from the courthouse prior to its being burned during Stoneman's Raid in December of 1864. Lewis Preston Summers, *History of Southwest Virginia, 1746–1786, Washington County, 1777–1870* (Johnson City, TN: Overmountain Press, 1989).

11. On April 18, 1863, word of 2,500 Federal soldiers raiding toward the area alarmed local citizens. The rumor eventually proved false. Shaffer, *Washington County*, 68.

12. Walter Beattie served as a hospital steward until his death on February 23, 1863. Fountain Beattie, seemingly not a brother to Walter as Colley indicated, later served with Mosby's 43rd Virginia Battalion. Driver, *1st Virginia Cavalry*, 150.

13. Susannah Cox, age 39 on the 1860 Census, taught at the Martha Washington College in Abingdon. "1860 United States Federal Census," Ancestry.com, 1997, accessed December 2, 2016, www.ancestry.com.

7. The Old Martial Fire Began to Burn in My Chest

1. Department of Western Virginia and East Tennessee encompassed an area from Abingdon to the Kentucky border, southward into Tennessee near Knoxville, and a portion of western North Carolina. George B. Davis et al., *The Official Military Atlas of the Civil War* (New York: Barnes & Noble Books, 2003), 385.

2. Warren Montgomery Hopkins served as aide-de-camp and, later, as assistant adjutant general to Brigadier General William E. Jones. Joseph H. Crute Jr., *Confederate Staff Officers 1861–1865* (Powhatan, VA: Derwent Books, 1982), 107–8.

3. Federals under the command of Colonel John Foster, hoping to open a route into southwest Virginia to hit the saltworks, engaged with Colonel James

E. Carter's Confederate force in Blountville on September 22, 1863. "Battle Summary: Blountville, TN," CWSAC Battle Summaries, accessed December 5, 2016, https://www.nps.gov/abpp/battles/tn019.htm.

4.   Brigadier General Felix Zollicoffer, killed during the January 19, 1862, Battle of Mill Springs in Kentucky. Eicher and Eicher, *Civil War High Commands*, 586.

5.   The 1860 Census lists a John S. Bradley in Washington County, Virginia, with over $45,000 in real estate and other holdings. "1860 United States Federal Census," Ancestry.com, 1997, accessed December 5, 2016, www .ancestry.com.

6.   Brigadier General Alfred Eugene Jackson, nicknamed "Mudwall," not to be confused with "Stonewall" Jackson's cousin, William Lowther Jackson, also with the moniker "Mudwall." Eicher and Eicher, *Civil War High Commands*, 314, 317.

7.   Robert M. Hickman, age 28, a druggist in Abingdon. "1860 United States Federal Census," Ancestry.com, 1997, accessed December 5, 2016, www .ancestry.com.

8.   Lieutenant Colonel Vincent A. Witcher of the 34th Virginia Cavalry Battalion served under General W. E. Jones in East Tennessee for a period. Sifakis, *Compendium: Virginia*, 138.

9.   Henry Preston, age 32, lived in Washington County, Virginia. "1860 United States Federal Census," Ancestry.com, 1997, accessed January 3, 2017, www .ancestry.com.

10. The 9th Michigan Cavalry Regiment, under Colonel James I. David, participated in the East Tennessee Campaign in the fall of 1863. *OR*, vol. 30, pt. 2, 555.

11. Lieutenant Colonel J. L. Bottles of the 26th Tennessee Infantry, home on leave in Washington County, Tennessee, joined in the pursuit of the Federals and received a mortal wound. John B Lindsley, ed., *The Military Annals of Tennessee Vol. I* (Wilmington, NC: Broadfoot Publishing Company, 1995), 412.

12. Major William B. Richards served as quartermaster in Gordonsville, Virginia. "Civil War Soldiers—Confederate—Officers," Fold3, 2016, accessed December 5, 2016, https://www.fold3.com/image/72102538/?terms =W.B.%20Richards.

13. On August 29, 1863, the Confederate Congress passed a Joint Resolution declaring "all able-bodied men in the service of the Confederate States as clerks, or employed in any other capacity in any of the quartermaster or commissary departments of the Government, should be put in active military service without delay, and that their places be filled with soldiers or citizens who are unfit for active military service." *OR*, series IV, vol. 2, 767.

8. I Did Not Volunteer to Curry Horses

1. Brigadier General William E. Jones and his force hit Rogersville, Tennessee, on November 6, repulsing the Federal forces there and capturing numerous supplies. Brian D. McKnight, *Contested Borderland: The Civil War in Appalachian Kentucky and Virginia* (Lexington: Univ. Press of Kentucky, 2006), 174.
2. On January 31, 1863, E. Boyd Faulkner received promotion to the rank of captain at the Quartermaster Depot in Gordonsville. He had previously served in the Rockbridge 1st Artillery Battery. "Compiled Service Records of Confederate Soldiers Who Served in Organizations from the State of Virginia," Fold3, 2016, accessed December 6, 2016, https://www.fold3.com /image/9003577.
3. The troopers in the 1st Virginia fought alongside the 2nd Virginia Cavalry in many of the same engagements.
4. The 8th Georgia Infantry Regiment mustered in on June 1, 1861, and served primarily in the eastern theater. In the fall of 1863, the regiment traveled west with Lieutenant General James Longstreet and fought at Chickamauga and Chattanooga before rejoining the Army of Northern Virginia in the spring of 1864. Stewart Sifakis, *Compendium of the Confederate Armies: South Carolina and Georgia* (Westminster, MD: Heritage Books, Inc., 2009), 199–201.
5. No records found on a Captain Poindexter at Charlottesville in 1863.
6. *Poll evil*: swelling of the ligaments in a horse's neck; *glanders*: a contagious bacterial disease impacting the respiratory system, generally fatal; *scratches*: also, cracked heel; *greasy heel*: dermatitis on back of horse's lower legs caused from standing in wet conditions. All in "Medical Dictionary," TheFreeDictionary.com, 2003, accessed December 6, 2016, http://medical -dictionary.thefreedictionary.com/. Identity of Major Preston unknown.

9. I Went Back

1. Private James Aldridge served in the 25th Virginia Infantry Regiment. The regiment formed on May 20, 1862, comprised of members of the former 59th Virginia Infantry Regiment. "Civil War Soldiers—Confederate—VA," Fold3, 2016, accessed December 7, 2016, https://www.fold3.com/image/ 271/10764978; Sifakis, *Compendium: Virginia*, 207.
2. Castle Thunder, a prison in Richmond capable of holding approximately 1,400 people, housed Confederate deserters as well as Federal prisoners. Speer, *Portals to Hell*, 93–95.

3. No records found for a Captain Broyles serving as provost.

4. Colley most likely referenced Stuart Hospital, a facility with 500 beds named for J. E. B. Stuart. The reference "Stuart at Windsor," possibly indicates confusion with Richmond's Winder Hospital, noted earlier. Colley convalesced at the Jackson General Hospital near Hollywood Cemetery. The facility eventually grew to 2,500 beds. "Stuart Hospital," Civil War Richmond, December 2, 2008, accessed December 7, 2016, http://mdgorman.com /Hospitals/stuart_hospital.htm; "Jackson Hospital," Civil War Richmond, February 5, 2008, accessed December 7, 2016, http://mdgorman.com /Hospitals/jackson_hospital.htm.

5. James Emmons, age 63 in the 1860 Census, lived in Culpeper, Virginia. "1860 United States Federal Census," Ancestry.com, 1997, accessed December 7, 2016, www.ancestry.com.

6. In February 1864, the Confederate Congress expanded the ages of able-bodied white males liable for conscription to those between 17 and 50. "Laws of Congress in Regard to Taxes, Currency and Conscription, Passed February 1864," Documenting the American South, accessed December 7, 2016, http://docsouth.unc.edu/imls/lawsofcong/lawsofcong.html.

7. Brigadier General Fitz Lee's cavalry force clashed with the Federal horsemen of Brigadier General David Gregg near Kearneysville, West Virginia, on July 16, 1863. William Morell, Joseph Pendleton, and Colonel James Drake numbered among the 13 Confederate casualties. *The Union Army: A History of Military Affairs in the Loyal States* (1908; repr., Wilmington, NC: Broadfoot Publishing, 1998), 6:798; Driver, *1st Virginia Cavalry*, 70.

8. Colonel Abraham Fulkerson of the 63rd Tennessee Infantry numbered among the "Immortal 600" prisoners held in Charleston and Savannah. Fulkerson served as president of the prisoner's association. Shaffer, *Washington County*, 60.

9. James W. Breathed served in Pelham's Battery rising to the rank of major in 1864; he eventually led the battalion. Driver, *1st Virginia Cavalry*, 154.

10. On February 29, 1864, Breathed's gunners met Brigadier General George Custer's cavalry at Rio Hill. Custer's force served as a diversion for the Kilpatrick-Dahlgren Raid. Brigadier General Judson Kilpatrick and Colonel Ulric Dahlgren rode toward Richmond with the goal of freeing Federal prisoners, and perhaps, per papers found on Dahlgren's fallen body, kill Jefferson Davis and other Confederate officials. One of the participants later recalled of the nature of Breathed's engagement. "There was not one rifle or carbine in the whole crew, a few pistols and one or two sabers composing all the dangerous arms; the rest of the men had sticks and clubs. Some of them

had pieces of fence rails, and all sorts of representative sabers and carbines on exhibition to make the command appear warlike, formidable, and dangerous." David P. Bridges, *Fighting with Jeb Stuart: Major James Breathed and the Confederate Horse Artillery* (Arlington, VA: Breathed Bridges Best, 2006), 198–204.

10. That Is the Last I Knew until My Foot Was Off

1. Confederate cavalry troops had to provide their own horses. If they lost one in battle and could not secure another, often they would return home to obtain one from their family.

2. The Battle of Cloyd's Mountain, fought May 9, 1864, involved the troops of Brigadier General George Crook on a raid to cut the Virginia & Tennessee Railroad. A Confederate force under Brigadier General Albert Jenkins intercepted them at Cloyd's Mountain. The victorious Federals burned the depot in Dublin, then destroyed the New River Bridge at Central Depot. Virginia Center for Civil War Studies, "Battle of Cloyd's Mountain," 2016, accessed December 8, 2016, http://www.civilwar.vt.edu/wordpress/battle-of-cloyds -mountain/. The following day, Brigadier General William Woods Averell's Federals battled Brigadier General W. E. Jones and his Confederates at Cove Mountain in Wythe County, Virginia. After four hours of fighting, the Confederates withdrew. Averell and company burned the New River Bridge the next day. *The Union Army*, 5:323.

3. Hay Turnbull, age 43 in the 1860 Census, ran a hotel in Franklin County, Virginia. "1860 United States Federal Census," Ancestry.com, 1997, accessed December 8, 2016, www.ancestry.com.

4. Stuart died on May 12, 1864, from a wound received the previous day in fighting at Yellow Tavern. McClellan, *I Rode with Jeb Stuart*, 416.

5. Brigadier General Fitz Lee, responding to a plea from the citizens of Charles City County—one also supported by General Braxton Bragg in Richmond—assembled 800 cavalry troops and rode toward Wilson's Wharf (also known as Kennon's Landing or Fort Pocahontas). The Federal garrison at Wilson's Wharf, African-American troops, operated under the command of Brigadier General Edward Wild. After an attack on the fort, one producing several Confederate casualties, Fitz withdrew his force. Longacre, *Fitz Lee*, 155–56.

6. When cavalry fought dismounted, which often proved the case, they would count-off, and every fourth man would remain behind, out of the line of fire, to hold the horses of the other three troopers.

7. On the May/June 1864 muster roll, Colley was listed first as 2nd Corporal, then 1st Corporal. "Compiled Service Records of Confederate Soldiers Who Served in Organizations from the State of Virginia," Fold3, 2016, accessed December 7, 2016, https://www.fold3.com/image/6793718.

8. John Haw III owned the farm and previously operated a facility manufacturing farm machinery. Gordon C. Rhea, "'The Hottest Place I Ever Was In:' The Battle of Haw's Shop, May 28, 1864," *North & South* 4 (April 2001): 42–57.

9. The Battle of Haw's Shop (Enon Church), fought May 28, 1864, marked Colley's final experience in the field during the war. On this day, as Grant maneuvered his forces away from the North Anna, Major General Philip Sheridan sent Brigadier General David Gregg's Division to Haw's Shop to hold the important position where five roads converged. Major General Wade Hampton had overall command of the Confederate forces on the field, and Brigadier General Williams C. Wickham led the brigade containing Colley and the balance of the 1st Virginia Cavalry. At some point during the seven hours of fighting, Colley and five other members of the 1st Virginia advanced to a fence line amid the dense undergrowth on the field, and Colley received the wound to his left foot, which surgeons later amputated. Rhea, "The Hottest Place I Ever Was In."

10. Capable of accommodating 2,500 patients, Jackson Hospital was the third largest hospital in the Confederacy. Rebecca Barbour Calcutt, *Richmond's Wartime Hospitals* (Gretna, LA: Pelican, 2005), 74.

11. An account from a Federal prisoner also states the land near the hospital was the farm of General Winfield Scott. John McElroy, *Andersonville: A Story of Rebel Military Prisons, Fifteen Months a Guest of the So-Called Southern Confederacy; A Private Soldiers Experience in Richmond, Andersonville, Savannah, Millen, Blackshear, and Florence* (Scituate, MA: Digital Scanning, Inc., 1999), 83.

12. Assistant Surgeon Josiah N. Boggs served in the Jackson Hospital during Colley's stay. "Compiled Service Records of Confederate Soldiers Who Served in Organizations from the State of Virginia," Fold3, 2016, accessed December 8, 2016, https://www.fold3.com/image/68814837.

13. On February 17, 1864, Congress changed the requirement to fifteen able-bodied slaves and required planters with exempted overseers to deliver one hundred pounds of bacon or its equivalent for every slave on the plantation to the government and to sell his or her surplus to the government or to soldiers' families at government prices. Susanna Michele Lee, "Twenty-Slave Law," Encyclopedia Virginia, accessed December 8, 2016, http://www.encyclopediavirginia.org/twenty-slave_law#start_entry.

14. Colley and the other patients heard the echo of salvos fired in the various engagements during the Federal advance on Petersburg. Steven E. Woodworth et al., *The Atlas of the Civil War* (Oxford: Oxford Univ. Press, 2004), 252.

15. Loosely based on a line from Shakespeare. "The Life and Death of Julius Caesar," The Complete Works of William Shakespeare, accessed December 8, 2016, http://shakespeare.mit.edu/julius_caesar/full.html.

16. The Virginia Secession Convention, meeting in Richmond, consisted of three factions. The immediate secessionists were eager to sever ties with the Union at all costs. On the opposite end of the spectrum sat the unconditional Unionists, delegates who remained loyal to the Union come what may. In the middle, and comprising the largest share of delegates, the conditional Unionists, those hoping for a compromise to avoid war. With the firing on Fort Sumter and President Lincoln's subsequent call for 75,000 volunteers to put down the rebellion, the pendulum swung in Richmond, and on April 17, 1861, the convention voted to secede, putting the issue before the residents of the Old Dominion for approval by popular vote on May 24, 1861. Shaffer, *Washington County*, 15–23.

17. Big and Little Otter Creeks in Bedford, Virginia. Friends of the Blue Ridge Parkway, "Peaks of Otter," December 6, 2016, accessed December 8, 2016, https://www.friendsbrp.org/discover-the-parkway/destinations /peaks-of-otter/.

18. Central Depot, current day Radford, Virginia.

19. Records indicate an "M. Littral" served in the Carrol County Militia. Historical Data Systems, Inc., "American Civil War Research Database," accessed December 8, 2016, http://www.civilwardata.com/active/hdsquery .dll?SoldierHistory?C&1394974.

20. During the Confederate retreat from Gettysburg, on July 10 near Funkstown, Maryland, the troopers of Brigadier General John Buford clashed with Stuart's horsemen. Edward G. Longacre, *The Cavalry at Gettysburg: A Tactical Study of Mounted Operations During the Civil War's Pivotal Campaign, 9 June-14 July 1863* (Lincoln: Univ. of Nebraska Press, 1993), 264.

11. Men and Women Went about Softly . . . Waiting and Dreading the End

1. Emory & Henry College, alma mater of J. E. B. Stuart and W. E. Jones, closed during the war as facility and students left to serve the Confederacy. Wiley Hall, the main building on campus, was used as a General Hospital. Shaffer, *Washington County*, 60.

2. On December 11, 1864, Major General George Stoneman assembled a force
    of 5,500, which included Major General Stephen Burbridge's command.
    Their target: the saltworks in Saltville, Virginia, and the lead mines near
    Austinville, Virginia. They put the salt works out of order for a few months
    but did little damage to the lead mines. The Second Battle of Saltville,
    fought December 20–21, yielded a victory for the Federals, as they over-
    ran the lightly defended works. Colley included Brigadier General Samuel
    Carter as one of the raid's participants, but Carter did not participate in the
    attack on Saltville. Perhaps Colley confused Carter's December 1863 raid
    into East Tennessee with this later action. Ibid., 80–85.

3. Captain James Wyatt with the 13th Tennessee Cavalry (US), a former
    resident of Abingdon, stayed behind after the balance of Stoneman's force
    continued their northward trek. Seeking vengeance on a local judge, with
    whom Wyatt had numerous run-ins as a troubled youth, Wyatt decided to
    burn the court house. Strong winds fanned the flames, which quickly spread
    to adjacent buildings. Ibid., 81–82.

4. Colley mentions the United States Colored Cavalry (USCC), which fought
    under Burbridge during the First Battle of Saltville, October 2, 1864. On the
    morning after the battle, Burbridge retreated into Kentucky leaving most
    of the wounded USCC on the field. According to accounts from witnesses,
    Confederate guerrilla fighter Champ Ferguson and company walked the
    field killing the wounded USCC. The actual number of troops killed during
    what came to be known as "the Saltville Massacre" remains unknown.
    Thomas D. Mays, *The Saltville Massacre* (Fort Worth, TX: McWhiney
    Foundation Press, 1998).

5. Reverend Thomas K. Catlett, age 64, listed as a Methodist preacher on the
    1860 Census. "1860 United States Federal Census," Ancestry.com, 1997,
    accessed December 9, 2016, www.ancestry.com.

6. Colonel James Brisbin led the 5th USCC, and Colonel James F. Wade the
    6th USCC. Both units fought in Colonel Robert Ratliff's Brigade during the
    October 2, 1864, First Battle of Saltville. Mays, *Saltville*, 27, 74.

7. Major General John C. Breckinridge and a couple thousand hastily assem-
    bled Confederate soldiers fought Stoneman's force of 5,000 for two days,
    December 17 and 18, in Marion, Virginia. Shaffer, *Washington County*, 83.

8. Captain James L. Cole initially served in the 37th Virginia Infantry, and later
    as quartermaster in Brigadier General Raleigh Colston's Brigade. Thomas M.
    Rankin, *37th Virginia Infantry* (Lynchburg, VA: H. E. Howard, 1987), 105.

9. Lieutenant Colonel Vincent A. Witcher of the 34th Virginia Cavalry
    Battalion (Sifakis, *Compendium: Virginia*, 138.); Colonel Henry L. Giltner
    of the 4th Kentucky Cavalry (Historical Data Systems, Inc., "American

Civil War Research Database," accessed December 9, 2016, http://www
.civilwardata.com/active/hdsquery.dll?SoldierHistory?C&240560); and
Brigadier General John C. Vaughn led Vaughn's Cavalry Brigade (Eicher and
Eicher, *Civil War High Commands*, 544).

10. Captain Harrison Ford of the 39th Kentucky Infantry. Historical Data
    Systems, Inc., "American Civil War Research Database," accessed December 9,
    2016, http://www.civilwardata.com/active/hdsquery.dll?SoldierHistory
    ?U&2247888.

11. Confederate prisoners who agreed to fight for the Union rather than remain
    incarcerated. Often, these "Galvanized Yankees" were sent to distant out-
    posts to fight Native Americans, rather than return to the active Civil War
    theaters and fight against their former comrades.

12. Andersonville Prison Commander Henry Wirz was hanged November 10,
    1865; Jefferson Davis was held at Fort Monroe.

13. In the immediate postwar period, many former Confederates continued
    to wear their uniforms in public. Eventually, US authorities forced them
    to remove rank insignia, badges, and buttons. William A. Blair, *Virginia's
    Private War: Feeding Body and Soul in the Confederacy, 1861–1865* (New
    York: Oxford Univ. Press, 2000), 138.

14. On March 2, 1867, the US Congress passed the First Reconstruction Act,
    placing each former state of the Confederacy, except Tennessee, in one of five
    military districts. Virginia comprised district one. Thomas C. Mackey, ed.,
    A Documentary History of the Civil War Era: Legislative Achievements, vol.
    1 (Knoxville: Univ. of Tennessee Press, 2012), 191–92.

12. Blessed be the Name of the Lord

1. Cosby was elected sheriff October 8, 1870. Summers, *History of Southwest
   Virginia*, 831.

2. Per the 1870 Census, several African Americans with the surname Ferguson
   lived in Russell County, Virginia, but none reported sharing the name of the
   notorious guerrilla fighter Champ Ferguson. "1870 United States Federal
   Census," Ancestry.com, 1997, accessed January 4, 2017, www.ancestry.com.

3. Daniel Trigg, an attorney in Washington County. Ibid., 837.

4. Theophilus P. Dunn, Town sergeant for Abingdon in 1872. Ibid., 661.

5. William G. E. Cunningham served Washington County in the Methodist
   Episcopal Church South, 1849–1852. Ibid., 844.

6. George Washington Ryan died August 15, 1872. "Charlene Roche Family
   Tree," Ancestry.com, 1997, accessed January 4, 2017, http://trees.ancestry
   .com/tree/40850494/person/20077933511/facts.

7. A native of Washington County, McCracken served the Methodist Church from 1879 until his retirement 30 years later. "Sketches of Holston Preachers," Photographs and Stories of Holston History, 2016, accessed December 9, 2016, http://holston.org/about/resources/photographs-and -stories-holston-history/resources/.

8. James Lewis Colley, born September 3, 1873, died on November 2 of the same year. "Charlene Roche Family Tree," Ancestry.com, 1997, accessed January 4, 2017, http://trees.ancestry.com/tree/40850494 /person/20074348422/facts.

13. I Have Wondered Up and Down in This Old World

1. Daniel Thomas Colley, born November 2, 1874. "Charlene Roche Family Tree," Ancestry.com, 1997, accessed January 4, 2017, http://trees.ancestry .com/tree/40850494/person/20074348422/facts.

2. William C. Edmondson, a prominent resident of Washington County, served in several positions during his lifetime. Summers, *History of Southwest Virginia*.

3. Leonidas Baugh served as deputy clerk of court in Washington County from 1869–1871; Connally F. Trigg worked as an attorney; L. Thompson Cosby served as clerk of court; Banghand not found. Ibid., 601, 837.

4. Fitzhugh Lee Colley, born October 5, 1876. "Charlene Roche Family Tree," Ancestry.com, 1997, accessed January 4, 2017, http://trees.ancestry.com /tree/40850494/person/20074348425/facts.

5. Thomas C. Lively of Wolf Creek, West Virginia. Age 24 on the 1870 census. "1870 United States Federal Census," Ancestry.com, 1997, accessed December 12, 2016, www.ancestry.com.

6. Hay mew: a stable with living quarters. English Dialect Society, *The English Dialect Dictionary: Being the Complete Vocabulary of All Dialect Words Still in Use, or Known to Have Been in Use During the Last Two Hundred Years*, ed. Joseph Wright (Oxford: OUP Australia and New Zealand, 1981), 445.

7. J. Lloyd of Glade Spring, Virginia. Age 35 on the 1870 Census; Landon King age 46 on the same census. Ibid.

8. Thomas and Eliza had 12 children. "Charlene Roche Family Tree," Ancestry .com, 1997, accessed December 12, 2016, http://trees.ancestry.com/tree /40850494/family?usePUBJs=true.

9. John Mullins Colley, born March 28, 1887, in Abingdon, Virginia. Ibid.

10. Mark Cross, listed in the 1880 Census as a resident of Saginaw, Michigan, employed as a "Land Looker." "1900 United States Federal Census," Ancestry. com, 1997, accessed December 12, 2016, www.ancestry.com.

11. James C. Porterfield, Washington County supervisor from Glade Spring. Summer, *History of Southwest Virginia*, 840.

12. T. Jeff Caldwell served in the 37th Virginia Infantry. Rankin, *37th Virginia*, 102.

13. John C. Summers served as commonwealth's attorney for Washington County, 1904–05. "A Guide to the Papers of Lewis Preston Summers 1814–1947 Lewis Preston Summers, Papers, 1814–1947 2781," Virginia Heritage, 2001, accessed December 12, 2016, http://ead.lib.virginia.edu/vivaxtf/view?docId=uva-sc/viu01394.xml.

14. Jonas S. Kelly, county supervisor from the Saltville District. Summers, *History of Southwest Virginia*, 840.

15. George W. Ward, a court judge in Abingdon. Ibid., 594.

16. D. A. Jones served as mayor of Abingdon 1870–72. Ibid., 660.

17. Charles W. Steele served as land assessor; no records on Allerson or Mullins. Ibid., 781.

18. A town in Spartanburg County, South Carolina.

19. The Methodist Church split in 1844 over the institution of slavery, thereby forming, in the slaveholding states, the Methodist Episcopal Church South. "The Slavery Question and Civil War (1844–1865)—the United Methodist Church," United Methodist Church, 2016, accessed December 12, 2016, http://www.umc.org/who-we-are/the-slavery-question-and-civil-war.

20. John W. Bishop, born in 1870, lived in Spartanburg County, South Carolina. "1880 United States Federal Census," Ancestry.com, 1997, accessed December 12, 2016, www.ancestry.com.

21. G. S. Coffin served as president of the Enoree mills. *Gaffney Ledger*, March 10, 1898, 6.

22. President William McKinley's Republican administration.

23. The Chichester Camp 905, formed in Enoree, found in the UCV camp listing of 1897, had William A. Hill as commander and Thomas W. Colley as adjutant. "Organization of 1026 Camps in the United Confederate Veteran Association Prepared Expressly for Use of Delegates to the Seventh Reunion and Meeting of the Association, Held at Nashville, Tenn., on June 22nd, 23rd and 24th, 1897," United Confederate, June 18, 2008, accessed December 12, 2016, https://archive.org/details/organizationof1000unit.

24. Captain Charles E. Chichester served with the South Carolina Gist Guard Artillery Battery. Sifakis, *Compendium: South Carolina and Georgia*, 19.

25. Diarrhea mixed with blood. "Medical Definition Of Bloody Flux," Merriam-Webster.com, last modified 2017, accessed June 8, 2017, https://www.merriam-webster.com/medical/bloody%20flux.

26. Dr. Julian H. Allen of Cross Anchor, South Carolina. "1900 United States Federal Census," Ancestry.com, 1997, accessed December 12, 2016, www .ancestry.com.
27. Susan Cox, age 60 on the 1880 Census. "1880 United States Federal Census," Ancestry.com, 1997, accessed December 12, 2016, www.ancestry.com.
28. James Ryan, age 59 in the 1880 Census, lived in Colley's home. Ibid.
29. Many Ackens lived in Spartanburg County, South Carolina, during Colley's time there. No "Eakens" found. "1900 United States Federal Census," Ancestry.com, 1997, accessed December 12, 2016, www.ancestry.com.
30. Washington Chapel United Methodist Church, for which Colley helped construct a new building, celebrated their 150th anniversary in 2016.
31. J. C. Sisk served as deputy treasurer of Washington County, 1899. Summers, *History of Southwest Virginia*, 838.
32. Henry C. Stuart, age 45, lived in Russell County, Virginia. "1900 United States Federal Census," Ancestry.com, 1997, accessed December 12, 2016, www.ancestry.com. C. F. Keller served in Barr's Light Artillery. Historical Data Systems, Inc. "American Civil War Research Database," accessed December 12, 2016, http://www.civilwardata.com/active/hdsquery.dll ?SoldierHistory?C& 377226.
33. Judge Francis Beattie Hutton served as judge of the Twenty-Third Judicial District; he was elected February 1903. Summers, *History of Southwest Virginia*, 772.

Appendix 1. Regimental History and Biographical Roster Sketch Contained in Colley's Journal

1. Note to readers: Colley did not enter all entries in alphabetical order.
2. Jenny: a female donkey. Merriam-Webster.com, last modified 2017, accessed January 4, 2017, https://www.merriam-webster.com/dictionary/jenny.
3. Fitzhugh Lee wrote to Colley on at least two occasions. In the first, dated January 26, 1895, Lee wrote: "Your kind letter received. I am glad that you are well, and that you take the proper view of life, with its burdens. We are all apt to have business misfortunes and domestic losses and troubles, but with brave hearts and clear consciences we can surmount them. Remember me to any of old Company D you may meet. Alas! We are all growing old now, and our ranks are being thinned rapidly, all of which should make us—the old soldiers of the State—cling closer and stand together in all things. I shall always be glad to hear from you." Lee's second letter to Colley, on October 22, 1896, stated: "I am always pleased to hear from [you] and

any of my old soldiers, particularly from those I am able to recall as having proved themselves good ones, and in that class I shall always place you." Thomas W. Colley, "T. W. Colley as a Soldier—1861 to 1865," *Confederate Veteran* 7 (January 1899): 12.

4. On June 9, 1863, the largest cavalry battle of the war took place at Brandy Station in Virginia.

5. Colley referred to a communication from Lieutenant General U. S. Grant regarding Hunter's destruction in the Shenandoah Valley. Of these actions, Grant said, "crows flying over it for the balance of this season will have to carry their provender with them." *OR*, vol. 37, pt. 2, 301.

6. Brigadier General William E. Jones fell mortally wounded during the June 5, 1864, Battle of Piedmont, Virginia. Shaffer, *Washington County*, 45.

7. Colley did not indicate Bluefield, Virginia, or West Virginia. Exact burial location of King not found.

8. Located outside Chicago, Camp Douglas first housed the Confederate prisoners from Forts Henry and Donelson. The prison eventually held a maximum of 12,000 prisoners. Speer, *Portals to Hell*, 71, 324.

9. Levi's-Barr's Artillery Battery served in the Department of Western Virginia and East Tennessee for much of the war. Sifakis, *Compendium: Virginia*, 45.

10. Emory & Henry College, founded in 1836, graduated several young men who would later fight for the Confederacy, including William E. Jones and J. E. B. Stuart. Shaffer, *Washington County*.

11. King's Company, Virginia Light Artillery, Saltville Artillery. "Battle Unit Details," Soldiers and Sailors Database, accessed January 4, 2017, https://www.nps.gov/civilwar/search-battle-units-detail.htm?battleUnitCode=CVAKINGCAL.

12. Fred's brothers—David, James, and Robert—also served in the regiment. Sifakis, *Compendium: Virginia*, 179.

13. A stable worker to care for horses.

14. Point Lookout in Maryland grew to become the largest Northern prison, holding over 22,000 at peak. Speer, *Portals to Hell*, 151, 329.

15. In General Robert E. Lee's General Orders No. 74, June 23, 1862, he noted: "In addition to the officers honorably mentioned in the report of the expedition, the conduct of the following privates has received the special commendation of their respective commanders: Privates Thomas P. Clapp [Theophilus M. Clapp], Company D, First Virginia Cavalry, and J. S. Mosby, serving with the same regiment." *OR*, vol. 11, pt. 1, 1042. Colonel Fitz Lee also noted Clapp killed a Federal officer (Ibid., 1043), but historian John Fox suggests Clapp possibly wounded "either Lieutenant [William] McLean or

Captain [William] Royal." John J. Fox III, *Stuart's Finest Hour: The Ride Around McClellan, June 1862* (Winchester, VA: Angle Valley Press, 2014), 134.

16. Duff fell during the Battle of the Wilderness in May 1864. Driver, *1st Virginia Cavalry*, 169.

17. Captain Hiram Bledsoe led his company of Missouri Light Artillery in the Western Theater. "Battle Unit Details," Soldiers & Sailors Database, accessed December 13, 2016, https://www.nps.gov/civilwar/search-battle-units-detail .htm?battleUnitCode=CMOHBLECAL.

18. Dr. Robert E. Grant, along with John Arthur Campbell, served as Washington County delegates to Virginia's Secession Convention. Shaffer, *Washington County*, 14.

19. In retaliation for the burning of wagons near Benjamin Morgan's home outside Berryville—and the death of several blue-clad soldiers—the Federals, most likely operating under orders from Brigadier General Alfred Torbert instead of Brigadier General George Custer, executed six of Mosby's men at Front Royal in September 1864. Mosby countered by hanging three of Custer's men. Jeffry D. Wert, *Mosby's Rangers* (New York: Simon & Schuster, 1990), 214–49.

20. Family members later donated the flag to the Museum of the Confederacy in Richmond.

21. Meadows, captured at Greencastle, Pennsylvania, in July 1863, succumbed to pneumonia in August 1863, while incarcerated at Fort Delaware prison. Driver, *1st Virginia Cavalry*, 207.

22. No Greenwell County exists in Virginia. A history of the regiment indicates a James W. Monday in the 1st Virginia Cavalry; this soldier hailed from Grayson County, Virginia. Ibid., 208.

23. Roe survived the war. Ibid., 221.

24. Colley confuses the dates and locations of the wounds Schwartz received. Schwartz was wounded at Gettysburg in July 1863 and at Todd's Tavern in May 1864. Robert O'Neill, note to editor, March 28, 2017.

25. The riot broke out in New Orleans on July 30, 1866, when a radical group attempted to reconvene the Constitutional Convention of 1864. When the shooting ended after confrontation in the streets, 38 dead and 146 wounded bodies lay strewn about. Donald E. Reynolds, "The New Orleans Riot of 1866, Reconsidered," *Louisiana History* 5, no. 1 (1964), accessed January 5, 2017, doi:10.2307/4230742, http://www.jstor.org.proxy.kennesaw.edu /stable/4230742.

faL

Appendix 2. Regimental History and Biographical Roster Sketch Written as a Separate Journal

1. In 1855, the US Army adopted *Hardee's Tactics* for officer instruction. William J. Hardee, *Hardee's Rifle and Light Infantry Tactics* (Silver Spring, MD: H-Bar Enterprises, n.d.).
2. Several of the troopers referred to the uniforms as "penitentiary cloths." Shaffer, *Washington County*, 32.
3. Camp Davis in Ashland. Ibid.
4. Hopkins died December 9, 1895. Driver, *1st Virginia Cavalry*, 187.
5. Edmondson died after a wound received in the May 7, 1864 fighting at Todd's Tavern. Ibid., 170.
6. 45th Virginia Infantry Battalion, Lieutenant Colonel Henry M. Beckley. Sifakis, *Compendium: Virginia*, 233.
7. Miles also died at Todd's Tavern. Driver, *1st Virginia*, 207.
8. The *Abingdon Virginian*, in their March 18, 1864, edition, reported on Bailey's altercation with Palmer, a reported member of the local conscript guard. Bailey supposedly called Palmer a "conscript catcher," which offended Palmer, thus leading to a confrontation. Bailey drew his sabre and Palmer shot him. "Distressing Occurrence," *Abingdon Virginian*, March 18, 1864, accessed January 5, 2017, http://chroniclingamerica.loc.gov/lccn/sn84025980/1864-03-18/ed-1/seq-2/#date1=1864&index=0&date2=1864&searchType=advanced&language=&sequence=0&lccn=sn84025980&words=Bailey+killed+killing+Thomas&proxdistance=5&rows=20&ortext=&proxtext=&phrasetext=&andtext=Thomas+Bailey+killed&dateFilterType=yearRange&page=1.
9. Baker fell at Todd's Tavern. Driver, *1st Virginia*, 148.
10. The *Abingdon Virginian*, in their February 26, 1864, edition, carried a story on Butt's death after a fall from his horse. "Death of John W. Butt," *Abingdon Virginian*, February 26, 1864, accessed January 5, 2017, http://chroniclingamerica.loc.gov/lccn/sn84025980/1864-02-26/ed-1/seq-2/#date1=1864&index=0&date2=1864&searchType=advanced&language=&sequence=0&lccn=sn84025980&words=Butt+John+killed&proxdistance=5&rows=20&ortext=&proxtext=&phrasetext=&andtext=John+Butt+killed&dateFilterType=yearRange&page=1.
11. Buskle was killed at Fredericksburg during the May 1863 Battle of Chancellorsville. Driver, *1st Virginia Cavalry*, 157.
12. Findlay died on January 2, 1915, in Washington County, Virginia. Ibid., 173.
13. Gray died August 31, 1900. Ibid., 179.

14. Lynch died of disease April 3, 1863. Ibid., 201.

15. James Sanders was called "Governor" by the residents of Saltville. Much of the October 2, 1864, battle took place on his property. William Marvel, *Southwest Virginia in the Civil War: The Battles for Saltville* (Lynchburg, VA: H. E. Howard, 1992), 100.

16. Colley referred to John Singleton Mosby's writings, which include *Mosby's War Reminiscences*, *Mosby's Memoirs*, and many letters written to colleagues and newspapers.

17. Roberts succumbed to disease on October 23, 1861 in a Richmond hospital. Driver, *1st Virginia Cavalry*, 221.

18. Russell died during the action at Raccoon Ford on October 11, 1863. Ibid., 223.

19. Williams died at Todd's Tavern. Ibid., 240.

20. Lizzie Hardin delivered the following comments to the Washington Mounted Rifles, as they prepared to leave for war. "In the ages when cowardice was a crime and courage the virtue of a God, the men armed and went forth to battle amid the exhortation of the women, to 'return with their shields or upon them.' To-day, the women of Abingdon would imitate their example, and though when you are far distant, amid the perils of war, many a heart here will be still with anguish—though full oft, from blood forsaken lips, shall be sent up for you, a cry to Him who is 'mighty to save,' yet, with a firm hand we would give you this banner, and in an unfaltering voice, we bid you bear it on to 'victory or death.' We would bid you in the day of the battle look upon it—think of your mountain homes, and remember 'tis for them you strike. Think of the mothers, the sisters, the wives you have left behind, and remember 'tis for them you draw the sword. Tamely, and for years have we submitted to insult and oppression, and shall we longer bow our necks, like slaves, to the yoke? Shall the descended of the men of '76 hear the clanking of their chains and fear to break them? God forbid! What though you perish in the attempt? 'The coward died a thousand deaths, the brave man dies but one!' Then men of Virginia, show yourselves worthy of the name you bear! From the women of your native mountains, take this flag beneath its fold, go forth to meet the oppressor, and fear not to die!" Shaffer, *Washington County*, 29.

21. Davidson died July 1, 1862, in a Richmond hospital. Driver, *1st Virginia Cavalry*, 166.

22. Fulcher died of typhoid fever July 4, 1862, in Richmond. Ibid., 175.

23. Horne, imprisoned at Fort Delaware, died April 19, 1862. Ibid., 187.

24. The Chain Bridge across the Potomac River, into Washington City.

25. Pendleton died at Todd's Tavern on May 6, 1864. Driver, *1st Virginia Cavalry*, 215.

Appendix 3. Short Historical Sketch of Officers from the
Washington Mounted Rifles Submitted for Publication

1. Rachel Cook, born May 1826. "1900 United States Federal Census," Ancestry
   .com, 1997, accessed December 14, 2016, www.ancestry.com. She was the
   wife of Alphonso F. Cook, lieutenant colonel of the 8th Virginia Cavalry.
   Historical Data Systems, Inc., "American Civil War Research Database,"
   accessed December 14, 2016, http://www.civilwardata.com/active/hdsquery
   .dll?SoldierHistory?C&387068.

2. As a form of punishment during the war, soldiers had to carry a fence rail on
   their shoulders in front of their comrades. Black, *Cavalry Raids of the Civil
   War*, 221.

3. Wyndham Robertson, a Washington County resident, served as Virginia's
   governor, 1836–37. Summers, *History of Southwest Virginia*, 766.

4. After the war, Blackford wrote an account of his experiences entitled *War
   Years with Jeb Stuart*.

5. Ancient Free and Accepted Masons. Ibid., 565.

Appendix 4. Wartime Letters

1. In this letter, Colley describes the action during the Battle of First Manassas
   /Bull Run. This and all subsequent letters are housed in the Thomas
   W. Colley Collection, Ms2003-017, Special Collections, Virginia Tech,
   Blacksburg, Virginia.

2. A Private Samuel McDaniels fought with the 3rd New Hampshire Infantry;
   no information found for the same name in a Vermont regiment. "Civil War
   Service Index—Union—New Hampshire," Fold3, 2017, accessed February 6,
   2017, https://www.fold3.com/search/#query=Samuel+McDaniel&ocr=1&dr
   _year=m,1861–1865&offset=5&preview=1&t=51,697,685,762,44,50,799,793,6
   96,834,790,821,811,818,803,798,813,695&p_place_usa=NH,none.

3. Colley relates details from the fighting at First Manassas/Bull Run, fought
   July 21, 1861.

4. Washington City's *National Republican* newspaper reported on "300 or 400
   hundred secession cavalry stationed in the neighborhood of Falls Church
   . . . ," in their August 27, 1861, edition.

5. George W. Mantz of Abingdon, listed as "shoemaker" on 1860 census. The
   same census also contained a saddler in nearby Scott County, Virginia,
   named Robert Dickerson. "1860 United States Federal Census," Ancestry
   .com, 1997, accessed February 6, 2017, www.ancestry.com.

6. A roundabout: a common jacket cut straight around the waist.

7. On November 18, Lieutenant Colonel Fitz Lee lost his horse during an engagement with Federal infantry near Falls Church. Driver, *1st Virginia Cavalry*, 25.

8. A fire of unknown origin destroyed several buildings in downtown Charleston on December 11, 1861. Brian Hicks, "Charleston at War: Charleston Beaten down by Great Fire," *The Post and Courier*, December 8, 2016, accessed February 6, 2017, http://www.postandcourier.com/news /charleston-at-war-charleston-beaten-down-by-great-fire/article _4c54dce2-de2e-591f-b6c4-357e1ec599ab.html.

9. Brigadier General J. E. B. Stuart engaged Brigadier General Edward Ord's force near Dranesville, Virginia, on December 20, 1861. The Confederates endured greater casualties, 194, compared to 68 for the Federals. Ron Baumgarten, "'A Splendid Little Affair' The Battle of Dranesville," Civil War Trust 2014, accessed February 6, 2017, http://www.civilwar.org/battlefields /dranesville/a-splendid-little-affair.html.

10. Battle of Seven Pines or Fair Oaks, fought May 31–June 1, 1862.

11. Colley describes Stuart's first ride around McClellan.

12. The Seven Days' Battles (June 25–July 1, 1862) began as General Robert E. Lee replaced the wounded General Joseph E. Johnston and proceeded to drive Major General George McClellan's forces away from Richmond. Colley references the fighting at Gaines' Mill on June 27.

13. Battle of Second Manassas, August 28–30, 1862.

14. Gravel: an infection of a horse's hoof, due to the penetration of a foreign object. "Horse Hoof Abscess: Treatment and Diagnosis," Horses and Horse Information, 1998, accessed February 6, 2017, http://www.horses-and-horse -information.com/articles/0398abcess.shtml.

15. Stuart conducted the Chamberburg Raid, also known as his Second Ride Around McClellan. See note 22 from chapter 4.

16. Inconclusive engagement at Morton's Ford, February 6–7, 1864, that pitted Brigadier General J. C. Caldwell's Federals against Lieutenant General Richard Ewell's Confederate force. "Battle Summary: Morton's Ford, VA," CWSAC Battle Summaries, accessed February 6, 2017, https://www.nps.gov /abpp/battles/va045.htm.

17. After failing to take Knoxville, Tennessee, Longstreet's troops wintered in upper east Tennessee. In the spring of 1864, General Robert E. Lee called the troops back to the Army of Northern Virginia, and on their way, they passed through southwest Virginia, collecting supplies as they went.

18. After his mortal wounding in Greeneville, Tennessee, on September 4, 1864, the Confederates brought his corpse to Abingdon, where he received

internment in an above-ground site in the Sinking Spring Cemetery. Brigadier General John Hunt Morgan's body, later removed as fear of Federal invasion mounted, eventually received two additional internments before reaching his final resting place in Lexington, Kentucky, after the war.

Appendix 5. An 1887 Account of His Wounding at Kelly's Ford

1. This account is housed in the Thomas W. Colley Collection, Ms2003–017, Special Collections, Virginia Tech, Blacksburg, Virginia.

BIBLIOGRAPHY

Primary Sources

MANUSCRIPT COLLECTIONS

Colley Journals, Private Collection

Colley Roster, Private Collection

Museum of the Confederacy. Richmond, VA.

Thomas W. Colley Collection, Ms2003–017, Special Collections, Virginia Tech, Blacksburg, VA.

W. L. Eury Appalachian Collection, Appalachian State University, Boone, NC.

ELECTRONIC SOURCES

"1860 United States Federal Census." Ancestry.com. 1997. Accessed November 28, 2016. www.ancestry.com.

"1863 Richmond Directory." Accessed November 29, 2016. http://www .mdgorman.com/Written_Accounts/1863%20Richmond%20Directory.htm.

Baumgarten, Ron. "'A Splendid Little Affair' The Battle of Dranesville." 2014. Accessed February 6, 2017. http://www.civilwar.org/battlefields/dranesville /a-splendid-little-affair.html.

Brock, Robert Alonzo. *History of Virginia from Settlement of Jamestown to Close of the Civil War*. Richmond, VA: H. H. Hardesty, 1888. https://books .google.com/books?id=fJJLAAAAYAAJ&pg=PA711&lpg=PA711&dq =%22Thomas+W.+Colley%22&source=bl&ots=342gVu_1AM&sig=JGaf1yqD _zJHQIvkaRuohrBcW6c&hl=en&sa=X&ved=0ahUKEwjqrK3y6 _zRAhXIiVQKHUoGDrg4ChDoAQgkMAQ#v=onepage&q=%22Thomas %20W.%20Colley%22&f=false.

"Civil War Service Index—Union—New Hampshire." 2017. Accessed February 6, 2017. https://www.fold3.com/search/#query=Samuel+McDaniel&ocr=1&dr _year=m,1861–1865&offset=5&preview=1&t=51,697,685,762,44,50,799,793,696 ,834,790,821,811,818,803,798,813,695&p_place_usa=NH,none.

Communications, United Methodist. "The Slavery Question and Civil War (1844– 1865)—the United Methodist Church." 2016. Accessed December 12, 2016. http://www.umc.org/who-we-are/the-slavery-question-and-civil-war.

Conference, Holston. "Sketches of Holston Preachers." 2016. Accessed December 9, 2016. http://holston.org/about/resources/photographs-and -stories-holston-history/resources/.

District of Columbia. Register of Wills and Conditions. "Probate Records (District of Columbia), 1801–1930." 2015. Accessed December 2, 2016. http://search.ancestry.com//cgi-bin/sse.dll?ti=0&indiv=try&db =usprobatedc&h=89109.

Downey, Brian. "The Battle of Antietam on the Web." December 23, 2016. Accessed January 3, 2017. http://antietam.aotw.org.

Fold 3. "Civil War Soldiers—Confederate—Officers." 2016. Accessed December 5, 2016. https://www.fold3.com/image/72102538/?terms=W.B.%20Richards.

———. "Civil War Soldiers—Confederate—VA." 2016. Accessed December 7, 2016. https://www.fold3.com/image/271/10764978.

———. "Civil War Soldiers—Confederate—VA." 2016. Accessed December 16, 2016. https://www.fold3.com/image/6793718.

———. "Compiled Service Records of Confederate Soldiers Who Served in Organizations from the State of Virginia." 2016. Accessed December 6, 2016. https://www.fold3.com/image/9003577.

Friends of the Blue Ridge Parkway. "Peaks of Otter." December 6, 2016. Accessed December 8, 2016. https://www.friendsbrp.org/discover-the-parkway /destinations/peaks-of-otter/.

Gorman, Michael D. "Jackson Hospital." February 5, 2008. Accessed December 7, 2016. http://mdgorman.com/Hospitals/jackson_hospital.htm.

——— "Stuart Hospital." December 2, 2008. Accessed December 7, 2016. http:// mdgorman.com/Hospitals/stuart_hospital.htm.

———. "Winder Hospital." July 17, 2008. Accessed December 2, 2016. http:// mdgorman.com/Hospitals/winder_hospital.htm.

Hicks, Brian. "Charleston at War: Charleston Beaten down by Great Fire." December 8, 2016. Accessed February 6, 2017. http://www.postandcourier .com/news/charleston-at-war-charleston-beaten-down-by-great-fire/article _4c54dce2-de2e-591f-b6c4–357e1ec599ab.html.

Historical Data Systems, Inc. "American Civil War Research Database." Accessed December 8, 2016. http://www.civilwardata.com/active /hdsquery.dll?SoldierHistory?C&1394974.

"Horse Hoof Abscess: Treatment and Diagnosis." 1998. Accessed February 6, 2017. http://www.horses-and-horse-information.com/articles/0398abcess .shtml.

Kambourian, Elizabeth. "Richmond Slave Trade." Accessed December 2, 2016. https://www.google.com/maps/d/viewer?mid=11AeMB-8ElBEyVEY

xHiFYTAeFtS8&hl=en&11 =37.55456919380494%2C-77.518049974182\1
3&z=12.

Lee, Susanna Michele. "Twenty-Slave Law." Encyclopedia Virginia. Accessed
    December 8, 2016. http://www.encyclopediavirginia.org/twenty-slave
    _law#start_entry.

Medical Dictionary. TheFreeDictionary.com, 2003. s.v. "Greasy heel." Accessed
    December 6, 2016. http://medical-dictionary.thefreedictionary.com
    /greasy+heel.

Merriam-Webster.com. "Jenny." Last modified 2017. Accessed January 4, 2017.
    https://www.merriam-webster.com/dictionary/jenny.

———. "Medical Definition of Bloody Flux." Last modified 2017. Accessed June
    8, 2017. https://www.merriam-webster.com/medical/bloody%20flux.

National Park Service. "Battle Summary: Blountville, TN." Accessed December 5,
    2016. https://www.nps.gov/abpp/battles/tn019.htm.

———. "Battle Unit Details." Accessed January 4, 2017. https://www.nps.gov
    /civilwar/search-battle-units-detail.htm?battleUnitCode=CVAKINGCAL.

———. "Battle Summary: Malvern Hill, VA." Accessed November 30, 2016.
    https://www.nps.gov/abpp/battles/va021.htm.

———. "Battle Summary: Morton's Ford, VA." Accessed February 6, 2017.
    https://www.nps.gov/abpp/battles/va045.htm.

———. "Battle Unit Details." Accessed December 13, 2016. https://www.nps
    .gov/civilwar/search-battle-units-detail.htm?battleUnitCode
    =CMOHBLECAL.

The Ohio State University. "Common Civil War Medical Terms." Accessed
    November 28, 2016. https://ehistory.osu.edu/exhibitions/cwsurgeon
    /cwsurgeon/commonterms.

"Organization of 1026 Camps in the United Confederate Veteran Association
    . . . Prepared Expressly for Use of Delegates to the Seventh Reunion and
    Meeting of the Association, Held at Nashville, Tenn., on June 22nd, 23rd and
    24th, 1897: United Confederate." June 18, 2008. Accessed December 12, 2016.
    https://archive.org/details/organizationof1000unit.

PBS. "THE WEST—Diggers." 2001. Accessed November 29, 2016. http://www
    .pbs.org/weta/thewest/program/episodes/three/diggers.htm.

Pulley, Angela F. "Elias Boudinot (ca. 1804–1839)." March 9, 2002. Accessed
    November 29, 2016. http://www.georgiaencyclopedia.org/articles
    /history-archaeology/elias-boudinot-ca-1804–1839.

Reynolds, Donald E. "The New Orleans Riot of 1866, Reconsidered." *Louisiana
    History* 5, no. 1 (1964): 5–27. Accessed January 5, 2017. doi:10.2307/4230742.
    http://www.jstor.org.proxy.kennesaw.edu/stable/4230742.

Roche, Charlene. "Charlene Roche Family Tree." 1997. Accessed December 12, 2016. http://trees.ancestry.com/tree/40850494/family?usePUBJs=true.

Shakespeare, William. "The Life and Death of Julius Caesar." Accessed December 8, 2016. http://shakespeare.mit.edu/julius_caesar/full.html.

Special Collections Dept., University of Virginia Library, "A Guide to the Papers of Lewis Preston Summers 1814–1947 Lewis Preston Summers, Papers, 1814–1947 2781." 2001. Accessed December 12, 2016. http://ead.lib.virginia.edu/vivaxtf/view?docId=uva-sc/viu01394.xml.

University of North Carolina. "Laws of Congress in Regard to Taxes, Currency and Conscription, Passed February 1864." Accessed December 7, 2016. http://docsouth.unc.edu/imls/lawsofcong/lawsofcong.html.

The Virginia Center for Civil War Studies. "Battle of Cloyd's Mountain." 2016. Accessed December 8, 2016. http://www.civilwar.vt.edu/wordpress/battle-of-cloyds-mountain/.

Published Primary Sources

Blackford, W. W. W. *War Years with Jeb Stuart*. Baton Rouge: Louisiana State University Press, 1993.

Davis, George B., US War Department, Leslie J Perry, Joseph W. Kirkley, and Calvin D. Cowles. *The Official Military Atlas of the Civil War*. New York: Barnes & Noble Books, 2003.

Hardee, William J. *Hardee's Rifle and Light Infantry Tactics*. Silver Spring, MD: H-Bar Enterprises, n.d.

Hubard, Lt. Robert T., Jr. *The Civil War Memoirs of a Virginia Cavalryman: Lt. Robert T. Hubard Jr.* Edited by Thomas P. Nanzig. Tuscaloosa: University of Alabama Press, 2007.

Kidd, James Harvey. *Custer's Michigan Cavalry Brigade in the Civil War*. Lexington, KY: Big Byte Books, 2016.

Lindsley, John B, ed. *The Military Annals of Tennessee*. Vol. I. Wilmington, NC: Broadfoot Publishing Company, 1995.

Mackey, Thomas C., ed. *A Documentary History of the Civil War Era*. Volume 1: *Legislative Achievements*. Knoxville: University of Tennessee Press, 2012.

McClellan, Major Henry B. *I Rode with Jeb Stuart: The Life and Campaigns of Major General J. E. B. Stuart*. New York: Da Capo Press, 1994.

McElroy, John. *Andersonville: A Story of Rebel Military Prisons, Fifteen Months a Guest of the so-Called Southern Confederacy; A Private Soldiers Experience in Richmond, Andersonville, Savannah, Millen, Blackshear, and Florence*. Scituate, MA: Digital Scanning, Inc., 1999.

Mosby, John S. *Mosby's Memoirs*. New York: Barnes & Noble Books, 2006.

———. *The Letters of John S. Mosby*. Edited by Adele H. Mitchell. n.p.: Stuart-Mosby Historical Society, 1986.

———. *Mosby's War Reminiscences and Stuart's Cavalry Campaigns—Primary Source Edition*. n.p.: Nabu Press, 2013.

———. *Take Sides with the Truth: The Postwar Letters of John Singleton Mosby to Samuel F. Chapman*. Edited by Peter A. Brown. Lexington: University Press of Kentucky, 2007.

Opie, John Newton. *A Rebel Cavalryman: With Lee, Stuart and Jackson*. Breinigsville, PA: Kessinger Publishing, 2010.

Robertson, Frank Smith. *In the Saddle with Stuart: The Story of Frank Smith Robertson of Jeb Stuart's Staff*. Edited by Robert J Trout. Gettysburg, PA: Thomas Publications, 1998.

Sheridan, Philip Henry H. *Personal Memoirs of P. H. Sheridan, General United States Army*. New York: Da Capo Press, 1992.

Trout, Robert J. *With Pen and Saber: The Letters and Diaries of J. E. B. Stuart's Staff Officers*. New York: Stackpole Books, 1995.

The Union Army: A History of Military Affairs in the Loyal States. Reprint. 9 vols. Wilmington, NC: Broadfoot Publishing, 1998.

United States War Department. *The War of the Rebellion: A Compilation of the Official Records of the Union and Confederate Armies*. 128 vols. Washington, DC, 1881.

United States War Department. *Supplement to the Official Records of the Union and Confederate Armies*. Edited by Janet Hewett, Noah Andre Trudeau, and Bryce A. Suderow. Wilmington, NC: Broadfoot Publishing, 1996.

Von Borcke, Heros. *Memoirs of the Confederate War for Independence, Volumes 1–3—Primary Source Edition*. n.p.: Nabu Press, 2013.

Secondary Sources

BOOKS

Allardice, Bruce S. *Confederate Colonels: A Biographical Register*. Columbia: University of Missouri Press, 2008.

Armistead, Gene C. *Horses and Mules in the Civil War: A Complete History with a Roster of More Than 700 War Horses*. New York, NY: McFarland & Company, 2013.

Black, Robert W. *Cavalry Raids of the Civil War*. Mechanicsburg, PA: Stackpole Books, 2004.

Blair, William A. *Virginia's Private War: Feeding Body and Soul in the Confederacy, 1861–1865*. New York: Oxford University Press, 2000.

Bluford, Robert. *The Battle of Totopotomoy Creek: Polegreen Church and the Prelude to Cold Harbor.* Charleston, SC: History Press, 2014.

Brandt, Dennis W. *Pathway to Hell: a Tragedy of the American Civil War.* Lincoln: University of Nebraska Press, 2010.

Bridges, David P. *Fighting with Jeb Stuart: Major James Breathed and the Confederate Horse Artillery.* Arlington, VA: Breathed Bridges Best, 2006.

Calcutt, Rebecca Barbour. *Richmond's Wartime Hospitals.* Gretna, LA: Pelican, 2005.

Cooke, Jacob B. *The Battle of Kelly's Ford, March 17, 1863.* 1887. Reprint, Delhi, India: Facsimile Publisher, 2016.

Crute, Joseph H., Jr. *Confederate Staff Officers 1861–1865.* Powhatan, VA: Derwent Books, 1982.

Davis, Burke. *Jeb Stuart, the Last Cavalier.* New York: Bonanza Books, 1957.

Dean, Eric T. *Shook Over Hell: Post-Traumatic Stress, Vietnam, and the Civil War.* Cambridge, MA: Harvard University Press, 1997.

Driver, Robert J. *First Virginia Cavalry.* Lynchburg, VA: H. E. Howard, 1991.

Dyer, Frederick H. *A Compendium of the War of the Rebellion.* 3 vols. New York: Thomas Yoseloff, 1959.

Eicher, John H., and David J. Eicher. *Civil War High Commands.* Boston, MA: Stanford University Press, 2001.

English Dialect Society. *The English Dialect Dictionary: Being the Complete Vocabulary of All Dialect Words Still in Use, or Known to Have Been in Use During the Last Two Hundred Years.* Edited by Joseph Wright. Oxford: OUP Australia and New Zealand, 1981.

Faust, Patricia L., ed. *Historical Times Illustrated Encyclopedia of the Civil War.* New York: HarperCollins Publishers, 1991.

Flannery, Michael A. *Civil War Pharmacy: A History of Drugs, Drug Supply and Provision, and Therapeutics for the Union and Confederacy.* New York: Pharmaceutical Products Press, 2004.

Fox, John J., III. *Stuart's Finest Hour: The Ride Around McClellan, June 1862.* Winchester, VA: Angle Valley Press, 2014.

Hagy, James William. *After the War Was Over: Reconstruction in Washington County, Virginia, 1865–1870.* n.p.: James W. Hagy, 2015.

Hennessy, John J. *Return to Bull Run: The Campaign and Battle of Second Manassas.* Norman: University of Oklahoma Press, 1999.

——— *The First Battle of Manassas: An End to Innocence July 18–21, 1861.* Lynchburg, VA: H. E. Howard, 1989.

Hewett, Janet B., and Joyce Lawrence. *Virginia Confederate Soldiers.* Wilmington, NC: Broadfoot, 1998.

Jones, Virgil Carrington. *Ranger Mosby*. McLean, VA: EPM Publications, 1997.

Kinard, Jeff. *Pistols: An Illustrated History of Their Impact* (Weapons and Warfare). Santa Barbara, CA: ABC-CLIO, 2004.

Krick, Robert K. *Lee's Colonels: A Biographical Register of the Field Officers of the Army of Northern Virginia*. Dayton, OH: Morningside House, Inc., 1992.

Lande, R. Gregory. *Psychological Consequences of the American Civil War*. Jefferson, NC: McFarland Publishing, 2017.

Longacre, Edward G. *Fitz Lee: A Military Biography of Major General Fitzhugh Lee, C.S.A.* Cambridge: Da Capo Press, 2004.

———. *Lee's Cavalrymen: A History of the Mounted Forces of the Army of Northern Virginia; 1861—1865*. Mechanicsburg, PA: Stackpole Books, 2002.

———. *The Cavalry at Gettysburg: A Tactical Study of Mounted Operations During the Civil War's Pivotal Campaign, 9 June–14 July 1863*. Lincoln: University of Nebraska Press, 1993.

Marvel, William. *Southwest Virginia in the Civil War: The Battles for Saltville*. Lynchburg, VA: H. E. Howard, 1992.

Mays, Thomas D. *The Saltville Massacre*. Fort Worth, TX: McWhiney Foundation Press, 1998.

McClurken, Jeffrey W. *Take Care Of The Living: Reconstructing Confederate Veteran Families in Virginia*. Charlottesville: University of Virginia Press, 2009.

McGrath, Thomas A. *Shepherdstown: Last Clash of the Antietam Campaign, September 19-20, 1862*. 5th ed. Lynchburg, VA: Schroeder Publications, 2016.

McKnight, Brian D. *Contested Borderland: The Civil War in Appalachian Kentucky and Virginia*. Lexington: University Press of Kentucky, 2006.

Miller, Brian Craig. *Empty Sleeves: Amputation in the Civil War South*. Athens: University of Georgia Press, 2015.

Nagel, Paul C. *The Lees of Virginia: Seven Generations of an American Family*. New York: Oxford University Press, 1992.

Nelson, Megan Kate. *Ruin Nation: Destruction and the American Civil War*. Athens, GA: University of Georgia Press, 2012.

Quarstein, John V. *The CSS Virginia: Sink Before Surrender*. Charleston, SC: History Press, 2012.

Ramage, James A. *Gray Ghost: The Life of Col. John Singleton Mosby*. Lexington: University Press of Kentucky, 2010.

Rankin, Thomas M. *37th Virginia Infantry*. Lynchburg, VA: H. E. Howard, 1987.

Schroeder-Lein, Glenna R. *The Encyclopedia of Civil War Medicine*. New Brunswick, NJ: M. E. Sharpe, 2008.

Sears, Stephen W. *George B. McClellan: The Young Napoleon*. New York: Ticknor & Fields, 1988.

———. *To the Gates of Richmond: The Peninsula Campaign*. Boston: Houghton Mifflin, 2002.

Shaffer, Michael K. *Washington County, Virginia, in the Civil War*. Charleston, SC: History Press, 2012.

Siepel, Kevin H. *Rebel: The Life and Times of John Singleton Mosby*. New York: Da Capo Press, 1997.

Sifakis, Stewart. *Compendium of the Confederate Armies: South Carolina and Georgia*. Westminster, MD: Heritage Books, Inc., 2009.

———. *Compendium of the Confederate Armies: Virginia*. Bowie, MD: Willow Bend Books, 2003.

Speer, Lonnie R. *Portals to Hell: Military Prisons of the Civil War*. San Francisco, CA: Stackpole Books, 1997.

Spratt, Thomas M. *Confederate Property and Material Suppliers in Virginia, 1861–1865*. Athens, GA: New Papyrus Publishing, 2003.

Summers, Lewis Preston. *History of Southwest Virginia, 1746–1786, Washington County, 1777–1870*. Johnson City, TN: Overmountain Press, 1989.

Thomas, Emory M. *The Bold Dragoon: The Life of J. E. B. Stuart*. Norman: University of Oklahoma Press, 1999.

Trout, Robert J. *They Followed the Plume: The Story of J. E. B. Stuart and His Staff*. Mechanicsburg, PA: Stackpole Books, 1993.

Wallace, Lee A. *A Guide to Virginia Military Organizations, 1861–1865*. 2nd ed. Lynchburg, VA: H. E. Howard, 1986.

Warner, Ezra J. *Generals in Gray: Lives of the Confederate Commanders*. Baton Rouge: Louisiana State University Press, 1997.

Wert, Jeffry D. *Cavalryman of the Lost Cause: A Biography of J. E. B. Stuart*. New York: Simon & Schuster, 2008.

———. *Mosby's Rangers*. New York: Simon & Schuster Adult Publishing Group, 1990.

Wilson, Gregory P. *Private John S. Mosby, First Virginia Cavalry: Picketing Fairfax County Before Becoming the Confederacy's "Gray Ghost."* North Charleston, SC: Createspace Independent Publishing Platform, 2015.

Wittenberg, Eric J. *The Union Cavalry Comes of Age: Hartwood Church to Brandy Station, 1863*. Washington, DC: Brassey's US, 2003.

Woodworth, Steven E., and Kenneth J. Winkle. *The Atlas of the Civil War*. Oxford: Oxford University Press, 2004.

NEWSPAPERS, MAGAZINES, JOURNALS

Brock, R. A., ed. *Southern Historical Society Papers*. Wilmington, NC: Broadfoot Publishing, 1990.

Civil War Times Illustrated Staff. "'Grumble' Jones: A Personality Profile." *Civil War Times Illustrated* 7 (June 1968)35–41.

Colley, T. W. "T. W. Colley as a Soldier 1861 to 1865." *Confederate Veteran* 7 (January 1899): 12.

Cosby, L. T. "Thomas W. Colley." *Confederate Veteran* 29 (July 1921): 309.

"Death of John W. Butt." *Abingdon Virginian*, no. 1864/02/26 (February 26, 1864). Accessed January 5, 2017. http://chroniclingamerica.loc.gov/lccn /sn84025980/1864-02-26/ed-1/seq-2/#date1=1864&index=0&date2 =1864&searchType=advanced&language=&sequence=0&lccn =sn84025980&words=Butt+John+killed&proxdistance=5&rows=20&ortext =&proxtext=&phrasetext=&andtext=John+Butt+killed&dateFilterType =yearRange&page=1.

"Distressing Occurrence." *Abingdon Virginian*, March 18, 1864. Accessed January 5, 2017. http://chroniclingamerica.loc.gov/lccn/sn84025980/1864-03-18 /ed-1/seq-2/#date1=1864&index=0&date2=1864&searchType =advanced&language=&sequence=0&lccn=sn84025980&words=Bailey +killed+killing+Thomas&proxdistance=5&rows=20&ortext=&proxtext =&phrasetext=&andtext=Thomas+Bailey+killed&dateFilterType =yearRange&page=1.

Gaffney Ledger. Gaffney, SC: Newspapers.com, 1898. https://www.newspapers .com/image/78047182/?terms=Enoree%2B%2B%2BCoffin.

"National Republican." 1861. Accessed February 6, 2017. https://www.newspapers .com/image/80559720.

Newborn, Horace. "A Wonderful Exploit: Jeb Stuart's Ride Around the Army of the Potomac June 12–15, 1862." *Blue & Gray* 15, no. 6 (1998): 6-21; 46–54.

Rhea, Gordon C. "'The Hottest Place I Ever Was In:' The Battle of Haw's Shop, May 28, 1864." *North & South* 4 (April 2001): 42–57.

Soodalter, Ron. "The Shock of War: 'Rage of Battle' Forever Haunted Some Veterans." *America's Civil War* (May 2017): 44–51.

Sword, Wiley. "Cavalry on Trial at Kelly's Ford." *Civil War Times Illustrated* 13 (April 1974): 32–40.

Wine, Winston B. "The One Who Brought the Flag Home." *The Historical Society of Washington County, Va, Bulletin* Series II, no. 30 (1993): 20–22.

Wittenburg, Eric J. "St. Patrick's Day Melee: The Battle of Kelly's Ford." *North & South* 11 (December 2009): 35–49.

INDEX